Paradoxes
of
Learning

PETER JARVIS

Paradoxes

of

Learning

ON
BECOMING
AN
INDIVIDUAL
IN
SOCIETY

Jossey-Bass Publishers · San Francisco

For sales outside the United States contact Maxwell Macmillan
International Publishing Group, 866 Third Avenue, New York,
New York 10022

Manufactured in the United States of America

The paper used in this book is acid-free and meets
the State of California requirements for recycled paper
(50 percent recycled waste, including 10 percent post-
consumer waste), which are the strictest guidelines
for recycled paper currently in use in the United States.

Library of Congress Cataloging-in-Publication Data

Jarvis, Peter, date.
    Paradoxes of learning: on becoming an individual in society/
Peter Jarvis. — 1st ed.
      p.   cm. — (The Jossey-Bass higher and adult education series)
(The Jossey-Bass social and behavioral science series)
   Includes bibliographical references (p.) and index.
   ISBN 1-55542-448-1 (alk. paper)
   1. Adult learning.   2. Social learning.   3. Adult education.
I. Title.   II. Series.   III. Series: The Jossey-Bass social and
behavioral science series.
LC5225.L42J37 1992
374—dc20   92-8186
                                             CIP

FIRST EDITION
HB Printing   10 9 8 7 6 5 4 3 2 1   *Code 9250*

A joint publication
in
The Jossey-Bass
Higher and Adult Education Series
and
The Jossey-Bass
Social and Behavioral Science Series

Consulting Editor
Adult and Continuing Education

Alan B. Knox
University of Wisconsin, Madison

Contents

Preface   xi

The Author   xvii

Part One: The Development of the Social Self

1. The Nature of Human Learning   3

2. The Paradox of Living and Learning in Society   17

3. Being and the Birth of the Self   33

4. Understanding Conscious Action   50

5. Learning and Action   68

6. Interests and Learning   86

**Part Two: Personal Growth
Through Lifelong Learning**

7. Being a Person   101

8. Authenticity, Autonomy, and Self-Directed Learning   119

9. Being and Having   143

10. Meaning and Truth   155

11. Learning, Personhood, and the Workplace   177

12. Aging and Wisdom   195

13. Learning and Change   209

14. The Political Dimension of Learning   221

15. Implications for Teaching and Education   235

References   249

Index   263

Preface

Interest in adult learning has increased dramatically in recent years, as growing recognition has been paid to the significance of adult education, human resource development, and continuing professional education. Many of the studies of learning have adopted a psychological perspective; to some extent, the study of learning has even been regarded as the preserve of psychologists. Naturally, learning is a field of psychological study, but it is much wider than that. Learning actually relates to the whole of human existence, and so it encompasses a variety of fields.

Paradoxes of Learning situates learning within the human experience and locates it in the paradox of the human condition. This paradox is summed up by the contradictions of living in society: there can be no freedom without constraint, no certainty without uncertainty, no truth without falsehood, no joy without sorrow, no sense of peace without the threat of war, and so on. Above all, there can be no learning without ignorance and no growth and development without learning. But even more important, people seek meaning for their lives and discover only that as one meaning unfolds, still more questions lie beyond it.

Humankind vacillates between animal existence and the higher qualities of the divine — for the serpent said to the woman in the Garden of Eden, "and you will be like God" (Genesis 3:5). Having read the manuscript of this book, Bob Brownhill, of the University of Surrey, England, commented that "our true essence is as animals but we would like to be gods" (personal communication, July 1991). Herein lies part of the paradox of learning: human beings are born as animals, but as the human essence emerges through learning, humankind grows and develops and learns to be. While this process is natural, it is not free. Its implications are problematic. Learning is constrained by the sociocultural milieu into which individuals are born, it is directed through pressures exerted by social structures, and it is subject to control by the power elites. Learning stems from the experiences of living in society, but paradoxically, there would be no society without people learning.

Audience

Paradoxes of Learning was written in response to the need to study human learning from a broad, interdisciplinary perspective. It is aimed, therefore, at all scholars and practitioners involved with any aspect of human learning. It is for those who work, or are being prepared to work, in all the so-called people professions: for educators, whatever the age group they teach; for trainers and human resource developers; for managers and other leaders; for psychologists, therapists, and counselors; for doctors and nurses; for sociologists, philosophers, and theologians. While the book is theoretical, its concerns are practical. It offers something of a practical nature to everyone involved with the learning process. It provides scholars with a different way of viewing learning and practitioners with an opportunity to reflect on the implications of learning in their own work situation.

Overview of the Contents

This book is a study of learning from both a sociological and a philosophical perspective. It is divided into two parts. Part One (Chapters One to Six) outlines the social context within which learning occurs. Chapter One sets the scene for the whole book. Chapters Two and Three examine the process of becoming a self in society, showing how both mind and self are socially learned phenomena. Chapters Four and Five develop theories of learning and action and point up the complex relationship between them. Chapter Six begins to outline some of the contradictions of individual and social interest.

Part Two (Chapters Seven to Fifteen) examines certain of the paradoxes in more detail, taking up themes that have been quite central to the history of human thought. Chapters Seven to Ten treat the topics of personhood; authenticity, freedom, and free will; being and having; and meaning and truth, respectively. Chapter Eleven focuses on learning in the workplace. Chapters Twelve and Thirteen deal with aging and changing, respectively. Chapter Fourteen explores the political aspect of learning. Finally, Chapter Fifteen examines the ramifications of the preceding discussion for teaching and education. While there is a certain sequence to the chapters in Part Two, few are totally dependent on any that appear earlier, so that they may be read individually. (All, however, build on the theoretical foundations laid out in Part One, especially in Chapters Two to Five.)

Background

Seeking to understand the complex process of learning has occupied a great deal of my time and thought over the past decade; *Paradoxes of Learning* reflects ideas that have developed gradually. Some of the ideas have been published elsewhere, although none in the form in which they appear here. Since the other publications are not referred to later in the book, it may be useful to mention a few of them now to show the development of my thinking.

Some of the ideas presented here were first discussed in my book *Adult and Continuing Education: Theory and Practice,* published in 1983. The opportunity to give a paper titled "Learning and Personhood: Towards a Social Philosophy of Education and Practice" at a conference on nurse education in Dublin in 1985 also stimulated my thinking. I have incorporated some of the resulting insights into Chapter Eleven of the present work.

In *Adult Learning in the Social Context* (1987), I pursued that line of thinking even further. At the time that book was published, I thought that I had concluded my investigation into adult learning. However, this was premature.

A few months after the book appeared, I prepared a paper titled "Being and Learning," which was published in Finnish as "Oleminen ja oppinminem" in *Aikuiskasvastus,* the Finnish adult education journal, in 1989. (This paper has not been published in English, although it was presented at seminars at the University of Georgia and the University of Tennessee.) Significantly, it set my thinking off in an existentialist direction. I also had a chance to develop my line of thought in an article titled "Learning, Being, and Aging," which was published in *Educational Gerontology* in April 1989. This article was substantially revised and published as "Experience, Learning and Ageing" in Glendenning and Percy's volume *Ageing, Education and Society* (1990). Some of the ideas from those papers now appear in Chapter Twelve of this book.

Later in 1989 I prepared "Self-Directed Learning: Toward a Theoretical Analysis," which was presented at the North American Symposium on Self-Directed Learning at the University of Oklahoma. The same ideas were developed further in "Free Will, Freedom, and Self-Directed Learning," which was to be presented at the North American Symposium in 1991. Personal circumstances prevented my attending, but Chapter Eight of this book has benefited substantially from this paper as well as the previous one.

Another paper, "Adult Education: Beyond Instrumentalism?," prepared in 1989 for a conference in the Netherlands, was published in Dutch as "Volvasseneneducatie — Het instrumentalisme voorbij?" Again the paper has not been published in English, but some of its material can be found in the discussion of rationality in Chapter Eleven. Finally, I presented a paper titled "To Be or to Have? That Is the Question for Adult Education" at the conference of the American Association of Adult and Continuing Education (AAACE) in Salt Lake City, Utah, in October 1990. That paper contained many of the ideas discussed in Chapter Nine.

As the foregoing chronology shows, this book was a long time in the writing, and I am enormously grateful to all those who provided feedback or otherwise contributed to the development of my thinking.

I have been privileged to work with practitioners and educators in several different professions and also to prepare educators for school teaching, adult education, and the professions; their interest in human learning has been a stimulus to this work. In particular, many students working with me who have been exposed to my ideas have entered into a critical dialogue with me, from which I have learned a great deal. Bob Brownhill of the University of Surrey read the whole manuscript and made many incisive comments, Brad Courtenay from the University of Georgia read six chapters and encouraged me to continue, and Alan Chadwick read Chapter Nine and was very supportive. Special mention should also be made of the fact that at the AAACE Conference in Atlantic City, New Jersey, in 1989 I had the fortune to engage in a public discussion with Jack Mezirow about learning and meaning. Preparing for that discussion was extremely beneficial to me; some of the results are reflected in Chapter Ten. Moreover, I have benefited enormously from the feedback of the reviewers whom Jossey-Bass asked to assess the manuscript. I am also most grateful for the assistance and support I received from Gale Erlandson, senior editor for the Jossey-Bass Higher and Adult Education Series, and from Alan Knox, consulting editor for adult and continuing education. In addition, I would like to thank Margaret Morgan, who spent considerable time assisting me with secretarial tasks in connection with the preparation of the manuscript.

Colleagues, students, and my family have consistently encouraged me in this quest to explore human learning. I am grateful to them for the support they have given me, and I can only hope that some of these thoughts will be useful to them and to others. But in the end, I acknowledge that I am fully responsible for the ideas presented here.

Guildford, England   Peter Jarvis
May 1992

The Author

Peter Jarvis is reader in the Department of Educational Studies at the University of Surrey, U.K. He is also adjunct professor at the University of Georgia in the United States. He received his B.D. degree (1963) from the University of London, his B.A. degree (1969) in sociology from the University of Sheffield, his M.Sc. degree (1972) in sociology of education from the University of Birmingham, and his Ph.D. degree (1977) in sociology of the professions from the University of Aston.

Jarvis's work has focused primarily on sociological and philosophical studies of adult education and adult learning. He has taught both teacher and adult and continuing education and has also been involved in a variety of research projects, some of them connected with nurse education. In 1988, he was awarded the Cyril O. Houle World Award for Literature in Adult Education for his book *Adult Learning in the Social Context* (1987); and in 1990, he was a fellow, at the University of Tokyo, of the Japanese Society for the Promotion of Science Research. His other publications include *Professional Education* (1983), *Adult and Continuing Education: Theory and Practice* (1983), *The Sociology of Adult and Continuing Education* (1985), *The Teacher-Practitioner in Nursing, Midwifery, and Health Visiting* (1985, with Sheila Gibson), and *An International Dictionary of Adult and Continuing Education* (1990). In addition, he has edited *Twentieth Century Thinkers in Adult Education* (1987), *Britain: Policy and Practice in Continuing Education* (1988), *Training Adult Educators in Western Europe* (1991, with Alan Chadwick), and *Adult Education: Evolution and Achievements in a Developing Field of Study* (1991, with John M. Peters and Associates).

Jarvis is founding editor of the *International Journal for Lifelong Education* and editor of two book series on adult education. He is a frequent speaker and lecturer on adult and continuing education in many parts of the world. Jarvis is currently working on a book about the state and the education of adults and editing two books—one on adult education in Europe and another on theological parallels to adult education theories.

Paradoxes
of
Learning

PART ONE

 The Development
of the Social Self

1

The Nature
of Human Learning

Learning is a subject worthy of study, not merely because by understanding it people can be encouraged to learn more effectively, but because it lies at the foundation of all human being. To study learning is, therefore, to study people — not people isolated in laboratories or in artificial situations, like classrooms, but people in time, space, and society. This task has preoccupied mythmakers and scholars from the time of Plato or even earlier, and so any individual study can only cast a little more light on this complex and important subject.

Such fundamental approaches to the study of learning have lost ground in recent years as the technology of learning, especially through behaviorism, has become more prevalent. Yet there have been signs that the basic questions of humankind are attracting renewed attention. Some writers have begun to emphasize a variety of humanistic concerns (Habermas, 1984) and even the humanistic and experiential nature of human learning itself (Kolb, 1984). In addition, they have also begun to recognize that professional practice is not the mindless application of knowledge acquired in the classroom but the use of a knowledge reflected on during the experience of professional work to learn more and to practice more effectively (Schön, 1983).

There has also been an increasing emphasis on training, which in some ways is the antithesis of the approach just described. Hence a fundamental paradox may be seen at the outset: learning is an individualistic enterprise, but society is organizational; therefore, learning also has to relate to the social nature of contemporary society. This book seeks to contribute to the discussion of these issues. The research it rests on comes not from the laboratory but from a consideration of the paradoxes of human, social living. Most studies of learning have been written from a psychological perspective. But this book has both philosophical and sociological orientations — with some psychological references — although it has been written from an adult education perspective. In approaching learning from a different perspective, it attempts to raise new and different questions. It *must* raise questions, since one of its main arguments is that learning begins with a fundamental disjuncture between individual biography and the socially constructed experience. This disjuncture leads people to ask questions and thus sets the learning process in motion. Yet the process of questioning is itself a paradox for an uncertain humankind in continual search of certainty (Jarvis, 1989).

The study is formulated within the framework of paradox, since the idea of self-contradictoriness in human existence is crucial: in life, there is death; in joy, sorrow; in freedom, a fear of freedom; in constraint, frustration; and so on. Indeed, the fact that individuals live in society causes some contradictions, because to enjoy their individuality, they need to be free of the constraints that relationships with others impose. But learning can be either conformist or creative, and so this also leads to paradoxical situations. Individuals can learn from the experience of life or learn to take life's experiences for granted. Learning, then, is not straightforward but complex and even contradictory.

One of the greatest of all paradoxes about learning, and perhaps one of the major reasons it has not been studied as extensively as, for instance, knowledge and behavior have been, is that it is taken for granted as an ordinary part of the process of human living. For instance, in a research project in the United

Kingdom examining why people do not participate in adult education, this point was brought out when a researcher noted that "the question on outcomes really flummoxed them because of the use of the word 'learning.' They didn't equate what they were doing with learning. I explored this in some detail with the writers' and photographers' groups, to find out why they found the word 'learning' so difficult. While they don't appear to view what they do as a hobby or practical activity, they wouldn't apply the word 'learning' or even 'education' to it either, because of the formal implications of those words" (McGiveny, 1990, p. 59).

Learning, then, is either part of the formal educational structure or is lost in the process of everyday life in informal and incidental experiences (Marsick and Watkins, 1990). The former has been studied extensively, but the latter aspect is also important. Though informal learning has often been explored, it has been treated under different names, such as *socialization*. Any study of learning *per se* must somehow focus on the human being in social living, which requires an interdisciplinary perspective.

But before this exploration can begin, it is perhaps worth looking back on some of the earlier thinkers in this area and trying to discover their understanding of human learning. Thus we start with a short historical excursus. This is followed by a discussion of the idea of learning throughout life. The chapter concludes with a section that locates experience and the human condition in a social framework.

Learning: Some Historical Perspectives

This section is included to demonstrate some of the problems that scholars in the past have tackled when they have considered the topic of learning. It also points the way to the analysis that follows: by touching on Plato's *Meno*, the story of the Garden of Eden, and the writings of Locke, it highlights some of the fundamental questions explored in this study. These sources are diverse, but they have been chosen to illustrate different aspects of this inquiry.

Plato asked questions about the nature of knowledge in his discussion with Meno, especially knowledge that was internalized and that enabled people to reflect and to question. But where did that knowledge come from? How did people seem to have the ability to reflect? For Plato, this remarkable human capacity existed because human beings carried over knowledge from a previous life. Therefore, learning was a matter of reminiscence — reflecting with the aid of knowledge that had been embedded in the soul from a previous existence, as Socrates is reported to have expounded:

> Thus the soul, since it is immortal and has been born many times, and has seen all things both here and in the other world, has learned everything that is. So we need not be surprised if it can recall the knowledge of virtue or anything else which, as we see, it once possessed. All nature is akin, and the soul has learned everything, so that when a man has recalled a single piece of knowledge — *learned* it, in ordinary language — there is not reason why he should not find out the rest, if he keeps a stout heart and does not grow weary of the search; for seeking and learning are in fact nothing but recollection [Plato, (fourth century B.C.) 1956, pp. 129–130; original italics].

Clearly this approach answers some of the fundamental questions that Plato might have posed but leaves others unanswered. It also rests on two controversial concepts: reincarnation and a mind-body dualism. While today many individuals in Western society may not be able to accept the idea of reincarnation, many peoples in other parts of the world take it for granted. Dualism — the idea that knowledge resides in a soul that is distinct from the body — is also problematic. We will return to this subject in Chapter Three in considering the development of mind and self. Our approach will be that these phenomena emerge from the body but are not distinct from it. This is in agreement with Ryle (1963), who addresses this problem most directly.

Those who composed the creation story in Genesis battled with a different set of questions. They took it for granted that animals lived in harmony with nature and apparently had little need to learn. But what made human beings different? For Adam and Eve were originally naked, innocent, and — like the animals — living in harmony with nature. But the myth goes on to say that they were free to eat from all the trees in the Garden except the tree of knowledge of good and evil. When they ate from that tree, they gained knowledge and they knew that they were naked. They had learned! Consequently, they were driven out of the Garden. Theologians have called this the Fall, but Archbishop William Temple once commented that if this was a fall, it was a fall upward! Perhaps this is the greatest paradox of all about human learning — the fact that something generally regarded as good has been intimately associated with a myth of the origin evil in the world. But this also points beyond the story to the fact that learning, and perhaps knowledge itself, has significant moral connotations. This is a point that we will return to continually as the study proceeds.

Doing things naturally after birth is part of the problem. When an animal is born it is soon up and about. People marvel at the rapidity with which it leaves its parents' protection and begins to forage for itself. It is not long, only a year or two, before the bird constructs its own nest and the animal its own lair. However, there is a major problem with this apparently idyllic existence. Instinctive behavior enables the animals to live in harmony with nature, but it inhibits them from learning and adapting to it in times of major change. Dinosaurs and many other species of animals and birds failed to cope with events such as climate change and other natural disasters and are now extinct. This does not mean that some animals cannot learn, only that there might be limitations on that learning. It is obvious, as the behaviorist B. F. Skinner has shown, that they can be taught.

What then is meant by instinct? Perhaps learning is a form of instinctive behavior? The concept of instinct is a difficult one to grasp, because there are many different definitions, containing a number of different elements. Reber's *Dictionary of Psychology* (1985, pp. 360–361), for instance, provides four main definitions:

An unlearned response characteristic of the members of a given species

A tendency or disposition to respond in a particular manner that is characteristic of a particular species. . .

A complex, co-ordinated set of acts found universally or nearly so within a given species that emerges under specific stimulus conditions, specific drive conditions, and specific developmental conditions. . .

Any of a number of unlearned, inherited tendencies that are hypothesized to act as motivational forces behind complex human behaviors

Whatever definition is adopted, it may be seen that instincts involve unlearned behavior, and if learning is instinctive, it would then create a nice paradox about learning itself being an unlearned human process. The idea that learning is instinctive is problematic for another reason: the first three definitions treat instincts within the context of species-specific patterns of behavior. But it would be difficult to claim with any certainty that learning is a species-specific form of behavior, especially one that is unlearned. Indeed, it would be difficult even to claim that learning is a pattern of behavior in precisely the same way that a bird's nest-building activity is a behavioral pattern, although it is one of behavior's constituent elements. Consequently, it would appear unwise to claim that learning is instinctive behavior. Instead, a clue to its origins might be discovered in the third and fourth definitions. Human beings possess drives and tendencies that are unlearned, and some of these may act as motivational forces underlying complex human activities like learning.

But more significantly, it is difficult to find any species-specific behavioral patterns in human beings. Unlike young animals, human babies do not soon leave their parents and undertake complex behaviors. They remain dependent on their parents for a considerable period of time — longer than any other animal baby. This is a fundamental difference between humankind and other animals. Humankind has reduced instinctive behavior to a minimum and in so doing has, to some extent, departed from the world of nature. Is this not one meaning of the mythological story of the Garden of Eden in the Old Testament?

The ancients, then, wrestled with this problem and enshrined their understanding of it in a beautiful story about learning in a garden of paradise. The paradise myth raises key questions that this investigation is concerned with. Specifically, the process of evolution entails a paradox. Instincts have had to decline for learning to emerge. Human beings have appeared with minimal instincts but with bodily drives and tendencies — and a brain — to propel them to perform complex sets of behaviors. Humankind has to live in a seemingly alien environment and has to learn how to cope with the problems of knowing about good and evil. Learning, then, is one of our most fundamental needs. Surprisingly, however, Maslow (1968) omits it from his hierarchy of human needs, as I have pointed out (Jarvis, 1983a).

Human beings have to learn through the experience of living. In *An Essay Concerning Understanding* ([1690] 1977), Locke argues that human beings are born as tabula rasa — just the opposite of what Plato contends — and acquire knowledge only later. For Locke, all learning derives from experience. Nowadays, some people might object to the idea of a tabula rasa; for instance, they might argue that genetic inheritance plays a role and also that babies do have experiences in their mothers' wombs. Even so, these points do not negate the fundamental idea that most learning begins with postbirth experience. This is something with which many later writers have also agreed; these include John Dewey (1916, 1938, and so on) and even more recent authors such as Kolb (1984).

From the idea of reincarnation, to the Fall, to the tabula rasa at birth — all of these beliefs about the nature of humankind have contained in them implicit assumptions about human learning, indeed about human being, and it is within this larger tradition that this book explores the subject of learning.

Learning Throughout Life

Lifelong learning is a term fraught with difficulties. Peterson (1983, p. 5) suggests that "lifelong learning is a conceptual framework for conceiving, planning, implementing, and co-ordinating activities designed to facilitate learning by all Americans throughout their lifetimes." On the surface, this definition seems both idealistic and feasible, albeit rather nationalistic. But like many other definitions, it entails a conceptual fallacy. This definition is not about learning, it is about lifelong education — about the provision of opportunities for Americans to learn throughout their lifetime. That is, it equates learning with education. Similar conceptual problems are to be found in other texts that purport to discuss lifelong learning. In *Learning to Be* (1972) that justifiably acclaimed report by Edgar Faure, the subject of nearly every section is education rather than learning. This report makes the point that the educational system should be reformed, so that it can provide a multitude of opportunities for individuals to learn. Obviously this is a laudable aim, and the emphasis of the report should be applauded. However, Faure and the other contributors would not deny that people 'learn to be' as a result of all their learning throughout life, not just learning that occurs within educational institutions. Other exponents of lifelong education also tend to limit learning to education. Lengrand (1986, p. 13), for instance, suggests that lifelong learning is "a very dynamic conception of education."

The point being made in this chapter is that however idealistic and commendable this picture of lifelong education is, it remains a limitation on the conception of learning itself. Learning is wider than education; education is only one social institution in which learning occurs, albeit the only one specifically directed toward it. Indeed, the reduction of human learning to the social institution of education is one of the typical features of the modern era. But all the social institutions together cannot contain learning, since learning is fundamental to human being and to life itself. These institutions exist only to facilitate the smooth functioning of the social system, and so they may often constrain learning. Without them, though, there would be a lot less opportunity for human learning and development; this is part of the paradox of being human. The distinction between human beings and the social system is quite fundamental to much of the ensuing discussion, and for the purposes of the remainder of this section, the emphasis is on learning throughout life and not on education.

But what is meant by life? No deep theological or metaphysical answer will be expounded here, although many underlying questions will be implicit in much of what follows. We will conceptualize human life as being within time, space, society, and relationship; it is within this framework that learning occurs. Life is about human experience, and without experience, there would be no human being. Learning, then, must in some way begin with that experience. But learning is not the same as living, since it is possible to think of situations in life when the consciousness of experiencing might be curtailed so that the potential for learning could be decreased. These situations include being asleep or unconscious or even being so preoccupied with an activity as to barely be aware of one's environment. In all these instances, learning might be minimalized.

It is assumed here that most learning occurs as a result of conscious experience, although this does not preclude the possibility that some events occurring at the periphery of experience and awareness are somehow internalized (Jarvis, 1987). Learning, then, is of the essence of everyday living and of conscious experience; it is the process of transforming that experience into knowledge, skills, attitudes, values, and beliefs. It is about the continuing process of making sense of everyday experience — and experience happens at the intersection of a conscious human life with time, space, society, and relationship. Learning is, therefore, a process of giving meaning to, or seeking to understand, life experiences. But it is more than merely reacting to these experiences, for often it is proactive, seeking to create experiences and to discover from them new knowledge, skills, attitudes, and so on.

Life is a temporal phenomenon, and so time becomes a factor in any understanding of human learning. As long as people's store of knowledge and skills gained from previous experiences is sufficient to cope with new experiences, life seems to go on in an unbroken and almost unthinking manner. People are often unaware of the passing of time. But when the situation is new, when the biographical store of knowledge is insufficient to respond to a new experience, then it is almost as if time stops. It is a "now" or a "then" — because the experience can be located within the flow of time. It is encapsulated within its boundaries. The experience is thought about, considered, experimented on, and so on, until a solution is found to enable daily living to continue. If the solution is successful and life is allowed to continue in a similar manner, then the way that that experience was dealt with — that is, what has been learned — is incorporated in the biographical store of knowledge. Memories of such situations enable people to deal with similar ones in the future in an almost unthinking manner. This brings out a profound paradox of human learning. People learn from an experience not only so that they can cope with that situation, but also so that they can respond to similar experiences in a similar manner in the future and not have to think about, or to learn from, them.

Time, then, becomes a constituent element in the construction of human biography. Over time, this biographical store of knowledge is built up, and this both affects the way people respond to future experiences and also what they may learn from them. It is clear that for most normal human beings, this process extends throughout the whole of life. Learning is a natural lifelong process, and people learn whether or not educational provision is made for their learning. But unless provision is made for learning, the experiences of everyday living may be restrictive, and learning may be limited to the primary experiences of life.

Everyday life occurs not only in time but in society and relationship. Heller (1984) makes the point that everyday life itself occurs within the structural framework of a society in which people reproduce both themselves and their social system, and yet that social system preceded them and will also continue after their lifetime. Hence there are pressures on individuals to learn unreflectively; at the same time, though, as the human essence emerges, it must be creative, and this leads to situations where reflective learning occurs. This is both part of the tension and part of the paradox of human social existence into which learning must be located. Thus the final section of this chapter is concerned with locating experience more explicitly in the social context.

Human Experience and the Social Context

Human beings have always lived within a social context; rarely, if ever, has the Robinson Crusoe–type existence actually been realized. But even if it were, few people are brought up in total isolation from the wider society. Feral children are extremely rare, if they have ever existed, and little is therefore known of what they might have learned. The great majority of people are born into a society at a specific time in history, and they acquire something of its culture. Even Robinson Crusoe was brought up within a society and had already internalized its culture before he was nearly isolated on his desert island. The reading of any historical diary (for example, Seaver, 1985) reveals how much of the prevailing knowledge, values, and attitudes are internalized by the people of the day.

Studying people from different cultures in the contemporary period also shows how human beings assimilate particular belief systems. It might be claimed that these patterns of cultural behavior are the product of genetic inheritance, but there is little evidence to suggest that complete cultural systems are transmitted this way. If they were, there would be little room for individuality and individual autonomy. Hence, it is maintained here that these cultural manifestations are learned, learned from the experiences of being brought up within different social frameworks. Mannheim (1936, p. 3) claims that "every individual is . . . in a two-fold sense predetermined by the fact of growing up in society: on the one hand he finds a ready-made solution and on the other he finds in that solution performed patterns of thought and of conduct."

People, then, live in societies, and they experience the patterns and routines of these societies. It is only through reproducing such patterns that societies can achieve stability and maintain continuity. Living in societies means having experiences of people, events, and places in time and space. Through these social experiences, people grow and develop (Jarvis, 1987). But while there is tremendous similarity between people of the same time period and culture, everybody's experiences are still unique to themselves, so that individual differences are also possible. The more open and complex the society as a result of the division of labor, among other things, the greater the likelihood that individuality will be manifest. Indeed, individualism did not appear early in the development of human thought and, with a few exceptions, really came to prominence only after the Reformation, the Industrial Revolution, and the ensuing growth in the division of labor in society. Even so, the actual process of learning has to be an individual one, although the context within which it occurs has always been social (Jarvis, 1987). In short, there is both commonality and difference between people of the same society. Though people are aware of their individual selves and their own unique biography, they may be less aware of those aspects of culture that make them similar to each other, because they take these for granted.

Through the process of internalizing the cultures that envelop them, individuals have become the people they are. One of the paradoxes of studying learning is that so many scholars who have tried to understand it have isolated their subjects from the social world, rather than seeking to understand the social process of learning that has made them what they are. This social process has two dimensions. There is direct experience that occurs through action and is experienced through the senses; this will be called *primary experience.* There is also a mediated or indirect form of experience that comes through communicative action; I will refer to this as *secondary experience.* Primary experience is practical, whereas secondary experience may be more theoretical. However, secondary experience can rarely occur without primary experience as well. It occurs when people interact and communicate information and ideas to each other through language and other modes of communication.

People are, to some extent, the sum total of their previous experiences. They bring their biographies to every new experience. Every time they have an experience, they use their store of knowledge to interpret that experience and, where necessary, to transform it into some new knowledge, skill, or attitude that helps them grow. This is a social phenomenon, as we have seen. Social human beings have experiences in social contexts, and this lies at the start of their learning.

All learning, then — not merely experiential learning —

begins with experience, both primary and secondary. But this is not experience for which the learners already have a solution or response, even though such solutions may exist in their society. Learning begins with experiences for which they have no preset responses. These individuals, with all their memories of previous experiences and their store of knowledge, are unable to respond to a specific situation in an unthinking manner. There is a disjuncture at a particular point in time between people's biographies — that is, their internalized cultural patterns of social living — and their experience, whether it be of a specific social situation or of new information in secondary experience. The continuous flow of time is interrupted and the moment becomes a "now" and then a "then": for the time being, the experience is recalled in the memory as a discrete event. At this point of disjuncture, individuals are forced to ask why this has occurred to them or what it means. These questions are located at the start and at the core of human learning. Only when they have made a response to the disjuncture, either through learning or by acknowledging that they cannot or do not wish to learn from the situation, can people again try to live in harmony with their culture.

It is important to note, though, that this is very different from the harmony that prevailed in the Garden of Eden, because culture is not a natural phenomenon. Until the Industrial Revolution and the French Revolution, it was generally thought that the social world was a divine creation, and so people could attribute wealth and poverty, power and powerlessness, and so on to the will of God or the gods. But after these two revolutions, the belief in a divine order was undermined and human beings themselves came to be seen as creating the social order. From this point of view, living in harmony with society means living in harmony not with a natural, or a divine, but with a human social construct. (Living in such harmony is not always ideal, though, as Freud's studies of the unconscious demonstrate. We will return to this problem later.)

The preceding remarks show why, in the study of human learning, we need to understand the social processes through which culture emerges; this helps us grasp how the disjuncture between existing patterns of social behavior and individual biography emerges. We should also recognize that human beings are complex animals, controlled in part by the unconscious, so that responses to that disjuncture do not have to be rational or obvious. Learning is not a simple or even necessarily a single process. It begins not with one but with two totally different forms of experience: primary experience, which relates to direct sense experience, and secondary experience, which is mediated and often linguistic.

Conclusion

This chapter began with certain philosophical questions and concluded with sociological and psychological ones. We have seen that learning is crucial to the process that links individual biography to the sociocultural world. The paradoxes of human learning revolve around the problems touched on in this chapter. To explore these problems further, it is necessary to shed further light on human learning and its social context. This is the task of the next three chapters. We begin with the process of becoming human in a social world.

2

The Paradox
of Living and Learning
in Society

The process of learning is located at the interface of people's biography and the sociocultural milieu in which they live, for it is at this intersection that experiences occur. It is important to understand the way human beings acquire that culture, and so this chapter examines the sociological process of becoming a human being.

When children are born, they are born into a society whose culture preceded them and will almost certainly continue after their lives are over. Culture, therefore, appears to be objective and external. But the children have inherited no, or minimal, instincts to help them live within society and conform to its culture; thus they have to acquire that culture. In the first instance, then, learning is a matter of internalizing and transforming something that is apparently objective to the individual. This learning always occurs within the complexities and paradoxes of social living, so that those research projects that have sought to relate it to animal learning or that have isolated people from their social situation in order to understand it have necessarily oversimplified the reality of their topic. This has been the case with some psychological approaches, such as behaviorism, although its results have been widely accepted in education —

especially in adult and continuing education. However, scholars in other disciplines, such as anthropology, sociology, and philosophy, have also tried to understand human learning and thinking, and their findings are as relevant to education as are those from psychology.

The purpose of this chapter is to locate learning within the social context. It first examines the process of internalization of objectified culture, then discusses the externalization of knowledge, and finally raises the question of legitimation — that is, the way truth value is assigned to knowledge.

Internalization

> Society is a dialectic phenomenon in that it is a human product, and nothing but a human product, that yet continuously acts back upon its producer. Society is a product of man. It has no other being except that which is bestowed upon it by human activity and consciousness. There can be no social reality apart from man. Yet it may be also stated that man is the product of society. Every individual biography is an episode within the history of society, which both precedes and survives it. Society was there before the individual was born and it will be there after he has died. What is more, it is within society, and as a result of the social processes, that the individual becomes a person, that he attains and holds on to an identity, and that he carries out the various projects that constitute his life. Man cannot exist apart from society. The two statements, that society is the product of man and that man is the product of society, are not contradictory [Berger, 1969, p. 3].

In this apparently self-contradictory situation, human beings are both taught and learn, conform and innovate, accept and rebel. It is a world of love and power, of cruelty and concern, of altruism and selfishness. It is a complex and paradoxical world, full of contingencies and often incapable of prediction; yet without patterns and predictability, there can be no society and no social living. This inherent dichotomy is the paradox of social existence. How can human beings be both the producers and the products of the social reality? How can there be no society without people and yet no human beings without society? In an earlier book (Jarvis, 1983a), I discussed these topics in considerable detail. I return to some of that discussion here, although this analysis takes a different and greatly extended form.

At birth, people are subject to the biological drives that sustain their physical entity as well as to the influences of their particular genetic heritage. They are human, but they do not exhibit the characteristics of fully fledged social human beings yet. They have no innate culture.

Every society has its own culture — that is, its own language, knowledge, skills, values, and beliefs. Culture is the sum total of all of these elements that make social living possible. These elements appear to be common to all the members of a social group, and this commonality helps to give it the appearance of external and unchanging objectivity. Yet it is not a thing — an empirical object. Nobody can cut out a piece of culture and hand it over to another person. It only has the appearance of objectivity. Throughout this study, therefore, culture is referred to as *objectified* rather than *objective*.

To take their place in society, children have to acquire this culture through socialization. They do this initially by copying the patterns of behavior of the significant others with whom they interact: parents, parent substitutes, and siblings. Children, like adults, often internalize the patterns of behavior they experience. Sometimes these patterns become so ingrained that they take them for granted, and then people appear to behave instinctively. This is how their worldview is formed. Figure 2.1 depicts the process of internalization, although it omits any consideration of time. (While only one semicircle is shown here, others could also have been included to indicate that people live and move in a variety of different subcultures simultaneously.)

The socialization process is often intended to produce conformity. Hence, the arrows in Figure 2.1 all converge on the

Figure 2.1. The Process of Internalization.

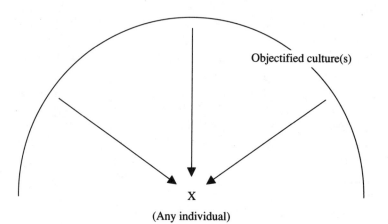

Objectified culture(s)

X

(Any individual)

individual. For some sociologists, this aspect of the process is predominant. This viewpoint is perhaps most common among those—such as Durkheim, Parsons, and others—whose perspective on society is holistic. Indeed, the functionalist approach to understanding individuals was very prevalent in sociology for a number of years immediately after World War II. People tended to be seen as a reflection of their culture and the self as a mirror image of the social forces that created it. Society regarded any form of deviance as a defect in the socialization process. Consequently, it is easy to see how learning becomes regarded as a process of acquiring and internalizing elements from culture. But learning is more than learning to conform.

In 1961, Dennis Wrong (1976) highlighted an error in this approach in his now-famous paper on oversocialization. Wrong pointed out that sociologists failed to take Freud into account when they thought of people as mere products of the social forces that acted on them. Nowadays, it could also be claimed that they neglected the significance of genetic inheritance. Harré (1979, pp. 10–18) provides an excellent sociobiological discussion of the socialization process. He notes that social life is maintained by ritual and convention — that is, by learned cultural patterns — rather than by biological processes. Nevertheless, some human behavior does have a genetic basis. He might also have emphasized the significance of language in the socialization process.

In some technologically simple societies, culture does appear to be rather monolithic and unchanging, so that anthropologists have been able to utilize a functionalist perspective to provide valuable insight. In these societies, people tend to learn and internalize their culture in a conformist manner, since the diversity that comes with pluralist cultures is absent. But with the introduction of more advanced technology, a division of labor emerges that begins to foster cultural differentiation. The development of the mass media, a high level of migration, the presence of political refugees, growing social mobility, and other factors have all contributed to the differentiation of national cultures. As a result, the functionalist approach has become less useful and has been discredited to a certain extent, although aspects of Parsons's thinking are beginning to reappear in the work of Habermas (1987) and others.

Highly differentiated industrial societies are characterized both by a common overall culture and by many forms of pluralism. There are enough similarities that citizens can be recognized as British or American or whatever, but in addition, differences exist that enable them to be seen as North Country British, Southern American, and so on. Geography is not the only relevant variable; children are also socialized differently depending on their gender and ethnic group, so that as adults, they are likely to have the attitudes and customs appropriate to those groups. The same is true with respect to social class. Bourdieu (1973) points out that there are certain inequalities in what children internalize. He (1973, p. 73) writes that "the statistics of theatre, concert, and, above all, museum attendance . . . are sufficient reminder that the inheritances of cultural wealth which has been accumulated and bequested by previous generations only really belongs . . . to those endowed with the means of appropriating it for themselves." He argues that people acquire "cultural capital" that is unequally distributed through the social system, with those in the upper echelons of society having more of it. All human beings' worldviews are formed through this process. It teaches them who they are, their place within the social structure, and some of their own behavioral patterns.

Children, then, are socialized into an objectified subculture that is bound to contain a variety of different perspectives. They learn behavioral patterns that reflect their social group or groups. But over time, they also mix with people from other subcultures, so that they are exposed to alternative interpretations of social reality. Being presented with alternatives means being free to make choices. Some of these choices will almost certainly reflect the initial socialization process, but others might originate elsewhere and could result in the children's differing from their parents and the other significant persons in the primary socialization process. Out of this synthesis of influences, the children's individuality emerges.

Individuality may be regarded in part as a product of modernity; thus, it is hardly surprising that ideologies of individualism have flourished at least since the Industrial Revolution. But one of the problems of this form of analysis is that culture might be regarded as simply being the result of contingencies that have no significant reason or purpose. This is a subject frequently discussed by modern philosophers, including Rorty (1989).

One of the paradoxes of human development is that as children mature, they are no longer merely the recipients of external pressures. Another process can also be detected: that of externalization. Habermas (1976, p. 9) claims that socialization processes "shape the members of the system into subjects capable of speaking and action." This is what is meant by externalization, which is the subject of the next section.

Externalization

At first, children tend to imitate the behavior they observe in and experience from interaction with their significant others — repetitive behavior. However, there comes a time when they begin to think for themselves, ask questions, and generally experiment. From Piaget (1929) onward, child psychologists have plotted this developmental progression. Children gradually become more independent; they usually develop a mind of their own and then process the external cultural stimuli and respond to them in a variety of ways. In this manner, the process of externalization begins. According to Heller (1984, p. 123), externalization has three dimensions; the first is bound up with implements and things, the second is embodied in systems of habit and custom, and the third involves language. Later in this chapter, I will show how the latter two dimensions are controlled in the legitimation process.

Individuals begin to act back on the social world that has formed them. Their actions, however, take specific forms and it is here that the first clue to the paradox of society can be found. Consider two people meeting for the first time. As they interact with each other, they gradually develop a mutual understanding that facilitates their interaction. When they meet a second time, their mode of interaction does not have to be completely rethought; both people share the general expectation that the norms that emerged during the first interaction will still be valid the second time around. At the third interaction, these norms appear to be even more fixed. Since the procedures of interaction have become accepted, the interaction occurs with an economy of effort. This is the process of habitualization, where a practice that has been found to be successful is again utilized in similar situations, until it is discovered to be no longer useful. This process occurs in most human action, whether it is proactive or interactive.

Habitualization helps make it possible to construct institutionalized norms and values, which lie at the heart of social living. If the two persons just mentioned, whose interaction processes have become fairly well worked out and agreed on, introduce another person into their group, they will probably expect that person to learn the norms they have already created. The norms appear to be almost objective to the newcomer, who will have to internalize them. The habitual behavior has thus become institutionalized. Berger and Luckmann (1966, p. 72) suggest that institutionalization occurs "whenever there is a reciprocal typification of habitualized actions by types of actors." In other words, whenever people in a similar position in society act in a similar manner in similar situations, institutionalization has taken place. This process is essential to social continuity. Comprehending it is crucial both to understanding the paradox of social living and also to understanding the paradoxes of human learning.

Social institutions, and the moral imperatives that accompany their formation, are the glue that holds society together; they are the vital essence of social living. Crucially, they also appear to be objective and unchanging, but they are not external objects that remain static throughout time. They are internal, they have been learned, and they help constitute the human person who acts in the social situation. They are not externalized in precisely the way that they are internalized, for as people develop, as was demonstrated above, they change and become individuals. Many stimuli are transformed in the transition from internalization to externalization in response to the changing circumstances of social existence. Thus the process depicted in Figure 2.1 may now be illustrated somewhat differently. In Figure 2.2, arrows point away from the individual toward the objectified culture, but the procedure has changed slightly (as the dotted line shows) as a result of the social processes of life itself. It is these changed processes that are transmitted to individuals in the next generation, so that the dimension of time must be included in this discussion. (As in Figure 2.1, each semicircle represents a variety of different intermeshing subcultures.)

Figure 2.2 illustrates the fact that if "individuals are to reproduce society, they must reproduce themselves as individuals" (Heller, 1984, p. 3). Yet the reproduction is not a perfect replica; rather, it is a slightly changed individual and a slightly different society with the passing of time. This diagram thus depicts one of the paradoxes of social living: that there are forces that engender conformity, but because human beings do not have instincts but learn, change is inevitable. The paradox is actually even more profound, because learning is both at the heart of all social conformity and also at the heart of all social change. Without the ability to learn, there would be no society and no humanity. But, paradoxically, it is learning that also helps generate some forms of change.

Figure 2.2. The Processes of Internalization and Externalization.

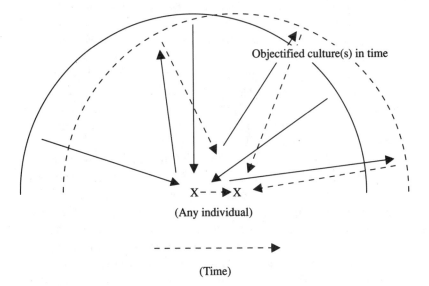

Since the propensity to conform is strong, social change is rarely revolutionary; it is most often evolutionary — slow and gradual. Social revolutions do occur, though only rarely, despite the frequency with which they are discussed. Since society rarely changes unrecognizably over a short period of time, people usually feel comfortable in the world they know. Yet when change does occur, either drastically or minimally, most people manage to adjust to it. Hence people are continually being recreated. But again, one of the paradoxes of learning becomes apparent: without learning, little or no change could take place; when change does occur, learning has to follow, so that other people can adapt to the new situation.

A significant point about habitualization and institutionalization is that, because change is often slow, the culture of a social group may appear to be unchanging and objective. The group's established patterns are maintained through socialization. But it might be asked why certain patterns have emerged in one society and not in another, and why these patterns are retained, despite the fact that they do not always appear to be beneficial to all of society's members.

This question suggests that these cultural norms have not merely arisen because they have gained general assent. They have emerged because certain groups have fostered their development and continued to maintain them, often to their own benefit. In society at large, those norms may have been established by the few rather than the many, in other words. Culture is not value free. It is generally accepted that the culture of a society favors its citizens, rather than those who migrate to it. Yet it is harder for those who are its citizens to recognize that the same process works in favor of those who exercise power in that society rather than to the benefit of all. Perhaps inequality is something that should be expected, since resources are scarce and are usually insufficient to meet everyone's needs. Hence, it may be seen that this objectified culture contains values, biases, and even knowledge that favor the few rather than the many.

Marx recognizes the significance of the process just described for knowledge and ideas. According to Marx and Engels ([1846] 1970, p. 64),

> The ideas of the ruling class are in every epoch the ruling ideas, i.e. the class which is the ruling *material* force of society, is at the time its ruling *intellectual* force. The class which has the means of material production at its disposal, has control at the same time over the means of mental production, so that thereby, generally speaking, the ideas of those who lack the means of mental production are subject to it. The ruling ideas are nothing more than the ideal expression of the dominant material relationships, the dominant material relationships grasped as ideas; hence of the relationships which make the one class the ruling one, therefore, the ideas of its dominance. The individuals composing the ruling classes possess among other things consciousness, and therefore think. Insofar, therefore, as they rule as a class and determine the ex-

tent and compass of an epoch, it is self-evident that
they do this in its whole range, hence among other
things rule also as thinkers, as producers of ideas,
and regulate the production and distribution of the
ideas of their age: thus their ideas are the ruling
ideas of the epoch.

The Marxist interpretation is not accepted here in its to-
tality since its model of society seems simplistic. From a Marxist
standpoint, society appears monolithic and a simple two-class
system prevails, with power being in the hands of the bourgeoisie. But while society may have a ruling class at one level,
it is also pluralistic at another, with different groups having their
own subcultures, their own varieties of language, and so on.
Each group may also have its dominant elite, so that there may
be factions within the bourgeoisie itself. Hence, the processes
of control are complex. However, in all situations, elites appear to encourage a great deal of repetitive behavior and the
accompanying nonreflective learning among the lower groups,
while they themselves are freer to indulge in more experimental behavior and the accompanying reflective forms of learning. This, then, is the process of creating cultural conformity
when individuals still feel that they are free. And so why, it might
be asked, is this not more widely recognized? Because another
process operates — that of legitimation.

Legitimation

Legitimation is the process of making things appear as if they
are natural and right; it is different from legislation, which means
making actions right in law. Legitimation requires social processes that give actions, beliefs, behavior, and so on the appearance that they are the right things to do, to say, and to think.
In other words, the presumptive behavior becomes viewed as
the only correct way to behave in a specific situation. These behavioral patterns then become external structures and constraints
on other people's social behavior. Many externalized aspects of
culture perform this function; a few are chosen here as examples.

To begin with, language — the mediator of much second-ary experience through which a great deal of learning occurs — plays a crucial role in the legitimation process. Language is not merely an arbitrary symbol representing some phenomenon, it is the major mode of communication. Once a phenomenon is captured by a word, it takes the form of a thing. A word sym-bolizes an apparent external reality, so that when children learn words, they seek, in the first instance, to equate them with ex-ternal things or beings. This is in part what Piaget means when he discusses the idea of concrete thinking: words symbolize ac-tual things, people, procedures, and so on. Adults also have a tendency to treat language in this concrete and repetitive man-ner. This is called reification — treating an abstract concept as if it is a concrete thing that is objective and unchangeable.

Language also contributes to the habitualization process in another conformist way. For instance, in discussing how they have learned to interact with each other, the two people described earlier might first say, "This is the way we do it," but after a while when introducing the new member to their group, they might say, "This is the way it's done." On the surface there ap-pears little difference, but to the listeners, the difference is sig-nificant. In the first case, the procedure seems to be subjective and changeable, so that it is open to personal interpretation. In the second case, though, the implication is that the proce-dure is objective and unchanging. The language now transmits a sense of authority, creating the impression that there is only one correct way to do things.

The existing members of the group do not want to change their behavior; the second approach allows them to maintain their economy of effort and to continue to act in a mechanical and presumptive manner. The process of objectification has oc-curred, and by making a social process appear objective, their own habitualized processes have been legitimated. Convention demands conformity by the new member. (This is one of the points Harré, 1979, made when critically assessing the contri-bution of sociobiology to an understanding of social living.) Con-sequently, we can see that language is not neutral; it tends to favor those who can use it to their own ends, but because it ap-pears neutral, it functions to legitimate their position.

Words alone are not sufficient to ensure that the social processes are always legitimated. Sometimes apparently stronger forces have to be employed; religion has frequently served this function (O'Dea, 1966). Why is one person born rich and another poor? Because, in the words of the hymn, God ordered "all their estate" — in other words, it is the will of God. Or why is one person born an untouchable and another a Brahmin? Because in a former life, one lived an evil life and the other a good life. And so on. Social inequities are legitimated by religious claims. Theology helps to guarantee that the privileged class retains its privilege, although this is not necessarily the intention of the theologians themselves. Religious precepts become embodied in a culture, and many people learn them uncritically. Theologies, therefore, reinforce the worldviews that give meaning to a socially constructed world, and in so doing, they provide an interpretation of the social world and legitimate it. However, the paradox is continued, since religion has also institutionalized and legitimated the function of the prophet, which is to denounce the present social structures and to announce a new age with new structures.

Like religious rituals, civil and occupational practices also play an important role in reinforcing social patterns. Elections, the installation of high-ranking officials, and the bestowal of honors on people of good standing may all serve the same function. For instance, it might be claimed that an election gives people the sense that they live in a democratic society, but usually all they do is to select the one others have chosen to exercise power overtly over them! Significantly, like religious rituals, these civic rituals purport to have other purposes, and they do, but they have a covert function of legitimating the status quo, or at least of helping to introduce change gradually. Above all, however, they suggest that the social structures are external and objective and they provide legitimacy for them, thus bringing pressure to bear on individuals to conform to them.

According to Althusser (1972), it is not only religion and politics that serve this function; institutions such as the family, education, law, the media, culture, and the labor unions may do so as well. While Althusser is concerned with society as a whole, we can also apply his argument to subgroups in society.

Within every social sector, these institutions transmit the accepted construction of social reality and reinforce the existing values and practices. Significantly for educators, Althusser argues that religion used to be the main agency of legitimation, but that now it is education. This is a claim that educators need to consider seriously. After all, a great deal of discussion about the need to generate critical thinking exists (Brookfield, 1987), but this is only rhetoric if the outcome of learning is always legitimation of the present. Hence, the place of education in this process has to be carefully examined and the political and ethical functions of education more thoroughly understood. It is within this situation that learning in education must be located.

The great majority of these processes function simultaneously, so that there is a mutual reinforcement of the objectified subculture. The pressures of social living function to make people view reality in a certain manner and then to ensure that they conform to it. But, paradoxically, their viewpoint has itself been learned, and they learn to conform to what they have learned. Most individuals have accepted this need to conform, acting presumptively within the social situation and merely monitoring their behavior; however, history is full of examples of "deviants" who have been persecuted because they did not, or would not, accept the prevailing norms. They have been condemned as witches, labeled insane, harassed as communists, and so on.

Thus far, the analysis suggests that those in power are reactive, insofar as they adopt the structures that are most beneficial to them and seek their legitimation. But they might be much more proactive than this; they might try to construct a society in which the processes and structures favor their position and then utilize the existing apparatuses of the state to legitimate it. In this way, they would try to persuade the people that these are the natural processes of society, or that "there is no other way" to achieve ends that are beneficial to everyone. Cohen (1975) refers to this as the management of myths—that is, of ideologies—and he highlights two distinctively different approaches, both of which fit into the above form of analysis. The first, which he calls cultural extension, occurs when the established groups seek to convince the people that they are merely extending widely accepted cultural traditions. The second, termed *cultural substitution,* occurs when the group seeking support purveys the myth of the need for new cultural practices to be introduced and learned.

Thus, we can see that a number of processes operate simultaneously in the creation of social reality. People create and habitualize their actions, and these actions then assume the appearance of objective reality. Other people tend to accept the objectivity of the culture into which they are socialized. But that objectified culture is not value free, nor does it operate in a neutral manner. It always tends to favor those who already exercise power within it, whether they are merely the existing members of a group or whether they are the power elite of society. This is why Marx speaks of a false class consciousness, and why other theorists, too, regard consciousness as something that is false and from which people have to be emancipated (Habermas, 1972; Freire, 1972b).

This may be too extreme a position. After all, the idea of falseness seems to imply the existence of a consciousness that is not false and therefore that is true. Such an implication is inconsistent with the point made earlier about the arbitrariness or lack of objectivity of culture. However, we also saw earlier that through the division of labor, migration and other forms of mobility, the emergence of the media, and so on, a variety of viewpoints become available from which people may choose. Thus, though culture may still not be neutral, the greater the number of alternative perspectives that are available, the greater the likelihood of intellectual freedom. Hence, people become somewhat free to learn and become creative agents in the social situation and to externalize their own interpretations and meanings, even if they contradict those that seem to be the objective truth with which they were socialized. Of course, pressures toward conformity still exist, so that individuals do not actually innovate often, even though they may feel they are free to act contrary to the prevailing norms if they wish to.

The above remarks have highlighted two interpretive paths. Some students of society emphasize the processes by which society functions — that is, they provide systems analyses — while others stress the power relationships in society, as is the case with Marxist analysis and critical theory. Both approaches illuminate the learning process.

Conclusion

For educators, perhaps the most significant implication of the preceding analysis is that all social processes are learned processes. People learn the objectified language of their culture and even learn to believe that it is value free, and they learn to conform to a wide range of beliefs and practices as if they are objective. They may also learn to feel free, even if they are not actually free of the inhibiting influences of the social structures. They may even grasp the fact that the social phenomena that constrain them are themselves the products of society and can be changed. But often those who exercise power in society find it to their advantage not to allow this change, and so the interests of the few prevail over the interests of the many. The dominant group often succeeds in creating the impression that this situation is just.

In short, learning can never be dissociated from power relationships in the social context. But within this context, individuals also learn to be themselves. This is the subject of the next chapter.

3

Being and the Birth
of the Self

To explore human learning further, we need to think about birth
and early childhood. This is, of course, because the self is not
something with which humans are innately endowed, but something gained — learned — through interaction with others. In the
last chapter, we examined this process from a macro perspective, as we considered how the individual is socialized into the
dominant culture. In this chapter, we apply a micro perspective in focusing on the birth of the self. The two chapters are
integrally related, since it is unrealistic to trace the emergence
of the individual without first having examined the social context of this process.

This chapter begins with the topic of being. In the first
section, we see that existence is changed into human essence
through the process of learning. In the second and third sections, which partly follow Mead's analysis, we concentrate on
how the mind and the self are created through the process of
learning from experience in social interaction. In the final section, we consider the concept of identity. The arguments in this
chapter are similar to those I have developed elsewhere (Jarvis,
1987). However, in the following pages I focus more specifically
on the process of learning than I did in the 1987 book.

Being

Being has occupied the minds of philosophers for centuries. However, we will not explore these profound philosophical debates here; for our purposes, it is enough to highlight a few findings that are significant for the study of human learning.

It can be claimed that at birth, children have being—that is, that they exist—but it would be imprudent to assert that they are full-fledged social beings. There is a significant difference between the concepts of being and existence. A stone might be said to exist, but it would be harder to claim that it has being. In contrast, it might be demonstrated that an insect has being—albeit in a lowly form—as well as existence. Existence, then, would imply some form of occupation of time and space in the world, whereas being would imply life. However, this simple distinction is not universally accepted.

Jaspers, for instance, seeks to relate existence to human life. Existence is, he suggests, "the unreflecting experience of our life in the world" (quoted in Macquarrie, 1973, p. 68). This is an important point, since a great deal of learning involves a nonreflective response to both primary and secondary experience. Jaspers goes on to claim that existence is potential being—that is, that "I do not have myself but come to myself" (in Macquarrie, 1973, p. 173). Ultimately, then, the individual becomes a self through a variety of learning processes in a culturally controlled social reality.

There is an implication in this discussion that existence is not something static, but dynamic. Indeed, Macquarrie (1973, p. 62) makes the point that the word *existence* formerly meant "to stand out" or "to emerge" from nothing. This concept is more closely related to the idea of a living, dynamic phenomenon than to the existence of a stone, for instance. However, the very idea that existence is dynamic immediately makes it difficult to distinguish from the idea of essence. The word *essence* denotes the fundamental characteristics of an object or phenomenon that differentiate it from another object or phenomenon. Thus, the essence of human-ness is what separates us from other species. Macquarrie (1973, p. 71) points out that for Heidegger, the essence of humanity is found in existence, whereas for Sartre, existence precedes essence. The position adopted here more nearly resembles that of Sartre than that of Heidegger: "human-ness" remains a potentiality within existence until it emerges from it as mind. This initially occurs as the result of a nonreflective learning process during the period that sociologists regard as primary socialization; later it happens through a combination of unreflective and reflective learning.

This might seem to be reminiscent of Cartesian dualism, which posits the existence of a separate mind within a physical body—the position that Ryle (1963) attacks as consisting of a "ghost in the machine." But I am proposing something different. Descartes gives primacy to the mind, as if it preceded and perhaps transcends the body. However, I am underscoring the primacy of existence, which is first manifest in the body. Thought processes of all types follow from existence. This implies that there are physical dimensions to learning as Bohm (1987, p. 90) argues: "Modern physics has already shown that matter and energy are two aspects of our reality," so that thought, energy, and matter are intimately connected.

Children are born into the world, they have existence in space and time, and they have life. Fundamentally, they are living human bodies with the potential of being. Through existence, those bodies may develop and eventually become full-fledged human beings. The role of the body in the learning process requires further discussion. Philosophers have perhaps paid less attention to the body than they might have, and theologians have maintained that at birth the baby has a soul as well as a body, and that personhood is constituted by the fusion of body and soul. However, it is not the intention to enter this theological debate here since that is a matter for individual faith, and the concept of the soul is not discussed further here.

The body is an important phenomenon in this discussion but also one which adds complexity to it. To have existence implies that there is a living body and that the body can be responsive to the social forces that act upon it. However, it also implies that individuals not only have bodies but are bodies.

We are both able to receive stimuli from and act on the

world because we have physical existence. But what is the relationship between the physical body and the human being? Heidegger (1962, p. 73) claims that "physical Being has nothing to do with personal Being." In light of the preceding claim that energy and matter are inextricably intertwined, Heidegger's position may be a little sweeping. Others, such as Mead, have explored the process through which body and self or existence and essence become fused in the human being. Mead writes that "the body is not a self, as such; it becomes a self only when it has developed a mind within the context of social experience" (Strauss, 1964, p. 161).

The body is responsive to the social forces that act on it, certainly from the moment of birth, but possibly even earlier, in the womb. The impressions of these encounters are stored in the baby's or child's brain and become a store of memories. The living human body is learning to become a human being. The title of Edgar Faure's (1972) famous UNESCO report on the future of education — *Learning to Be* — takes on new meaning in light of the fact that the body actually has to learn to become human. However, that body is not only the passive recipient of experiences; it soon seeks to initiate them in creative and reflexive action. The human essence is creative, and the results of those acts are also stored in the mind. These memories form the foundation on which the self develops through continual learning.

Mind

According to Mead (1934), mind and self are additions to the body that are acquired through the process of social living; that is, they are both learned phenomena. He believes that the birth of the self occurs only after mind has developed. We will follow the same sequence in our discussion.

At birth, when there is existence without a great deal of human essence, children have human bodies that contain brains but that do not have fully developed minds. As Peters (1965, p. 102) writes, "No man is born with a mind; for the development of mind marks a series of individual and racial achievements. A child is born with an awareness not as yet differentiated into beliefs, wants, and feelings. All specific modes of consciousness, which are internally related to types of objects in the public world, develop *pari passu* with the pointing out of paradigm objects." It is with the development of mind, and thereafter the self, that the essential human characteristics emerge. From the previous chapter, it is clear that children are the recipients of social experiences. Consciousness initially arises in children's reaction to these experiences and later develops through social interaction, since they memorize their perceptions of the experiences. Learning is nonreflective at first, but as the store of memories grows, a basis for reflective learning emerges. Soon children also initiate experiences as experimental and later repetitive acts. Giddens (1979, p. 56) regards this process as the "reflexive monitoring of action," where action is the experience from which learning occurs.

Mead argues that consciousness emerges as a result of social behavior. Indeed, social action is the precondition of consciousness. Hence, small children develop awareness only through the process of social interaction. The nature of this social interaction varies, however, since the social structure in which the interaction occurs may take different forms. Thus, the development of mind can be constrained by social forces.

Mead (Strauss, 1964, p. 162) says that "if . . . you regard the social process of experience as prior (in rudimentary terms) to the existence of mind and explain the origin of minds in terms of interaction among individuals within that process, then . . . the origin of minds . . . ceases to seem mysterious or miraculous. Mind arises through communication by a conversation of gestures in the social process or context of experience." Gesture, according to Mead (Strauss, pp. 157–158), is "that phase of the individual act to which adjustment takes place on the part of other individuals in the social process of behavior." Without gesture or interaction, there could be no mind.

People gain the necessary tools to develop the ability to think through the acquisition of language, though this does not mean that thought and language are synonymous. However, very young children have no language and only a rudimentary way of understanding their primary experience of other people's actions. The fact that human action tends to be repetitive and patterned makes it possible for children to learn nonreflectively the patterns of behavior that occur and the physical rewards that accompany those actions. In addition, children learn to give meaning to those experiences. Hence, both subjective meaning and emotive reaction become associated with certain behavioral patterns. These impressions may be carried in the brain; the beginnings of mind can be found in this store of memories of previous experiences. Memories of others' responses to the actions that people themselves initiate are also retained. Those actions gradually change from being experimental to repetitive to presumptive as people gradually learn what is acceptable and what is not.

Obviously, there is a physiological or neurological basis on which mind develops, and there are certainly bodily drives that interact with the mental processes in specific ways. However, mind is a concept, not a "thing," and no surgeon could undertake an operation on the mind. That happens on the brain. This store of memories in the brain is socially constructed: it is the cultural capital that Bourdieu highlighted, varying from subculture to subculture, advantaging some and disadvantaging others. The mind, then, reflects and contains the experiences of the specific social situation of each person; it is both the basis of individuality and a reflection of the way culture is structured and biased. But this remains a rudimentary process until such time as gesture and (later) language is learned. Mead (Strauss, 1964, p. 127), for instance, says that "it is important to recognize that that to which the word refers is something that lies in the experience of the individual without the use of language. Language does pick out and organize the content of experience. It is an implement for that purpose."

Children's experiences are initially of a direct, primary nature. They recall those experiences and gradually learn to attach meaning to the repetitive patterns of behavior they encounter. However, when the medium of communication is abstract language, the form of the experience changes, for while the experience of receiving linguistic communication is primary and the communicants can still attach meaning to that experience, a secondary meaning is carried through the language. This changes the nature of the experience and consequently the nature of the ensuing learning, because there are two simultaneous learning processes. This double aspect of learning, involving both primary and secondary experience simultaneously, is reflected in certain curriculum theories in education. When educators refer to the "hidden curriculum," they are speaking of the primary experiences children have in school while they are also acquiring other forms of knowledge and skills. In secondary experiences, learning can be more cognitive and grounded less in action, but this favors those whose linguistic capacity is the most extensive.

It will be recalled from Chapter Two that language, like culture in general, is not value free. It reflects both historical time and social culture, so that the language that people use becomes one of the signs by which others can locate them in history and in the social structure. For instance, at one time or another most people have tried to guess where somebody else comes from. Social as well as geographical origins can be detected. Bernstein (1971, p. 78) emphasizes that "associated with the organization of social groups are distinct forms of social language." He goes on to demonstrate that children from a non-manual class background have usually acquired an elaborated speech code as well as a restricted code, while those from a manual class background have only a restricted code.

Freire also focuses on the social significance of language. He shows how language has been used to reinforce the political domination of the elite. Referring to postcolonial Africa, for example, Freire (1978, pp. 13–14) writes as follows:

> The inherited colonial education had as one of its principal objectives the de-Africanization of nationals. It was discriminatory, mediocre, and based on verbalism. It could not contribute anything to national reconstruction because it was not constituted for this purpose. . . . Divorced from the reality of the country, it was, for this very reason,

a school for the minority, and thus against the majority. It selected out only a very few who had access to it, excluding most of them after a few years and, due to continued selective filtering, the number rejected constantly increased. A sense of inferiority and inadequacy was fostered by this "failure."

This system could not help but reproduce in children and in youth the profile that colonial ideology itself had created for them, namely, that of inferior beings lacking all ability; their only salvation lay in becoming "white" or "black with white souls." The system, then, was not concerned with anything related closely to nationals (called "natives"). Worse than the lack of concern was the actual negation of every authentic representation of national peoples — their history, their culture, their language. The history of those colonized was thought to have begun with the civilizing presence of the colonizers. . . . Culture belonged only to the colonizers.

These remarks illustrate the social nature of thought. Like Marx and Engels, Freire believes that the thought patterns of the people are those of the dominant elite. Thus, he recommends that all books and other reading materials be purged of the ideology of the colonizers. Only by learning a different language can the oppressed be freed from the strictures of the colonial world.

It is perhaps Mannheim (1936, pp. 1–11) above all who has highlighted the social nature of thought and therefore of mind. He observes (1936, p. 22) that "only in a quite limited sense does a single individual create out of himself the mode of speech and of thought we attribute to him. He speaks the language of his group; he thinks in the manner in which his group thinks. He finds at his disposal only certain words and meanings. These not only determine to a large extent the avenues of approach to the surrounding world, but they also show at the same time from which angle and in which context of activity objects have hitherto been perceptible and accessible to the group or the individual." In short, many of an individual's initial experiences are influenced by class, gender, ethnicity, and other social variables. This means that the learning processes that undergird the development of mind are related to the social structures within which people live. Thus, people's minds — their biographies — are the sum total of their learning within social situations. People from similar social backgrounds are likely to have had similar learning experiences, to have developed a similar language and therefore to have similar minds. Consequently, they may appear to think similar thoughts and act in similar ways. This similarity allows for intersubjectivity and empathy to be exercised more easily within the subcultural boundaries than beyond them. By contrast, people from a different social background, even though they are of the same society, may have developed minds that are different from those of other social backgrounds, even though there will be similarities that reflect the nature of the wider society in which they all live.

But is mind merely the reflection of the social background? Is there no independence of thought? Clearly people are not perfect reflections of their subculture; they do have some individuality. This individuality starts with the physical differences at birth and continues to develop as people respond to the wide variety of experiences that are inevitable in a modern pluralistic, technological society. Minds develop independently as they acquire "an organized set of attitudes" (Mead, in Strauss, 1964, p. 192) or universe of meaning. Independence does not imply a dualist position — that mind and body are totally separate phenomena — but that mind has in some way transcended the body and can act independently of it.

Since gesture only has relevance when it actually does communicate meaning from one person to another, it is not always certain that people from different social backgrounds will communicate precisely with each other, because the words they employ may not signify exactly the same meaning. Meaning, therefore, is a social construction and relates to the subculture, or subcultures, within which people live, according to Mead:

> Gestures become significant symbols when they implicitly arouse in an individual making them the

same responses which they explicitly arouse, or are supposed to arouse, in the other individuals, the individuals to whom they are addressed. In all conversations of gestures within the social processes . . . the individual's consciousness of the content and flow of meaning involved depends on his thus taking the gestures of the other toward his own gestures. . . . Only in terms of gestures as significant symbols is the existence of mind or intelligence possible; for only in terms of gestures which are significant symbols can thinking — which is simply an internalized or implicit conversation of the individual with himself by means of such gestures — take place [Strauss, 1964, pp. 158–159].

Hence, mind develops through learning. The fact that mind is learned has implications for other human variables, including self and intelligence. Before we turn to the subject of self, a few comments on intelligence may be useful.

Mead suggests that intelligence is related to the same social constraints as mind and thus that intelligence may also be learned — or partly so. It is possible to argue that intelligence is the ability to respond to experience, so that different types of intelligence may involve the ability to respond to different experiences. Many educators and others are aware, for instance, that so-called intelligence tests have a middle class bias, and so it is hardly surprising that people from this background do especially well on them. Furthermore, it is well known that if people practice on them, they perform better, and so successful completion of such tests may also be indicative of acquired skill through practice.

It has also been recognized that certain forms of intelligence increase with age (Cross, 1981, pp. 157–164), which adds support to the idea that intelligence is based on the ability to respond to life's experiences. Cattell (1963), for example, distinguishes between fluid and crystallized intelligence. The former is intelligence that has a biological basis, whereas the latter relates to experience, which again suggests that intelligence is learned and social as well as biological.

The brain is a neurological system, but mind and intelligence are not constituents of the brain from birth. Mind is not a static phenomenon; it is always emerging. Mead says: "We must regard mind . . . as arising and developing within the social process, within the empirical matrix of social interactions. We must, that is, get an inner individual experience from the standpoint of the social acts which include the experiences of separate individuals in a social context wherein the individuals interact" (Strauss, 1964, p. 195). Essence emerges from existence into humanity, and mind and intelligence are learned during this process and continue to develop throughout life. As essence emerges from existence, the human characteristics are soon apparent in the child, and they develop as the person develops. But the person is more than merely body and mind; the person is also a self.

The Birth of the Self

The self is learned and formed in the context of social interaction. As Mead (Strauss, 1964, p. 42) puts it, "A self can arise only where there is a social process within which this self has had its initiative. It arises in that process. For the process, the communication and the participation . . . to which I have referred is essential. That is the way that selves have arisen. That is where the individual is in a social process in which he is part, where he does influence himself as he does others."

Mead emphasizes that no self can develop before language emerges, since it is only through the use and recognition of arbitrary symbols (language), as well as other forms of communication, that people can become conscious of themselves as social human beings. Only when this consciousness exists can the self become an object to itself, which makes it distinct from other living beings that may have no self-awareness. In this instance, self is both subject and object. This is a significant point in Mead's analysis, and he illustrates it with the example of a person being chased by someone else. He claims that during the chase, the person being pursued is so preoccupied with running away that the individual has no consciousness of action at all. Yet Mead may not be correct: a person being chased may be very conscious of self, and action for the consciousness might be aroused and stimulated, since both the chase and the desired escape present it with problems.

However, there are situations where the self is not self-conscious. This is true in situations that are taken for granted. For example, people driving along a long stretch of empty road and listening to the radio may be so engrossed either in the radio program or in the trip that they are not conscious of the process of driving. This is the type of situation that Bergson (1920) described as *durée*. It is depicted in the learning processes model in the following chapters as presumptive action and nonlearning—a taken-for-granted response to a potential learning situation.

The self arises in social interaction, rather in the individualistic type of situation described in the foregoing example. There are two stages in its development, according to Mead: the first is through interaction with significant others in which learning occurs, and the second is through learning about the generalized other. In the first stage, children interact with significant others and learn these attitudes in a nonreflective manner. However, their world soon becomes broader than that of interaction with significant others alone.

Through play, children learn to extend their understanding of the world. Mead points out that children first play by themselves, then there is side-by-side play, and finally there is interactive play. Through play children learn about the phenomena of the world around them, and through role play they begin to learn about the experience of others. Later play turns into games, and then, Mead says, "the rules are a set of responses which a particular attitude calls out. You can demand a certain response in others if you take a certain attitude. These responses are all in yourself as well" (Strauss, 1964, p. 216). Thus the actions of others in play is an essential precondition for the development of the self:

> At this stage we speak of a child as not yet having a fully developed self. The child responds in a fairly intelligent fashion to the immediate stimuli that

come to him, but they are not yet organized; he does not organize his life as we would like to have him do, namely, as a whole. There is just a set of responses to the type of play. The child reacts to a certain stimulus and the reaction in himself is called out in others, but he is not a whole self. In his game he has to have an organization of roles, otherwise he cannot play the game. The game represents the passage in the life of the child from the taking of the role of others in play to the organized part that is essential to self-consciousness in the full sense of the term [Mead, in Strauss, 1964, p. 216].

Eventually, however, the larger society provides the backdrop against which the self develops some form of independence. Mead regards the organized society, or community, as the generalized other; "the attitude of the generalized other is the attitude of the whole community" (p. 218). His generalized other represents an oversimplification, since society is not monolithic but is subdivided by socioeconomic class, gender, and so on. He is aware that subcultural differences exist:

If the given individual is to develop a self in the fullest sense, it is not sufficient for him merely to take the attitudes of other human individuals toward himself and toward one another within the human social process and to bring that social process as a whole into his individual experience merely in these terms. He must also, in the same way as he takes the attitudes of other individuals toward himself and toward one another, take their attitudes toward the various phases or aspects of the common social activity or set of social undertakings in which, as members of an organized society or social group, they are all engaged. He must, then, by generalizing these individual attitudes of that organized society or social group itself as a whole, act towards different social objects [Strauss, 1964, p. 219].

Nevertheless, Mead looks beyond the concrete situation to something of the commonality of social living. This commonality can only occur after people have developed language, which makes it possible to communicate to and receive communication from others. As Mead (pp. 224–225) emphasizes, "Language in its significant sense is that vocal gesture which tends to arouse in the individual the attitude which it arouses in others, and it is this perfecting of the self by the gesture which mediates the social activities that gives rise to the process of taking the role of the other." Mead (pp. 213–214) uses the example of Helen Keller and says: "As she recognized, it was not until she could get into communication with other persons through symbols which could arouse in herself the responses they arouse in other people that she could get what we term a mental content, or a self." Hence, the second stage in the full development of the self occurs when "that self is constituted not only by an organization of these particular individual attitudes but also by an organization of the social attitudes of the generalized other or the social group as a whole to which he belongs" (Strauss, 1964, p. 222).

For Mead, the self comprises two elements — the *I* and the *Me*. The former is the learned response of the organism to the attitudes of others, while the latter encompasses the organized set of attitudes of others that the self assumes or learns. Mead's position is somewhat similar to Freud's. Freud sees the self as consisting of the id, the ego, and the superego. The id is the reflex action for the fulfillment of bodily drives, a subject that Mead does not discuss. The ego is the reality principle in which mental processes such as discrimination, memory, judgment, and reasoning emerge. The superego comprises the attitudes of others, often significant others, that have been internalized (Hall, 1954, p. 41). The strength of Freud's position is that he emphasizes the subconscious and the bodily drives, whereas the advantage of Mead's approach is the emphasis he places on social interaction, especially with respect to the use of gesture in the formation of both mind and self.

Hence, the self — like the mind — is essentially cognitive in Mead's thinking. Like mind, it is not present in the individual at birth but is learned through interaction and eventually manifests itself through socially constrained but individual identity. Mead recognizes that there is a certain similarity in his thinking about self to the theological concept of the soul, which some theologians might argue is within an individual at birth, although Mead (Strauss, 1964, p. 115) cautions that the two ideas should not be confused: "If we abandon the conception of a substantive soul endowed with the self of the individual at birth, then we may regard the development of the individual's self, and of his self-consciousness within the field of his experience, as the social psychologist's special interest."

Earlier we noted that Ryle (1963, p. 61) rejects the dualist notion of the soul, "the ghost of the machine." (However, he equates it with mind, rather than distinguishing self and mind in the way Mead does — and as we are doing here.) Luckmann takes a different position; interpreting religion broadly, he views the development of the self as a profoundly religious phenomenon. He suggests (1967, p. 49) that as the human organism transcends its biological nature, a religious phenomenon occurs. In this respect, Luckmann's approach resembles that of Teilhard de Chardin (1965), who suggests that individuals go through a process of personalization. What is significant about Luckmann's (1967, p. 50) analysis is his point that an organism becomes, or acquires, a "self" by constructing with others an "objective and moral universe of meaning" — that is, it is a learned phenomenon. Unlike the mind-body dualists, however, Luckmann regards this learned phenomenon that is called a self as an entity in the cerebral cortex; he does not equate it with the Christian idea of soul.

From a different standpoint, we have seen that the culture within which the self develops is not value free but is biased toward those who exercise power and influence. Since initially mind is formed through nonreflective learning processes, those biases are built into the learning. The same biases occur in the language used by those with whom people interact. Consequently, the self develops with built-in biases. And if biases exist in the formation of mind and self through this initial learning, then they will affect future action and learning. We will return to this topic in Chapter Six.

Identity

People acquire an identity through social interaction, then. Berger (1966, p. 117) summarizes this point nicely: "Identity is not something 'given,' but is bestowed in acts of social recognition. We become that as we are addressed [by others]. The same idea is expressed in Cooley's well-known description of the self as a reflection in the looking glass." People first internalize the identity that others ascribe to them — as child, son or daughter, and so on. Individuals acquire other identities as they progress through life. This is because modern society has become so complex that it is no longer possible to retain a single identity. Berger, Berger, and Kellner (1974) suggest that there are four facets to modern identity; it is open, differentiated, reflective, and individuated. Each of these is important in any consideration of learning in modern society. With respect to openness, they comment (1974, p. 73) that "the modern individual is . . . peculiarly 'unfinished' as he enters adult life. Not only does there seem to be a great objective capacity for transformation of identity later in life, but there is also a subjective awareness and even readiness for such transformations. The modern individual is not only peculiarly 'conversion-prone,' he knows this and often glories in it."

Berger, Berger, and Kellner point out that one result of the pluralistic nature of modern society is that people have become more aware of the subjective basis of their identity. Pluralism forces individuals to be reflective, so that the emphasis on reflective learning might be seen as a symbol of modernity. This form of society has also resulted in individuated, autonomous individuals — another point that we will return to, in Chapter Eight.

Conclusion

We have observed that mind, self, and identity are phenomena learned in a social context. People initially learn from their primary experiences, and this learning is nonreflective. With the incorporation of gesture and language, those experiences become more complex. As the store of memories grows, the mind develops. Eventually, the store of memories develops into a biography that acquires a self and an identity.

Since culture is not homogeneous, children are bound to have some experiences that contradict previous experiences. Therefore, they are forced to make conscious choices in both action and learning. In this way, they develop into individual selves. The more individual choices that are made, the more that individuality develops. But as self-identity increases, it may not be in accord with the apparent best interests of the social group that actually helped to mold it. This creates the potential for conflict — but also for innovation.

Many values and practices, however, become taken for granted as a result of nonreflective learning, through which people learn to conform to the cultural environment into which they are born. This is the world into which mind and self easily fit and action becomes presumptive. A paradox then occurs: individuals who have mind and selves, which are learned phenomena, seek harmony with the value-oriented cultural world so that they can act presumptively, in a nonlearning manner. From existence, essence has emerged — through a process of learning — and essence consists of those characteristics of humanness that contribute to a person's fundamental makeup.

So far, we have emphasized that learning occurs through the processes of everyday living and communicating. A better understanding of the relationship between learning and action is necessary before we can move on to other issues.

4

Understanding
Conscious Action

In the first three chapters, I have shown that human beings emerge as a result of learning in a social context: the mind and the self are learned phenomena, and people are socialized into the dominant culture. The whole process is a complicated one of learning through action and interaction with fellow human beings in the social-cultural milieu. People can experience the world directly through action and reaction, which represents primary experience, but they can also experience it indirectly through language in communicative interaction, which constitutes secondary experience. We will consider both forms of experience, and other forms of mediations, in this chapter. The purpose of the chapter is to focus on conscious action, so that its relationship to learning can be discussed later on. However, since the idea of action implies that there can be nonaction and since this may also be related to learning, or nonlearning, we will discuss it as well.

The chapter has four main sections. The first introduces the concept of action. In the second, the idea of conscious action is explored. The third presents a typology of action. Communicative interaction is the topic of the fourth.

The Concept of Action

An action is an occurrence effected by a human agent rather than by a previous event, so that acting is regarded here as a process of doing something, usually as a result of previous thought. Action is a process or an abstract phenomenon. An action is a complete process. Actions are nearly always meaningful to the actors, whereas behavior does not carry the same connotation, since there are alienating and pathological situations where this is simply not true. No major conceptual distinction, therefore, is made here between act and action.

A sequence of actions is regarded here as a performance (Harré, 1979, p. 48). Performances frequently occur in the course of daily living; a conversation would be an example. On occasion it is difficult to distinguish between an action and a performance, since a sequence may either be short or long and different actions may sometimes tend to flow into each other. Schön (1983) highlights this problem in his discussion of reflection-in-action.

Actions are performed in space. Most performances are public — that is, open to the appraisal of others and potentially controlled by other agencies. But some are private — that is, performed in solitary situations or in ones in which only relatives and friends are present. Many private performances occur in space that is either owned or controlled by the actors themselves, while all other actions are performed in space owned or controlled by others: either public space or organized private space. The meaning of public performances is assumed to be common to those people occupying the space, although there are instances when this meaning is not fully communicated to others. Because actions are performed in such an arena, the actors are not necessarily in complete control of their actions, and other people can deflect them from their original purpose or even prohibit their performance completely.

The concept of action does presuppose that there is a certain freedom to act within the bounds of human social relations, however. Existentialists (Macquarrie, 1973, p. 173), for example, would claim that action implies that the actor is free, a perspective that educationalists, such as Knowles (1980) and Rogers (1969), assume. But more radical theorists—Freire (1972a, 1972b), among others—imply that the human beings are not entirely free but are constrained by social structures, so that they need to be emancipated through learning. Indeed, Berger (1966, p. 171) suggests that freedom "presupposes a certain liberation of consciousness." Giddens (1979, p. 55), however, incorporates the concept of power into his theory of action, since agency refers to action but always "as events in the world." He stresses (1979, p. 61) the fact that action occurs within the structures of social relationships—that is, often in the public sphere or in controlled private space. Giddens makes another important point: that social relationships imply power relationships. He asserts (1979, p. 91) that "power . . . is centrally involved with human agency; a person or party who wields power *could* 'have acted otherwise,' and the person or party over whom power is wielded *would* have acted otherwise if power were not wielded." Power is not only wielded by external agents. Some thinkers suggest that while people may assume they are free, there is nothing worse than being imprisoned behind bars built within the mind itself.

Since action presupposes the existence of an agent who wills that the occurrence take place, it is just as possible for an agent to will that no action occur. Hence, the concept of nonaction need not be regarded only as a negative idea. Nonaction can imply that an actor was unaware of the possibilities of action, or that the actor decided that no action was necessary, or even that the actor was prevented from acting by another's exercise of power. These ideas suggest a relationship between nonaction and consciousness, and clearly a similar connection exists between action and consciousness.

Toward an Understanding of Conscious Action

Actions are rarely mindless, although Heidegger (1968, p. 4) once suggested that "it could be that prevailing man has for centuries . . . acted too much and thought too little." Consequently, it is important to recognize the significance of consciousness in action. Consciousness is used here in the sense of thinking and planning, rather than in the sense of false class consciousness and so on.

Daily living is itself a matter of thinking, planning, acting, and learning, so that it is perhaps surprising that thus far there have been few efforts to develop a theory of action in which both thinking and learning from experience might be located. (See, however, Argyris and Schön, 1974; Argyris, 1982; Habermas, 1984.) Indeed, much of the work on learning from experience does not concentrate on either action or experience, despite the fact that experience occurs in the actions that make up daily life. Greater insight into conscious action may contribute to a better understanding of the relationship between theory and practice, which is complex, as Argyris and Schön (1974) and Cervero (1991), among others, demonstrate.

Learning occurs throughout the life span, at the points where conscious living intersects with time, space, and relationships. Life-span learning means, for Berger, Berger, and Kellner (1974, pp. 70–77), that planning future actions becomes a significant aspect of daily living. Dewey uses the term *consciousness* to denote "meanings actually perceived, *awareness,* being wide awake, alert, attentive to the significance of events, present, past, future." He regards consciousness as something that is undergoing *transitive transformation* — in other words, that is constantly changing. Some events do not cause consciousness to change, but still, there is an ongoing transformative process throughout the whole life span. Conscious action and the taken-for-granted behavior of a conscious person raise some important questions. Within modern society, for instance, consciousness is shaped by major social institutions such as technology and bureaucracy, which are the carriers of contemporary culture. And it will be seen throughout this study that some of the paradoxes of learning revolve around these symbols of modernity.

According to Schutz (1970, p. 129), before we carry out conscious action, "we have a picture in our mind of what we are going to do." Schutz is concerned here with forethought to the action rather than with other aspects of consciousness; in this respect he echoes Kelly's (1963) concept of a human being as a researcher into life who is trying things out and experimenting. However, there are other aspects of consciousness relating to actions: there is a monitoring of the action and a looking back at it after its completion. Consequently, the following discussion is divided into three parts: thought before action (planning), thought during action (monitoring), and thought after action (retrospecting). We will also touch on reflection, a particular type of thinking that can emerge from either monitoring or retrospecting.

Planning

Planning is the form of consciousness referred to in the preceding quotation from Schutz. It is familiar to adult educators and human resource specialists, who see it as an element of problem-solving education. Many exercises are assigned in management training, for example, to help people consider all the options before acting and then plan a strategy or a campaign of action. Planning is also the type of action that occurs in everyday life when people just stop and think before they act; it is the antithesis of impulsiveness. For Berger, Berger, and Kellner (1974, pp. 67–72), however, planning refers to the total life plan, and it is the method through which a great deal of contemporary knowledge of society is organized into people's consciousness. They regard this type of rational action as a feature of modern society.

The idea of planning is also central to Weber's (1947) well-known discussion of rationality, since rationality presupposes that people plan in order to achieve certain ends. Weber (1947, p. 115) distinguishes between four types of rational thought. The first is *Zweckrationalität,* which means a "rational orientation to a system of discrete individual ends"; the second is *Wertrationalität* or "rational orientation to absolute value"; the third refers to emotional actions; and the fourth involves traditional, long-established practice. Each of these forms of rationality is important to developing an understanding of the relationship between action and learning.

Planning is also central to Habermas's (1984) first form of action — teleological (that is, intended to bring about certain ends). He describes (1984, p. 85) it in the following way: "The actor attains an end or brings about the occurrence of a given state by choosing means that have promise in being successful in the given situation and applying them in a suitable manner." Habermas's dramaturgical action (action that seeks to give an impression of the actor to others) could be said to be teleological as well, in the sense that the actors also seek to create an impression through a rational application of their actions. However, for the purposes of this study, planning is not regarded as a different form of action — merely as a part of the process of acting consciously in contemporary society. We might note, too, that Weber's second form of rationality refers to ethical behavior. This forms the basis of Habermas's (1984, p. 85) second form of action — normatively regulated action — where people act rationally according to their values.

Once an action is planned and begun, it is then monitored.

Monitoring

Giddens (1979, p. 56) argues that agency involves the "reflexive monitoring of action." This in turn also relates to the intentionality of human behavior. Here the actor is fully conscious of the ongoing process of the action or performance and is keeping every aspect of it under review, although there are varying levels of consciousness. For instance, a person performing a frequently occurring action, such as shifting gears while driving a car, may be less conscious of the action than of one being performed for only the second or third time, or individuals talking together may be barely conscious of the environment in which they are conversing. But in all cases, the action and the thought about the action are continuous, almost as if they are one. Giddens believes that the ability to monitor and adapt behavior in either an innovative or a conformist fashion is something that distinguishes human action from that of other animals, which live in harmony with nature and act instinctively within that context. However, we noted in Chapter One that human beings also seek to achieve this state with their sociocultural world, so that they can act in a taken-for-granted manner and not have to monitor their actions so consciously.

Retrospection

To shed light on this process, it is helpful to turn to the work of Schutz again. He suggests (1970, pp. 127–128) that "only when the action has been accomplished, when in the suggested terminology it has become an act, he may turn back to his past action as an observer of himself and investigate by what circumstances he has been determined to do what he did. The same holds good if the actor grasps in retrospection the past initial phases of his still on-going action. This retrospection may even be anticipated *modo futuri exacti.*" In distinguishing the completed act from the ongoing act, Schutz makes an important distinction, because he emphasizes that actors may stand back from their action, encapsulate it within the boundaries of past time, and analyze it. Retrospection is distinguished here from reflection, since the former implies looking back, whereas the latter suggests a process of analysis that occurs when the level of consciousness is very high and as a result of which change may occur.

Reflection

Reflection has become one of the central tenets of modernity. Boud, Keogh, and Walker (1985, p. 11) suggest that reflection has at least three attributes: it is undertaken by the learner, it is purposeful, and it involves both cognition and feelings. There is a sense, then, that reflection is a rational process. Paradoxically, reflection is both private and social. It is this process that, according to Habermas (1972, p. 310), releases people from their "dependence on hypostatized powers." In places, he argues that this release is determined by an emancipatory self-interest, although his later work seems to have jettisoned much of his initial thinking on emancipation and reflection as he has moved on to consider communicative action.

In addition, people carry out actions with varying levels of consciousness, from a mere awareness that an action is happening to a heightened concentration on an action or its outcome. For a variety of reasons—possibly because the anticipated ends were not achieved through an action—either the monitoring or the retrospection might result in a situation being problematized. At this point, the process of reflection starts that sets learning in motion. People often say they did something that turned out unsatisfactorily and so they thought about it and did it differently the next time. This process of reflecting on an experience and learning from it is essential to everyday life in contemporary, differentiated society, since this kind of society constantly demands adjustment to new and complex conditions.

Toward a Typology of Action

Using the criteria given earlier, it is possible to specify many forms of action to describe different types of behavior. This exercise has been undertaken in workshop situations, with thirty or forty different terms being noted. However, with the exception of moral and other qualitative actions, which can be described in a variety of ways, most types of action appear to fall into five categories: experimental/creative, repetitive, presumptive, ritualistic, and alienated. These terms are drawn from Merton's (1968) classification of modes of human adaptation to organizational behavior. Adaptation is only one outcome of learning, although Merton (1968, p. 194) comes close to considering the connection between action and learning. His main concern is with understanding how people adapt to the constraints of society's expectations, rather than with relating the process to a wider discussion of learning within both the life span and its social context. Merton produces a fivefold classification of adaptation: conformity, innovation, ritualism, retreatism, and rebellion. Some of his terms are used here, with slightly different connotations. These five are listed in the sequence of habitualization. Berger and Luckmann (1967, pp. 70ff) point out that habitualization occurs naturally:

All human activity is subject to habitualization. Any action that is repeated frequently becomes cast into a pattern, which can be reproduced with an economy of effort and which, *ipso facto,* is apprehended by its performer *as* that pattern.

Action is not the only possible response to an experience; nonaction is also conceivable. Three forms of nonaction were implied in the previous discussion: anomic, preventive, and nonresponse. Together with the five types of action, these are presented in Table 4.1, which relates responses to potential learning experiences to levels of consciousness.

Table 4.1. A Theoretical Analysis of Conscious Action.

Category of response to potential learning experiences	*Level of consciousness*		
	Planning	*Monitoring*	*Retrospecting*
Nonaction			
Anomic	None	None	High
Preventive	Low — high	None	None — high
Nonresponse	None — high	None	None — high
Action			
Experimental/creative	High	High	High
Repetitive	High — none	High — low	High — none
Presumptive	None — low	None — low	None
Ritualistic	None	None — low	None — high
Alienating	None	None — low	None — high

Nonaction

We first discuss the three forms of nonaction.

Anomic. The concept of anomie has been popularized in sociology through the work of Durkheim (1964), who applies it to a condition where the harmony or solidarity between individuals and their social situation has broken down. He regards this condition as pathological. Merton (1968) also uses the term *anomie,* but with a slightly different meaning. He distinguishes (1968, p. 217) between simple and acute anomie. The former involves the disintegration of the value systems of a group, whereas the latter involves a conflict of value systems that causes the group's breakdown.

In the present context, I use the adjective *anomic* more or less in Durkheim's sense, to denote a lack of harmony between people and their sociocultural environment. This is a normless and meaningless situation because the disjuncture between the individuals' biographies and their sociocultural situation is too large to be bridged. They are forced to retreat into their own private space because they know that they are incapable of acting meaningfully in a public or controlled arena.

An extreme example of such a situation might occur when individuals without any technological training find themselves in a technological research laboratory with scientists who are unaware of their ignorance and who try to converse with them about their work. Another example might involve tourists in a foreign country who understand neither the language nor anything about the culture. We could cite many more trivial examples of situations that seem meaningless to those involved. In these cases, meaningful public action becomes impossible. The result is nonaction. The only other possible response in such an anomic situation is to retreat from the situation itself into the private sphere.

Preventive. We noted earlier that Giddens incorporates the power dimension into his discussion, so that certain situations can be envisioned where an actor wants to respond to a situation but is unable to do so because those who exercise power over the situation prevent this. In the work situation, management may block action, but there are many social situations in which the group has this inhibiting function. Most people can think of social situations where another person has prevented them from acting, and a number of experiments in social psychology have illustrated the constraining power of the group (Asch, 1955). A final nonaction situation may occur when people feel constrained

by the hidden forces of culture, even though they are not necessarily aware of any external pressure acting directly to restrict
their behavior. Crutchfield's (1955) research illustrates the strength
of these internalized pressures to conform. In these preventive
situations of nonaction, the very process of prevention creates
a learning process for those whose action is being inhibited.

Nonresponse. This final form of nonaction occurs when individuals are acted on by outside pressures but fail to react. For
whatever reasons, people sometimes choose to ignore the stimuli
they are receiving. It may be because they are oblivious to the
pressures or because they are intent on another form of action.

Types of Action

Having examined the three forms of nonaction, we now need
to consider the five forms of action.

Experimental/Creative. Kelly's (1963) theory of human behavior
assumes that behavior is like scientific action; it resembles an
experiment where the actors might know what they are doing,
although neither the means nor the outcome of the act is assumed or assured beforehand. This creates a need to establish
a connection between action and reason — that is, a need for planning. Planning is central to creative activity, which in turn is
fundamental to human being itself.

An experience may either be accepted at face value or
problematized; the subsequent action is dependent on the way
the experience is perceived. It is here that the difference between
Argyris and Schön's (1974) Model 1 and Model 2 behavior begins,
for the first accepts the validity and inevitability of the experience while the latter questions the context in which it occurs.
The form of action that follows this type of experience rarely
has a definite outcome; indeed, it might be mere reasoning or
a type of action that is "trial and error." When the action is completed, the outcome is considered. If it is acceptable, it is internalized and a form of learning has occurred; if it is not acceptable, it is rejected and another form of learning has taken place.

Clearly this approach to social living is one that occurs

often, when the actors fully understand the social situation but yet do not know precisely what the outcome of their action will be. The action might be only a slight adaptation of a previous performance, but it could also be an entirely new and creative form of behavior. The amount of deviation from the previous thought or action does not matter so long as the new idea or action is experimental in some way. This form of action can occur in both public and private space. In all cases, a disjuncture between biography and experience occurs, although the disjuncture is not so great as to make the experience anomic and meaningless. Finally, the experimental behavior may result in either innovative or conformist conclusions about how to think and behave. In other words, one of the outcomes of experimental action is almost certainly retrospection, which will probably lead to learning.

Repetitive. Repetitive behavior usually begins as a new form of cognition or action—that is, as something that has to be learned, as in trying to memorize a sequence of procedures in a vocational preparation program or a series of historical dates or other similar information. It may be either intended proaction or enforced reaction; such action-oriented learning has been called drill, practice, or training. In the last case, the British philosopher R. S. Peters (1966, pp. 29–30) has suggested that education is more cognitive, while training is more skill oriented. However, for the purposes of this discussion, both forms of behavior—cognitive and psychomotor—may become repetitive.

When the behavior has become repetitive, there is no innovation or experimentation, and both the process and the outcome of the action tend to be conformist, although the behavior is still carefully monitored because it is not yet taken for granted. Indeed, the intention of the action is to reproduce whatever has been, or is to be, learned rather than to change it. Merton (1968) regards conformity as acceptance of both the processes and the goals of the action. Argyris (1982, p. 42) points out that people will slow down an action and repeat it if it is not as skillful as they think it should be, and then practice it until it produces the results they want, which is indicative of careful monitoring.

This form of repetitive behavior is the precursor to presumptive behavior. It can and does occur in individual and social situations, it is also both cognitive and psychomotor, and it has the added benefit that it limits choices of behavior in complex and pluralistic societies. In both cognitive and psychomotor forms, the actions are meaningful and may be freely performed. However, many repetitive acts are not freely performed, as Giddens and Freud point out, and in these situations repetitive behavior may be a prelude to ritualistic or alienating behavior. Giddens concentrates on power external to the actor, but Freud also highlights the power of those inner forces that compel people to conform, even though they feel that they should be deviant. As repetition proceeds, the behavior is increasingly taken for granted, even though this might be at the cost of dulling the inner voice of the superego.

One other form of repetitive action is reflexive. This is the involuntary type of act that occurs when the human reflexes respond to a stimulus. It is meaningless, often noncognitive and nonsocial, and makes little reference to an individual's biography. Thus it is a different form of action from all the others discussed here and will not be referred to further.

Presumptive. When the actors fully understand the social situation within which actions are carried out, they often perform the actions automatically — in either public or private space — since they have habitualized them. That is, they carry out the actions in a meaningful but almost unconscious way and time seems to flow in an uninterrupted manner, a state that Bergson (1920) calls *durée*. Here the harmony between the actors and the social world is established and perpetuated through presumptive action. Argyris (1982, p. 42) regards this form of action as an automatic response to a situation, almost reflexive in character. Schutz and Luckmann (1974, p. 7) describe meaningful action that is taken for granted as follows: "I trust that the world as it has been known by me up until now will continue further and that consequently the stock of knowledge obtained from my fellow-men and formed from my own experiences will continue to preserve its fundamental validity. . . . From this assumption follows the further and fundamental one: that I can repeat my past successful acts. So long as the structure of the world can be taken as constant, as long as my previous experience is valid, my ability to operate upon the world in this and that manner remains in principle preserved."

This form of action is meaningful since it reflects the lifeworld of the individual actor; it presumes that the world is unchanging, so that it is possible to act in an unthinking manner. This is not unlike the situation in the Old Testament paradise myth or the situation of animals in nature. But there is one major difference: the world with which the actors are in harmony is not a "God-given" world; it is one created by people and biased by their own interests and concerns. There is a sense in which individuals feel that they are free to change their behavior but they also feel no need to, since they are in harmony with the world. They can act, not only in their own private space but also in the public space which they inhabit in an apparently free and unthinking manner. Whether their actions are actually free is another matter, since this type of behavior often emerges as a result of habitualized and oft-repeated actions that enable actors to act in this way.

In Argyris and Schön's (1974) terms, the fact that the actors feel in harmony with their social world might reveal a gap between the actors' theory in use and their espoused theory. The more people have to think about their performance, the less likely, it seems, that there is disjuncture between the two theoretical perspectives Argyris and Schön have identified. Presumptive behavior, however, is repetitive in nature and essential to the smooth functioning of social life itself, and the apparent inability of the external powers to coerce people into conformity merely illustrates the actual power and influence of those who exercise power within society. This is what Gramsci refers to as *hegemony* (see Entwistle, 1979, pp. 10–16.)

Ritualistic. Ritualistic action is meaningful action (although the level of its conscious monitoring is very low) in which both the norms of the act and the outcome are known in advance. Merton (1968, p. 205) describes it as that "mode of adaptation of individuality seeking a *private* escape from the dangers and frustrations which seem . . . inherent in the competition for major cultural goals by abandoning these goals and clinging all the more closely to the safe routines and institutional norms." In the present study, ritualism does not have quite the same implications, although it is recognized that it can be both proactive and reactive. For our purposes, ritualism is the process of "going through the motions." It occurs where the actors choose to undertake repetitive forms of behavior (such as driving a car along an interstate highway) to produce a desired result, or it may involve a reaction to a power situation in which actors are expected to conform, even though they would have chosen to act in another way if this were possible.

Alienating. *Alienation* is a term popularized by Marx, although Fromm (1966) points out that the idea can be traced back to the Old Testament concept of idolatry: when human beings worship inanimate objects of their own creation, they become estranged from their life-forces. Marx employs the concept in opposition to creative work — labor, he believes, is creative and of the essence of humanity. By contrast, repetitive work — such as work on an assembly line — is so mechanical that it destroys the essence of humanity. Seeman (1959) discusses five variables that scholars have often cited as features of alienation: meaninglessness, powerlessness, normlessness, isolation, and self-estrangement. To begin with meaninglessness, in one sense alienating situations are usually meaningful, inasmuch as the actors know why they are doing what they are doing, although they are powerless to change it. Normlessness is similar to the situation that we are describing as anomic. Action that is repetitive and frequently controlled by others can be isolating. It is the antithesis of the type of action that engenders growth and development, which is why it leads to self-estrangement.

Consider the following possibility: normal presumptive behavior suddenly results in an unexpected outcome to which the actors cannot respond with the low level of planning and monitoring that had preceded it. Suddenly they are forced to think, to plan their next action, and even to reflect on the previous one. Perhaps there is nothing unusual in this in the process of normal living, since one type of action is often followed by another of a different type; in fact, levels of conscious awareness change from one situation to another. (People driving along a highway may be acting ritualistically and not monitoring their behavior with a very high level of consciousness. But if they come across an automobile accident, their level of awareness of their own driving changes.) Furthermore, it is not unusual to engage in retrospection on a previous action. But the significant thing about this change is that suddenly the actors' own stock of knowledge is insufficient to cope with the new situation, so that they are forced to plan a new action as well as to reconsider a previous one. It is at this point that the possibility, even the probability, of learning occurs.

Communicative Interaction

Quite central to the argument about the birth of the self was the point that children are socialized through interaction with their parents and significant others. This argument was based on Mead's understanding of mind, self, and society. It emphasized the importance of relationships through which linguistic communication and therefore learning occurs. However, communication is more than linguistic; nonverbal communication also plays a key role in the socialization process. Nonverbal communication can only occur when there are both primary (direct) and secondary (mediated) experiences, although there are occasions when the latter can occur without the former. When two persons converse, they have a direct experience of interacting with each other, but they also have a secondary experience gained as a result of the information, knowledge, and so on acquired in the interaction. Secondary experiences—a form of communicative interaction—can happen whenever any of the five forms of action just discussed occur in relationships. In addition, they can occur in more impersonal situations, when people receive communications through books, the media, and so on. In these instances, no primary interaction needs to happen at all, although communicators using the media often try to produce situations that appear to be personal. In many forms of distance education, for instance, local centers are established in order to create some primary experiences. When this is done, the educational process is more successful.

This approach to communicative interaction is similar to but not the same as Habermas's (1984) theory of communicative action, which Mezirow (1991; also see Mezirow and Associates, 1990) employs in his more recent writing about adult learning and perspective transformation. Habermas's position here is closer to the idea of the universality of hermeneutics than to emancipation; Giddens (1985, p. 96) suggests that Habermas has moved away considerably from the position he expounds in *Knowledge and Human Interests* (1972). It is now necessary to examine his position.

Habermas's position on communicative action is essentially dialogical. He believes (1984, p. 95) that social interaction is at the heart of communicative action: "Only the communicative model of action presupposes language as a medium of uncurtailed communication whereby speakers and hearers, out of the context of their preinterpreted lifeworld, refer simultaneously to things in the objective, social, and subjective worlds in order to negotiate common definitions of the situation."

People negotiate with each other to reach common ground because they cannot always take the content or the meaning or the validity of the communication for granted. In such situations, some form of implicit questioning arises and the potential for learning exists.

Habermas suggests that the actors relativize their utterances to facilitate a genuine dialogue. But this might not be the only possible response, since one person could accept unquestioningly the validity of the truth claims of another's utterance. Habermas goes on to discuss the validity claims of the utterance and then states (1984, p. 100) that "it is the actors themselves who seek consensus and measure it against truth, rightness, and sincerity, that is, against the 'fit' or 'misfit' between the speech act, on the one hand, and the three worlds to which the actor takes up relations, on the other." These three worlds are the objective, the social, and the subjective. Habermas (1984,

p. 100) claims that "understanding takes place against the background of a culturally ingrained preunderstanding." Here, then, he indicates the learning possibilities of the communicative act. In this area, he has undoubtedly produced a major shift in sociological theory, although his emphasis on consensus and mutual understanding is perhaps a little too idealistic. Clearly, Habermas's orientation is now hermeneutic, that is, concerned with interpretation and understanding, which places a greater emphasis on both reason and rationality and less on the idea of emancipation of the individual through critical reflectivity.

It is beyond the scope of this study to explore Habermas's position further or to enter the current debates about it. Suffice it to say that communicative interaction is an important basis for learning; it encompasses the secondary mode of experience through which learning occurs.

Conclusion

This chapter has outlined a theory of conscious action that contains three forms of nonaction and five of action. In presumptive, ritualistic, and alienating situations, the only action possible is of a conformist nature, although in the repetitive situation, the actors might be practicing a new behavior. Innovative action is only possible in experimental situations. After the type of action has occurred, the outcome can be repeated in a process of learning. Only in reflective situations can the actors learn from their experiences in a conscious manner; in all other situations, they memorize the action, either consciously or unconsciously. The basic point is that learning and action are inextricably intertwined.

5

Learning and Action

In the previous chapters, the emphasis has been on action rather than learning. Now, however, it is important to focus on the latter concept. A theory of learning developed more fully elsewhere (Jarvis, 1987) forms the basis of this chapter. The first section of the chapter describes a pertinent research project. This is followed by a section that explicates three main categories of learning. The next section links the types of learning to the types of action and nonaction outlined in Chapter Four. In the final section, the concept of disjuncture is examined.

Understanding Learning: A Research Project

Over a period of about fifteen months in 1985 and 1986, I carried out a project to discover something more about the way adults learn. All the participants were first invited to write down a learning incident in their lives. They were asked to state what started the incident, how it progressed, and when and why they concluded that it was completed. Having undertaken this exercise, they were then paired so that they could discuss their different learning experiences with a partner. (They were encouraged to examine the similarities and differences in their experiences.)

After that, the pairs were combined into groups of four, and the individuals again discussed their respective learning experiences within these groups.

The first time this exercise was conducted, the groups were asked to feed back their ideas at this point for a general discussion. Afterward, they were given a diagram of Kolb's (1984) learning cycle and were encouraged to adapt it so that it related to the four experiences that formed the basis of their group discussion. Kolb's learning cycle is shown in Figure 5.1.

Figure 5.1. Kolb's Learning Cycle.

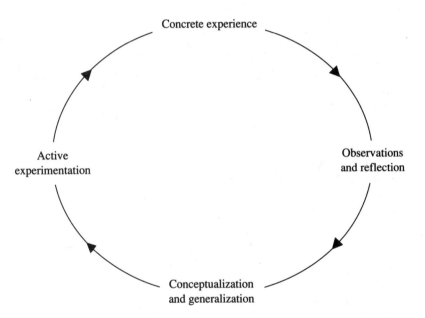

Participants were told that the cycle was not necessarily correct and that they were free to adapt it in any way they wished. Based on the feedback from the first set of groups, a more complex model of learning was constructed by modifying the learning cycle in Figure 5.1 so that it reflected these groups' learning experiences. Whenever this exercise was subsequently repeated, the last stage each time was to modify the adaptation of Kolb's cycle that had emerged from the previous time the exercise had been carried out.

This exercise was conducted on nine separate occasions both in the United Kingdom and the United States. Participants were teachers of adults and teachers of children, university lecturers and adult university students who were teachers of adults in their normal occupation, younger people and some not-so-young participants, men and women. In all, about two hundred people participated in the exercise, although the sample was middle class and not tightly controlled. A complex model of learning was constructed as a result of the research. This model was subsequently tested in seminars over another nine-month period, again in both Europe and the United States, with some two or three hundred people participating in them.

It might be claimed that the use of Kolb's cycle invalidated the project, since it is an experiential cycle, which would tend to favor learning experiences that occurred in the action mode. But the subjects were asked to write down their learning experience before they were introduced to Kolb's learning cycle. And in any case, many of the experiences that the subjects described occurred in the communicative mode. (I determined this by occasionally asking them if their learning experience was of a cognitive or a practical nature and whether or not they had a teacher.)

The model of learning that emerged is depicted in Figure 5.2. This model is much more complex than Kolb's learning cycle; its features will be clarified in the following paragraphs. Subsequent to the publication of that work, the theory of learning which evolved from this research has been discussed quite fully by Marsick and Watkins (1990), Kontiainen (1991), and Merriam and Caffarella (1991).

Three Categories of Learning

The definition of learning that is central to this book emphasizes the connection between learning and experience. Learning might be regarded as a response to an experience or even as a response to an experience created through an action. Basically

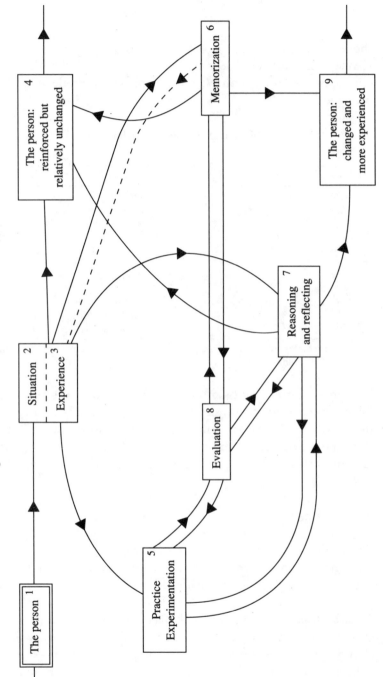

Figure 5.2. A Model of the Learning Processes.

The person [1]

Situation [2]
Experience [3]

The person:
reinforced but
relatively unchanged [4]

Practice
Experimentation [5]

Evaluation [8]

Reasoning
and reflecting [7]

Memorization [6]

The person:
changed and
more experienced [9]

there appear to be nine possible types of responses to an experience, and these can be grouped into three overarching categories: nonlearning, nonreflective learning, and reflective learning (see Table 5.1).

Table 5.1. A Typology of Learning.

Category of response to experience	Type of learning/nonlearning
Nonlearning	Presumption
	Nonconsideration
	Rejection
Nonreflective learning	Preconscious learning
	Skills learning
	Memorization
Reflective learning	Contemplation[a]
	Reflective skills learning[a]
	Experimental learning[a]

[a]Each of the reflective forms of learning can have two possible outcomes, conformity and change.

It is possible to think of situations where two or more of these forms of learning occur simultaneously, especially when both modes of experience are considered. The next three sections of this chapter discuss each of these types individually, however, and in each instance a suggested route through Figure 5.2 is indicated.

Nonlearning

People do not always learn from their experiences. This is why we start with a discussion of nonlearning responses to experience: presumption, nonconsideration, and rejection.

Presumption. Presumption is the typical response to everyday experience. It involves a sense of trust that the world will not change and therefore that successful acts can be repeated, as Schutz and Luckmann (1974, p. 7) emphasize in the passage quoted in Chapter Four. While this appears almost thoughtless and mechanical, it is the basis of a great deal of social living. It would be quite intolerable for people to have to consider every word and every act in every social situation before they performed it.

(With respect to presumption, the route through Figure 5.2 is 1 through 4.)

Nonconsideration. Nonconsideration is another response to potential learning experiences that occurs commonly in everyday life; its effect on the actors varies depending on the circumstances. People do not respond to a potential learning experience for a variety of reasons. They may be too busy to think about it, may be fearful of the outcome, or may not be in a position to understand the situation they are in. Thus, though they might recognize the potential for learning from the experience, they may not be able to respond to it.

(In terms of nonconsideration, the route through Figure 5.2 is 1 through 4.)

Rejection. Some people have an experience but reject the possibility of learning that could have accompanied the experience. For instance, think of an older person (or a young one) experiencing the complexity of the modern city and exclaiming, "I don't know what this world is coming to!" Here is a possible learning experience, an experience of the complex modern world, but instead of probing it and seeking to understand it, some individuals reject the possibility. In a sense, these people are in the anomic situation described in the previous chapter. All those who look at the world and say that they will not have any of their opinions or attitudes changed by it because they are sure they are right are in this situation. Rejection may actually serve to confirm them in positions they already hold.

(In this case, the route through Figure 5.2 is 1 through 3 through 7 to either 4 or 9.)

Sociologically, the significant thing about any response to experience is that no one is totally individuated; everyone lives in a society. What, then, are the effects of nonlearning? The most significant fact might be that society and its structures are unaffected by the people's experiences. (But it might be argued that any failure to affect the structures of society might hinder later changes, and so it would be wrong to suggest that nonaction does not have some consequences.) In addition, little change is likely to occur in the actors because people's knowledge, skills, and attitudes do not change when they do not learn. There is an advantage to this situation, though. People who go through life often approaching things presumptively, or even from a position of nonconsideration, experience considerable freedom because their life unfolds in the expected manner. This sense of freedom results from the fact that society does not seem to be pressuring them to do anything they do not want to do. By contrast, when individuals reject the possible learning opportunity, then social pressures which inhibit that opportunity often appear oppressive. Yet there is still a sense of individual freedom — freedom not to respond to the social pressures that appear to be operating. It is a negative freedom, which enables them to stand back and reject the social forces that are exercised on them. Hence, people might still feel free to act as they desire, even though circumstances seem oppressive.

Nonreflective Learning

The three types of learning that constitute nonreflective learning — preconscious learning, skills learning, and memorization — are the types that are usually thought of as learning proper. They share the feature that they do not involve reflectivity.

Preconscious Learning. Preconscious learning is often called *incidental learning*, though this term is inadequate because it does not convey the idea of a learning process that passes into the mind without the learner's conscious awareness. This form of learning occurs at the edge of consciousness or the periphery of vision. Typically, individuals monitor their actions, albeit with a low level of consciousness, and memorize those actions. People driving are not usually conscious of all the incidents that occur during their trip, but when discussing the trip with somebody who asks a specific question, they might respond, "I think

I vaguely recall something like that." If pressed, they might even be able to remember something quite specific. They have learned, but the learning has not necessarily become conscious knowledge.

Preconscious learning is not likely to occur as a result of experiencing in the communicative mode, although it can take place while the two modes of experience are happening simultaneously and the recipient is concentrating on the secondary rather than the primary experience. For instance, in carrying on conversations, people are not always concentrating on their environment; they may see things out of the "corner of their eye" or may be "vaguely aware" that something else is going on. For further discussion of preconscious learning, see Beard (1976, pp. 93–95), Mannings (1986), Reischmann (1986), and especially Marsick and Watkins (1990).

(In the case of preconscious learning, the route through Figure 5.2 is 1 through 3 through 6 to 4.)

Skills Learning. Skills learning is usually associated with such forms of learning as training for a manual occupation or the acquisition of a high level of physical fitness through training. But some learning in preparation for a manual occupation is certainly not nonreflective. Thus this term has to be further restricted to the learning of simple, short procedures, such as those that somebody on an assembly line might be taught. These skills are often acquired through imitation and role modeling.

Skills learning is another form of learning that occurs in the action mode of experience rather than in communicative interaction. There is a significant relationship between skills learning and knowledge: learners might watch a demonstration and claim that they now know how to carry out a task. However, they only know cognitively and indirectly (through memorization) until they have actually performed the task for themselves.

(With respect to skills learning, the route through Figure 5.2 is 1 through 3 through 5 to 8 to 6 to either 4 or 9.)

Memorization. Memorization is perhaps the most commonly known form of learning. Children learn their mathematical tables, their language vocabularies, and so on. When adults return to higher education, they sometimes feel that this is the most important type of learning expected of them, and so they try to memorize what the instructor has said or what such and such a scholar has written in order to reproduce it on an examination. The authority speaks and every word of wisdom has to be learned and memorized. This form of learning, therefore, occurs in the communicative interaction mode of experience. Memorization can also occur as a result of past successful acts, memories of which are stored away and form the basis of planning for future action. Thus, it also relates to direct action experiences.

(For memorization, the route through Figure 5.2 is 1 through 3 to 6, then possibly to 8 to 6, and then to either 4 or 9.)

The significance of preconscious learning, skills learning, and memorization in the wider social context becomes clear. They represent a process of social reproduction. Society and its structures remain unquestioned and unaltered. When people learn this way, they are learning to fit into the larger organization or the wider society; they are learning their place, as it were.

Reflective Learning

Thus far it has been shown that learning tends to be culturally reproductive, simply because that is the way it is frequently defined. It was suggested that nonreflective learning inevitably reproduces the social structures of society, but this is not true of reflective learning. Freire (1972a, 1972b), Gadamer (1975, 1976), Mezirow (1977, 1981, 1991), Argyris (1982), Schön (1983, 1987), Kolb (1984), Boud, Keogh, and Walker (1985), and others have examined the process of reflection. Because of Freire's work, it might be assumed that all reflective learning has to be revolutionary or critical, but this is not the case. Reflective learning is not automatically innovative, but Gadamer (1976, p. 38) does claim that "only through hermeneutical reflection am I no longer unfree over against myself"—that is, that individuals are able to stand back, make decisions, and evaluate their learning. It was suggested earlier that reflective learning is itself a symbol of modernity. But before we can discuss these issues, we need to consider the three main types of reflective learning: contemplation, reflective skills learning, and experimental learning.

Contemplation. Contemplation is a common form of learning. The behaviorist definitions of learning make no allowance for contemplation, and yet it could be viewed as a very intellectual approach to learning, because it involves pure thought. It is the process of thinking about an experience and reaching a conclusion about it without necessarily referring to the wider social reality. Contemplation (the word, with its religious overtones, was carefully chosen) can involve not only meditation but also the reasoning processes of the philosopher, the activities of the pure mathematician, and even the thought processes of everyday life. What distinguishes contemplative learning from the process of thinking itself is the fact that a conclusion is reached.

(With regard to contemplation, the route through Figure 5.2 is 1 through 3 to 7 to 8 to 6 to 9—with the two-way processes operating throughout the latter part of this path.)

Reflective Skills Learning. In an earlier book (Jarvis, 1987, pp. 34–35), I referred to reflective skills learning as *reflective practice.* This is one of the forms of learning that Schön (1983) has in mind when he points out that professionals in practice tend to think on their feet. In the course of responding to unique situations, they often produce new skills. In fact, many skills are learned in a totally unthinking manner, and so this may be regarded as a more sophisticated approach to learning practical subjects. It involves not only learning a skill but also learning the concepts that undergird the practice. This makes it possible to know why the skill should be performed in a specific way.

(In this case, the route through Figure 5.2 is 1 through 3 to 5, 7, and 8 and then loop as many times as necessary in both directions out from 5 to 8 to 6 to 9.)

Experimental Learning. In experimental learning, theory is tried out in practice, and the result is a new form of knowledge that captures social reality. This approach to learning relates very closely to Kelly's (1963) understanding of human beings as scientists who are always experimenting on their environment and acquiring new knowledge from it.

(With respect to experimental learning, the route through Figure 5.2 is 1 through 3 to 7, 5, and 8 and then loop as many times as necessary in both directions out from 7 to 8 to 6 to 9.)

We have noted that these three forms of learning do not always have to be innovative. The fact that the word *learning* can be used to denote both conformist and innovative outcomes seems paradoxical. Learning can result in agreement and conformity or disagreement and innovation. It is, perhaps, the second set of outcomes that makes a consideration of power crucial to any understanding of learning.

From the typology of learning, it is apparent that it re- √ lates very closely to the typology of action produced in the previous chapter. The next section of this chapter endeavors to illustrate their interrelationship.

Learning and Action

This section explores the relationship between learning and action. This relationship is complex; we will approach it from several directions.

Learning and Habitualized Action

We have observed that action is not a simple phenomenon but may take a number of different forms. One way of analyzing it is to relate it to the process of habitualization, which was touched on in Chapter Two. Berger and Luckmann (1966, p. 71) argue that "in terms of the meanings bestowed by man upon his activity, habitualization makes it unnecessary for each situation to be defined anew, step by step. A large number of situations may be subsumed under its predefinition." In other words, as actions become more familiar, there is less need to learn from them. The process of habitualization consists of a number of stages, as the typology of action presented in Table 5.2 suggests.

Table 5.2. Types of Action/Nonaction and the Learning Situation.

Action/nonaction	Learning situation
Anomic	Nonlearning situation
Preventive	Potential learning situation
Nonresponse	Potential learning situation
Experimental/creative	Learning situation
Repetitive	Potential learning situation
Presumptive	Nonlearning situation
Ritualistic	Minimal or nonlearning situation
Alienating	Minimal or nonlearning situation

It will be seen that there were three forms of nonaction and that in at least two of them there lies a potentiality for learning. However, the experimental/creative situations are those in which individuals try out what they think will work, often as a result of careful planning, and if it does, then they tend to repeat the action on future occasions. It is a situation in which actors have to monitor, retrospect, and even reflect upon their action and evaluate it, while in repetitive action there is a tendency to think less and presume more; the final three forms of action are minimal or nonlearning situations. The first is the situation in which actors take for granted the situation and perform almost unthinkingly, the second is when the presumption becomes merely going through the motions, and the final one is where ritualistic action becomes oppressive and/or meaningless. Only when the end results of the action are other than expected will these latter forms of action produce potential learning situations.

It is important to note that the habitualization process is normal and can even be regarded as one of the goals of training. After all, if workers do not have to think about a task, they can do it more quickly and efficiently. Consequently, when mechanical procedures need to be carried out, it may be appropriate for people to function in action forms that are essentially nonlearning processes.

Learning, Thought, and Action

In Chapter Four, three forms of thought were discussed: planning, monitoring, and retrospecting. These will form the basis of the following analysis of the connection between learning, thought, and action. In addition, because both monitoring and retrospection can easily turn into reflection, we will also touch on the subject of reflection.

Planning. This form of consciousness does not involve any action in itself, although it may well result in future action. It is basically a process of reasoning, although it can include other types of thought, such as imagining and predicting. There are only two types of learning that can occur during the planning stage: memorization and contemplation. Planning becomes learning when the planning processes not only look forward to the next act, but when a conclusion is reached. The knowledge acquired is of a rational-logical nature. Memorized learning can be recalled in such a way that it guides future action, or else a belief or hypothesis is acquired that needs to be tested through some form of experimental action.

Monitoring. Monitoring occurs in the process of conscious action, where the action itself forms the basis of the experience from which learning becomes possible. One form of learning — preconscious learning — seems to occur as a result of an almost unconscious monitoring of action; it is only recalled by the conscious mind at a later time and in a new experience. It could occur during all types of action situations, perhaps even those that are classified as nonlearning situations in Table 5.2. In addition, monitoring is at a high level of consciousness in skills learning, since the learners are constantly aware of the practice process. This high level of consciousness also occurs *during* the reflective skills and experimental learning processes, for it will be recalled from the preceding discussion that in these two forms of reflective learning, the action is part of the learning process itself. For the most part, therefore, monitoring occurs in forms of learning that are related to direct action experience rather than communicative interaction.

One form of action that has not been fully discussed so far is presumptive action. In this case, harmony exists between the social world and the actors' biographies and action can occur in an almost instinctive manner. This almost thoughtless action is usually monitored with a very low level of consciousness, as is shown by the fact that it is possible under certain conditions to recall presumptive behavior. For the most part, time seems to flow smoothly and in an almost unnoticed manner. The stock of knowledge people have assimilated enables them to make sense of their world. This is, as Schutz and Luckmann (1974, p. 3) claim, humankind's "fundamental and paramount reality." Meaning itself comes from understanding behavior: "It is only in explication that my own behavior becomes meaningful to me. But again too, the behavior of my fellow man becomes 'intelligible' to me through the interpretation in my stock of knowledge of his bodily performances, of his expressive movements, and so on, whereby I simply accept the possibility of his meaningful behavior. Further, I know that my behavior can be explicated by him as meaningful in his acts of interpretation, and 'I know that he knows that I know.' The everyday lifeworld is therefore fundamentally intersubjective; it is a social world" (Schutz and Luckmann, 1974, p. 16).

In commenting on Schutz and Luckmann's views, Habermas (1987, pp. 130–135) claims that the lifeworld is unquestioning, intersubjective, and apparently almost unchanging. Thus it may be seen that when a situation is almost automatically meaningful, it is because it corresponds to people's paramount reality and enables them to act presumptively, repetitively, ritualistically, and even in an alienated manner. As a result, there is little planning, little monitoring, and little reflection, and so this is a classic nonlearning situation. This situation is fundamental to all social living; people act and interact on the assumption that they can anticipate the outcome of their behavior. If they did not have this confidence, social living would not be possible, and yet when this confidence is disturbed, disjuncture — and thus learning — occurs. It is a paradox of learning that nonlearning is essential to social life, but the converse is also true.

Retrospection. Rather like the process of monitoring, retrospection is common at the end of conscious action and normally results in a storing away of a memory of an act or a series of actions that have been performed. Again, the learning process accompanying the thought is nonreflective. But when the act has been disturbed in some way, time appears to stop as the act is located within the boundaries of time and reflected on.

Reflection. When presumptive action is no longer possible, people experience disjuncture. Harmony between the actors and their social world is destroyed, because people become conscious that their stock of knowledge (their biographies) is insufficient to cope with, or is prevented from responding to, their action experience. They are no longer able to act unthinkingly or in the monitoring mode. Instead, they are forced to reject the possibility of learning from the situation or else to reflect on their previous actions or plan for future ones. At the point of disjuncture — which can occur after any form of action and also in the situations of the first two forms of nonaction (anomic and preventive) — any type of learning can begin.

Communicative Interaction and Learning

Communicative interaction is linguistic and mediates a secondary experience. In precisely the same way as with primary experience, actors bring their biographies to the situation and have an experience; they enter into communication. Communication has at least two prerequisites: first, that the actors understand what is being communicated, and second, that the content of the communication is in some manner shared. Since the experience is essentially cognitive, only certain forms of learning and nonlearning can occur in this mode, such as memorization and the three forms of reflective learning. However, this is not to deny that the information being communicated might have practical implications; it is to deny that it is practical knowledge. Practical knowledge can only be learned in primary experience, so that the actors have to use their newfound information to practice, experiment, and so on in practical action.

It is categorically not a transfer of knowledge or skills to the practical situation, but it is the learning of new knowledge and skills through primary experience.

Therefore, communicative interaction is in itself limited to only three forms of learning — those that are cognitive. In the nonreflective learning situation, the learners memorize what they are told, what they read, and so on and then reproduce it at a relevant time. This is an extremely common form of learning, especially in many educational establishments! By contrast, the reflective forms of learning can occur as a result of encouragement within the interaction, perhaps due to a feeling of equality between the actors, or because there is a disjuncture between what is already known and what is being communicated that leads to reflection on it.

In addition, nonlearning can occur in communicative interaction when what is being communicated is already known. "Perfect" communication, in one sense, can occur because the actors are totally in agreement. This seems to be what Habermas (1984, p. 100) is seeking when he includes the idea of consensus in his discussion of communicative action and when he suggests that an agreed-on definition of a situation can establish order. But paradoxically, it is a *lack* of agreement that results in learning. For this reason, it is now necessary to discuss the concept of disjuncture in a little more detail.

Disjuncture

Disjuncture occurs whenever there is lack of accord between the external world experienced by human beings and their internal biographical interests or knowledge. It was suggested in Chapter One that when the dwellers in the Garden of Eden ate of the tree of the knowledge of good and evil, they were no longer in harmony with nature. Disjuncture came about, forcing them (and us) to try to recapture this harmonious relationship.

Disjuncture makes learning possible. The paradox is that if harmony is fully established, there can be no learning situation. However, modern society is undergoing change at such a rapid rate that lack of total accord between the internal and external worlds is inevitable. In addition, in dyadic relationships, even of the most harmonious kind, changes in one person create disjuncture within the relationship, and so learning occurs as the two people seek to reestablish the lost harmony. Change, then, is one of the conditions of the modern world, and these conditions themselves are fuel for the fire of lifelong learning.

This highlights the major paradox in human learning: interpersonal harmony is considered extremely desirable, and learning is also considered a laudable goal. However, to achieve the best conditions for learning, the ideal state of harmony has to be disturbed and disjuncture has to occur between the learners and their natural world, or their sociocultural world, or both.

Disjuncture is not limited to primary experience. It can also occur in communicative interaction, which Gadamer (1976, p. 19) regards as the "universal phenomenon of human linguisticality." In this mode, people experience a wider range of phenomena indirectly. But only if there is disjuncture between the store of knowledge in the mind and the information being presented in discourse can the conditions exist for learning. By contrast, if the information being transmitted is already known, then there need be no disjuncture and no possibility of learning.

A secondary experience rarely occurs without a primary one happening simultaneously. However, disjuncture does not need to take place in both modes simultaneously. Disjuncture in communicative interaction, which can result in learning, does not have to cause disharmony in the primary experience. Indeed, in good teaching, the primary relationship should be maintained and developed to help people learn from any disjuncture that occurs in the secondary mode. Teachers who get angry or frustrated with their learners when they are unable to understand the lecture material should recognize that this is the necessary state in which learning can occur, rather than considering their students unintelligent and unable to learn.

Conclusion

We have observed that learning—the process of thinking and acting and drawing a conclusion—occurs when presumptive action is impossible. Only in contemplative learning is there no action; the other learning processes involve a relevant and important action component. Learning has come to be regarded as a cognitive process and thus as the preserve of psychologists. There is no question that learning has a major cognitive component, and yet the action element in learning points beyond the psychological to other aspects of social living. Paradoxically, though learning is intimately bound up with action, a potential learning situation arises only when action cannot be performed unthinkingly. But we have noted that disjuncture does not have to result in learning, since potential learners can reject the opportunity to learn. They may not regard learning or changing to be in their best interest. The concept of interest constitutes the focus of Chapter Six.

6

Interests and Learning

While the ideas of dominant culture and conscious action were discussed in earlier chapters, it is necessary to continue to synthesize these ideas in exploring the way the person emerges through the process of learning in society. Only after we have explicated these concepts will we be able to analyze in depth some of the existential problems that surround the learning process. Thus this chapter first explores the ideas of consciousness and false consciousness, then relates them to interest and need, and finally discusses Freire's understanding of conscientization.

Consciousness and False Consciousness

It was argued earlier that mind, the self, and identity are social constructs, learned through experience. People who have similar experiences may have similar perspectives on the world. Thus we can speak not only of individual consciousness but also of some forms of group consciousness, including a class consciousness, a gender consciousness, and so on (though these imply similarity rather than uniformity). Individuals from the same class may have a similar understanding of social events, women may have interpretations of experience that are more similar to those of other women than they are to those of men, members of ethnic groups may see the world differently from other groups, and so forth.

The process of becoming, therefore, does not occur in isolation, nor is it neutral and unbiased. Some groups seek, either consciously or otherwise, to control or influence the culture into which people are socialized. Some Marxists would claim that this exercise is intended, overt, and malevolent. Gramsci (see Entwistle, 1979) would claim that it is a hegemonic process in which the bourgeoisie tries to influence society without apparently exercising direct force over it — in other words, that this is a covert influence rather than an overt one. Few would claim that no pressures are exerted and that every aspect of culture has an equal chance of being transmitted to everyone. The human essence does not emerge in egalitarian surroundings.

Power, therefore, should not be omitted from any discussion of learning — or teaching — because, however democratic or pluralistic society appears to be, the process of control or influence occurs in every society and organization and affects everybody's consciousness. The extent to which this happens in various societies differs. But it is clear that these processes are related to the learning that takes place in society, and so it would be unwise to neglect them in any analysis of it.

Marxists claim that people in the lower classes have a false class consciousness because they have been socialized into accepting many of the cultural values and interpretations of reality that reflect the ideological domination of the upper classes. Similarly, radical feminists might argue that many women have a false gender consciousness, because they have been influenced by the dominant male culture. Habermas, however, has rejected the idea of false class consciousness, although he does employ the idea of false consciousness in other contexts. He regards (1987, p. 234) false consciousness as either "collective or interpsychic, in the form of ideologies or self-deceptions," and he believes that this is accompanied by restrictions that people experience as repressive.

As noted earlier, though, there is a major problem with the concept of "falseness," since it implies that there is a "true" or "valid" consciousness—something that is impossible to attain because there are no unbiased sociocultural environments. Because there can be no true or valid consciousness in this sense, every interpretation might be regarded as ideological—based on the perceived interests of those who are making claims. From this standpoint, the use of words like *true* and *false* may be no more than a linguistic ploy to convey approval or disapproval of specific ideological interpretations of the world.

In a not-dissimilar approach, Sartre, who does not consider the influence of the cultural on the individual, examines the concept of "bad faith." For him, bad faith occurs when people lie to themselves: "Bad faith . . . has in appearance the structure of falsehood. Only what changes everything is the fact that in bad faith it is from myself that I am hiding the truth. Thus the duality of the deceiver and the deceived does not exist here. Bad faith on the contrary implies in essence the unity of a *single* consciousness. This does not imply that it cannot be conditioned . . . like all other phenomena of human reality, [but] bad faith does not come from outside to human reality" (Sartre, 1958, p. 49).

Implicit in the claims of false consciousness is the distinction between ideology and rationality. This is of fundamental concern when considering planning, learning, or acting in the social context, since the social world has itself apparently become a more "rational" world. Sartre's position, however, is that the unconscious forces operate to ensure that people deceive themselves about reality.

Even so, in one sense everybody's consciousness is true or accurate because it has developed as a result of what they actually experience. But there is another sense in which the idea of false consciousness is suspect in many societies, and this is rooted in the structures of society itself. Even self-deception might stem from the same social processes. If society is pluralistic, people are presented with a variety of interpretations of social phenomena; being presented with a choice means that they can reflect and that they have some freedom to choose which interpretation of reality to accept, or whether to accept any at all. This process of making choices means that people are not totally molded by social processes controlled by others. But not all societies are pluralistic, so that in some more totalitarian societies, or under more deprived social conditions, the diversity of information open to people may be much more limited. Consequently, their social experiences and their social identities are more constrained. An implication of this conclusion is that social analyses of specific situations may not be generalizable, so that, in terms of learning theory, the considerable insights of Freire (1972a, 1972b) might be less valid in some situations than in others. Before examining Freire's analysis, we need to introduce two other terms that have implications for an understanding of human learning.

Interest and Need

The concept of interest plays a less important role in learning theory than that of need. However, the two concepts are intimately related, as the following analysis will demonstrate.

Interest

People are conscious of their own interests as a result of their perception of both themselves and their world. They think they know what is in their best interest, even though the process through which their consciousness was formed was influenced to some extent by those who exercise power in society. When, for instance, politicians claim that a decision or a law is in the national interest even though it clearly penalizes some groups, they (the penalized) may accept it as being beneficial, or at least necessary, even though they suffer as a result of it. In other words, the people may have a false perception of their own interests because they have learned nonreflectively to accept what those in authority tell them is in their best interest or in the best interest of the nation. The more knowledge they have about their social situation, however, the more likely they are to be aware of their "real" interests. Indeed, Geuss (1981, p. 54) suggests that the only way people will ever know their real interests is for them to have perfect knowledge and perfect freedom, a situation that is most unlikely to occur. Human authenticity can be fully realized only when people know their true interests, and so the process of learning functions as a humanizing one in which the self grows, develops, and becomes more authentic.

Without perfect knowledge, individuals might decide what is in their interest but not reach the most informed decision, although the extent to which this is false consciousness or merely ignorance is a matter for debate. Indeed, if they had perfect knowledge they would be gods! In more totalitarian societies it might be more realistic to view it as false consciousness, while in more pluralistic societies as ignorance. By contrast, when others decide what is in the interest of the people, and they may do so from the very best of motives, their decision needs to have been taken in the light of both perfect knowledge and perfect altruism for it to be a correct decision, and neither might be particularly perfect! In other instances, it might be altruistic but based on incomplete understanding or be ideological, and so on. However, in situations where decisions are made and implemented then power has been exercised in an ideological manner, however well-intentioned the motives. In addition, the people might well experience these acts as repressive in the manner to which Habermas referred but, by contrast, they might accept them unreflectively and continue to conform to the social situation in which they find themselves.

In an earlier discussion that he seems to have departed from somewhat in more recent writings, Habermas (1972) employs the term *interest* in a slightly different, but still important, way. He accepts the idea that a break has occurred between the natural and cultural worlds and that people develop in an objectified sociocultural environment. He is at pains to destroy the idea of an objective world that can be studied from a positivist perspective. But people have cognitive interests — that is, interests that guide their approach to reality. These interests are the "mediators between life and knowledge" (Ottmann, 1982, p. 82) and relate directly to human experience. Habermas (1972, p. 313) writes: "The specific viewpoints from which, with transcendental necessity, we apprehend reality ground three categories of possible knowledge: information that expands our power of technical control; interpretations that make possible the orientation of action within common traditions; and analyses that free consciousness from its dependence on hypostasized powers. These viewpoints originate in the interest structure of a species that is linked in its roots to definite means of social organization: work, language, and power."

Hence, Habermas postulates three forms of interest: the technical cognitive interest of the empirical-analytical sciences, the practical one of the historical-hermeneutic sciences, and the emancipatory one grounded in psychoanalysis and critical theory. Self-reflection that can emancipate the thinker, or reflective learning in the sense discussed earlier in this study, can occur only in the final form. For Habermas, the critical self-reflection occurs as a result of psychoanalysis rather than from any sense of experience of pluralism. Having undertaken a full analysis of Freud's work, especially that on dreams, he concludes (1972, p. 223) that "the restricting agency that controls speech and action by day slackens its domination during sleep because it can rely on the suspension of motor activity. We can assume that this agency suppresses motives of actions." Hence, psychoanalysis overcomes blocks in the consciousness and penetrates false objectifications, so that "analytic knowledge is self-reflection" (p. 233). Indeed, the ancients used to believe that dreams reveal the truth. Habermas (p. 287) goes on to claim that "in the case of an objectivation whose power is based only on the subject not recognizing itself in it as its other, knowing it in the act of self-reflection is immediately identical with the interest in knowledge, namely in emancipation from that power." Habermas thinks that unlike Marx — who he feels does not extend his theory sufficiently — Freud provides a basis for understanding false consciousness and a way that individuals can be emancipated from this type of consciousness through analysis.

Habermas is clearly trying to get outside of the problems raised by the ideas of false consciousness and people's failure to know their own interests. He is trying to show how the natural processes through which people suppress their understanding of their own experiences and distort their own biographies can be revealed through psychoanalysis and self-reflection. Hence, he has apparently provided a logical basis for a form of reflective learning. But while he has highlighted some important aspects of psychoanalysis, his claims for it might be too sweeping. He has been criticized strongly for this approach (see McCarthy, 1981; Thompson and Held, 1982). He has come under especially strong attack for his claim that in self-reflection knowledge and interest are identical, since, as Geuss (1981) points out, people can know their true interests only when they have absolute knowledge, and psychoanalysis cannot produce that! Habermas has modified and extended his analysis in his formulation of a theory of communicative action. It was, however, his earlier work that led Mezirow (1981) to introduce the idea of critical theory into adult learning, even though Mezirow (1991) has now utilized communicative action in his own theory of perspective transformation.

This discussion of interest might logically lead to a consideration of human rights, a topic I have addressed elsewhere (Jarvis, 1991). But since there are major differences between the concepts of interest and right, this would lead us too far astray.

Need

The greater importance that educational theory attaches to need than to interest is reflected in the work of Maslow (1968), Bradshaw (1977), and others. The preceding arguments are just as applicable to an analysis of need as they are to one of interest, although need does have certain positive moral overtones that interest does not. Interest gives some impression of self-seeking, whereas need implies that its fulfillment is an imperative.

These connotations explain why need can be used in an ideological fashion: people "need" to have a high standard of living and so on. Consequently, the problems with the concept of need are at least as great as they are with the idea of interest and possibly even greater. Like interest, need has no empirical basis, so that it can always be judged as a deficit against some norm. That norm might be perfect knowledge, or it might be a greater or lesser degree of ignorance, but justifying norms is nearly always problematic since they are not empirical. The process is invariably an ideological one that is worked out within the context of power relationships, even though many educators may undertake their needs assessment from a totally altruistic standpoint. Illich (1977, p. 15) says: "Educators . . . tell society what must be learned, and are in a position to write off as valueless what has been learned outside of school." He claims (1977, p. 22) that need "became the fodder on which professions were fattened into dominance."

McKnight's (1977) attack on the professionals' prescription of needs is even more critical. Illich and his associates wrote at a time when the professions were under attack, and indeed they contributed to the decline in confidence that people had in professionals. Now management and consultants prescribe — perhaps from a similar ideological basis — and no doubt before long their prescriptions will also be attacked as being ideological, as in fact they are. The point at issue here is that need is as much an ideological concept as is interest, so that the concept of learning needs is a problematic one. From the perspective of the manager, for example, the organization may be seen to have deficiencies that might be rectified if certain workers could perform functions that they cannot perform now. Therefore, in the interest of organizational efficiency, these individuals need to learn. And from a personal perspective, they might need to learn certain things because they perceive it to be in their best interest to do so. Hence, the concept of need appears to be based on that of interest. This does not overcome any of the problems raised in the initial analysis.

Throughout this study, it has been argued that the human essence only emerges as a result of learning from experience in either of its modes. Consciousness of interest and need clearly plays a significant part in molding the experiences that people have, and so, like perceptions of meaning, truth, identity, and so on, perceptions of interest and need form part of people's biographies. Disjuncture is broader than interest and need; it grows out of the relationship between biography (subjective assessment of what is known, what is of interest, or what is needed) and the experience (perception of what is required — either that

of the subject or that of the other involved in the interaction).
One possible result of the reflective learning that can follow dis-
juncture is emancipation from false consciousness. This is what
Freire concentrates on.

Conscientization

Freire's (1972a, 1972b, 1974) most significant writing on learning
emerged when he was working in Brazil, among people whose
own culture had been denigrated by the powerful European elite.
The great likelihood of false consciousness and false identity in
this situation made a Marxist approach seem especially relevant. Freire's concept of conscientization should be understood
against this background. Conscientization is "the process in
which men, not as recipients, but as knowing subjects, achieve
a deepening awareness both of the socio-cultural reality which
shapes their lives and of their capacity to transform that reality" (Freire, 1972b, p. 51).

Freire is concerned with the "culture of silence" that prevails among the poor in Brazil. He suggests (1972b) that "the
dependent society is by definition a silent society. Its voice is
not an authentic voice, but merely an echo of the voice of the
metropolis—in every way, the metropolis speaks, the dependent society listens."

That the voice of the people is not authentic reflects the
idea that it is not a voice that articulates the people's own interests. There is a level of falsity about what they express; those
who control the infrastructure of society speak and so everybody else repeats what they hear. But people have to realize
their own humanity and become conscious of their own interests
and identity:

> Many participants in these debates [in the literacy
> program] affirm happily and self-confidently that
> they are not being shown "anything new, just re-
> membering." "I make shoes," said one, "and now
> I see I am worth as much as the Ph.D. who writes
> books."

> "Tomorrow," said a street-sweeper in Bra-
> silia, "I'm going to work with my head held high."
> He had discovered the value of his person. "I know
> now that I am cultured," an elder peasant said em-
> phatically. And when he was asked how it was that
> he knew himself to be cultured, he answered with
> the same emphasis, "Because I work, and working,
> I can transform the world" [Freire, 1974, pp. 47–
> 48].

People become conscious of their own humanity; they
become aware that they have their own culture and that it has
its own value; they become aware of the value of their work
and the way it can transform the world. Thus it may be asked
whether their false consciousness was still not an actual consciousness, and the response must be in the affirmative. However, this consciousness was distorted in terms of their own
interests, and when they achieve conscientization, they see the
world through new eyes. They become "beings of relation":
"By their characteristic reflection, intentionality, temporality,
and transcendence, men's consciousness and action are distinct
from the mere *contracts* of animals with the world. The animals'
contracts are a-critical; they do not go beyond the association
of sensory images through experience. They are singular and
not plural. Animals do not elaborate goals, they exist at a level
of immersion and are thus a-temporal" (Freire, 1972b, pp.
52–53).

Through the process of conscientization, people learn to
exist rather than merely live in the world. The richness of conscientization in Freire's thought might best be summarized with
the following experience: "It is striking . . . to observe how this
self-depreciation changes with the first changes in the situation
of oppression. I heard a peasant leader say in an *asentamiento*
(a production unit) meeting 'They used to say we were unproduc-
tive because we were lazy and drunkards. All lies. Now that
we are respected as men, we're going to show everyone that we
were never lazy or drunkards. We were exploited!'" (Freire,
1972b, p. 39).

At the point of conscientization, people are able to reflect critically on the world. Through praxis — a term Freire uses to refer to a process of critical reflective thought and the ensuing action — they can transform the world. But this is a paradoxical process: "The process of transforming the world, which reveals this presence of man, can lead to his humanization as well as his dehumanization, to his growth or his diminution. These alternatives reveal to man his problematic nature and pose a problem for him, requiring that he choose one path or the other. Often this very process of transformation ensnares man and his freedom to choose. Nevertheless, because they impregnate the world with their reflective presence, only men can humanize or dehumanize. Humanization is their utopia, which they announce in denouncing dehumanizing processes" (Freire, 1972b, p. 55).

As people become more aware of their humanity and their own interests, they can seek to transform the world. While Freire (1985, p. 170) was fully aware of the political implications of this process, he neither elaborated a theory of agency nor one of the state. Hence his theory, while exciting in many ways, appears strangely incomplete.

Conscientization is a reflective learning process, involving either a sudden discovery or else a gradual process of reflecting on experience in either the primary or the secondary mode. That approach to learning has also been employed with other oppressed groups, such as women (Thompson, 1983) and ethnic minorities. Thompson (1983, p. 181) quotes a woman who had taken a Second Chance course (another educational opportunity) for women: "By helping me to see my life and society in general in a different way, the course has helped me to revalue myself and my relationship with my husband. Before Second Chance I considered myself a failure, not only academically but in personal relationships in life generally. . . . I am now inclined to believe . . . that . . . I haven't done such a bad job." Whether this and other experiences described by Thompson might be regarded as conscientization or perspective transformation, or whether there is any difference between them, is a significant point.

Mezirow admits to having been influenced by Freire; his own early research was with returning women students. Perspective transformation, therefore, has a similar theoretical basis to conscientization. Mezirow (1990, p. 14) defines perspective transformation as "the process of becoming critically aware of how and why our presuppositions have come to constrain the way we perceive, understand, and feel about our world; of reformulating these assumptions to permit a more inclusive, discriminating, permeable, and integrative perspective; and of making decisions or otherwise acting upon these new understandings." Like Habermas, Mezirow believes that self-reflection itself is sufficient for transformative learning, which he regards as a process through which meaning perspectives are changed. Also like Habermas, he focuses on communicative action, or secondary experience, so that he is more concerned with meaning than with primary experience and the practical knowledge of action.

Transformative learning is clearly important to the process of becoming a self. People of all ages and backgrounds can have transformative experiences, which change their understanding of the world, their understanding of themselves, and their self-identity. In pluralistic societies, such experiences are especially common, since people often exchange the meaning perspective of one group for that of another. This underscores the importance of being critical. Learners should always be skeptical about the position they hold, recognizing that all positions are to some extent ideological.

Conclusion

This chapter has shown that in the same way that mind and self are influenced by the social milieu in which they emerge, an awareness of interest and need are also socially influenced. But when individuals become conscious that their interests and needs are not necessarily being met, or that their own experiences of them differ from their expectations, they may change their minds. In other words, they may experience perspective transformation, or even conscientization and may see things differently. In so doing, people reflect back on their society, transcend their social environment, and demonstrate their individuality. They are products of a modern world.

PART TWO

 *Personal Growth Through Lifelong Learning*

7

Being a Person

Human beings are always in the process of becoming—of incorporating into their biographies current learning experiences and thus creating new, but social being. Being is, therefore, transitory; it is always a manifestation of the "now" in the process of becoming. Time does not stand still, and so the process of becoming continues for as long as there is life. Becoming implies not only a future but a potential—development into something more than what already exists. Words like *being* and *becoming* are relatively rare in the educational vocabulary because few existentialists have concerned themselves with education; growth and development are much more common concepts in this field. Being and becoming provide the focus of this chapter, as we consider the subject of being a person.

In the chapter, we first explore what it means to be a person in the world, then turn to the process of personal development. Finally, we take up the topic of authenticity and growth, focusing both on the relationship between the authentic person and reflective learning and on the connection between the inauthentic person and nonreflective learning.

On Being a Person in the World

Individuals live and act in the social world; in it, the self develops as a result of learning from both modes of experience. Without a sociocultural milieu, therefore, there could be no self and no person. The social world is crucial to personal development, and certain religions and political ideologies have recognized this in their attempts to formulate ideal types of societies in which heaven could be achieved on earth. Studies such as *God's Blueprints* (Whitworth, 1975) have examined the groups of people who have sought to create a utopia on earth. The religions of the world have always had their own picture of perfection — their understanding of an ideal state of being in the world toward which they urge their followers to strive.

But the actual world is not the ideal one. The social world is fragmented by class, gender, race, and language and by differences in values, attitudes, and expectations. In this world, people are not totally free to develop in any direction; to a great extent, they learn to become the type of person that their social environment dictates. In Western society, this process is controlled by the values of technological capitalism, bureaucracy, the mass media, and so on. This is brought out in Simmel's (1908) analysis of the metropolitan mind. He writes ([1908] 1971, p. 84) that "the metropolis has always been the seat of the money economy. . . . Money economy and the intellect are intrinsically connected. They share a matter-of-fact attitude in dealing with men and things; and, in this attitude, a formal justice is often coupled with an inconsiderate hardness. . . . Money is concerned only with what is common to all; it asks for exchange value, it reduces all quality and individuality to the question: How much? All intimate emotional relations between persons are founded in their individuality, whereas in rational relations man is reckoned like a number." In relating rationality to the growth of technological capitalism, Simmel ([1908] 1971, p. 85) claims that the modern mind has become "more and more calculating."

Mind, then, is learned, or as Marx puts it, the self is the product of society rather than vice versa. In some ways, people inevitably reproduce the society into which they were born. This does not obviate the possibility of human freedom; it just means that we are less free than we sometimes think. And in any case, people have to understand the world before they can reproduce it. This points to the fact that a great deal of learning is either conformist reflective or nonreflective, the latter being the focus of this section.

Among the most common phenomena in modern society are technology, mass production, and bureaucracy. In these the worker is dispensable and replaceable by anybody else, which breeds a form of consciousness that is particular to contemporary society. Berger, Berger, and Kellner (1974, p. 31) note that "a correlate of mechanisticity is *reproductibility*. No action in the work place is in principle unique. It can be reproduced and indeed must be reproducible, either by the same worker or another with comparable training."

In addition, bureaucracy has devised standardized procedures and functions most efficiently when people learn these procedures and practice them. Learning within these organizations is, therefore, a nonreflective memorization of procedures, and action is a repetition of what has been learned. Modern society determines to a considerable extent the type of person that is necessary to fit into its structures, and in some ways the prevailing norms appear to be contrary to the types of religious ideals of a bygone age.

The decline of the significance of organized religion has led to a variety of formulations about being a person in the contemporary world. Nietzsche, for instance, believing that "God is dead," inquired about how individuals should live in the new era. For him, they need to learn to live authentic lives. But what, then, is authenticity? Without exploring Nietzsche's philosophy in any depth (see Cooper, 1983), we can make a few relevant points. In discussing Nietzsche's work, Cooper identifies two imperfect models of authenticity. Cooper (1983, pp. 8–25) calls these the Polonian and the Dadaist models. Polonius said to his son, "To thine own self be true," while the Dadaist claims that "the only requirement for the authenticity of a person's actions and commitments is that these issue from spontaneous choices, unconstrained by convention, opinion, or his own past" (Cooper, 1983, p. 10). In an effort to determine the lowest common denominator in these two positions, Cooper suggests that both revolve around self-concern: the former implies that human essence precedes existence and so the injunction is to live in accordance with the essential nature of human beings, while the latter emphasizes that what is essential to people is whatever distinguishes them from others, and so people have to be true to themselves. In these instances, inauthenticity occurs when the self is in some way inhibited from expressing itself—either in its alleged essence or else in what it has become. Some strengths and weaknesses of both of these formulations will become apparent later in this chapter.

Other existentialist writers, such as Buber and Marcel, have tended to play down the significance of the individual self and have focused on interaction as the ideal in human existence. Marcel's (1976) analysis of the interpersonal emphasizes the availability of one person for another. Macquarrie (1973, p. 111), in commenting on Marcel's work, suggests that availability means that "one person is *present* to another"; that is, people are constantly engaging themselves with others. Buber emphasizes that the fundamental human relationship is not an I-It relationship, but an I-Thou one. He asserts (1961, p. 244) that "the fundamental fact of human existence is neither the individual as such nor the aggregate as such. Each, considered by itself, is a mighty abstraction. The individual is a fact of existence in so far as he steps into a living relationship with individuals. The aggregate is a fact of existence in as far as it is built up of living units of relation. The fundamental fact of human existence is man with man."

It is only in human interaction that the values society most highly prizes can be manifest: without it, love, truth, peace, justice, and so on could not exist. But likewise, there could be no hatred, untruth, injustice, and so forth. For these philosophers, authenticity is to be discovered in persons acting in the world and enabling others through relationships to manifest their own personhood. The paradox of the human condition may be seen here: isolated individual existence is not possible, and yet existence with others can only be judged authentic inasmuch as it allows others to become the unique persons they are. Inauthenticity occurs when relationships are dehumanized, when the individuality and excellence of the other is in some way suppressed, when the richness of human relationships — through which the human essence emerges — is in any manner defiled. However, the impersonal bureaucracy of contemporary society denies the personal interaction of authentic persons, and in this situation people may find it difficult to be true to others and to themselves in the face of such impersonality. This, then, is the paradoxical exception to the Polonian position.

While these formulations are similar, they also contain profound differences. For example, for Marcel and Buber, the highest manifestation of the human essence involves giving up one's autonomy in relationships with others, while the other scholars mentioned here concentrate on the self and believe that its expression is the most significant manifestation of the human essence. In each of these positions, there are underlying normative interpretations; authenticity is never value-free action, and so the learning process must always have normative connotations.

It is perhaps significant that when there is interaction in which the values of love, truth, and so on are manifest, primary and secondary experience unite and ideal communication occurs. In this relationship, the idealism inherent in Habermas's (1984) communicative action can be discovered.

Few learning theorists have related learning to being, but there are two notable exceptions in adult education — Kidd (1973) and Rogers (1961, 1969) — and one in initial education, Peters (1966). Kidd (1973, p. 125) argues that being and becoming are both what living is about and that they are also the chief objectives of learning. He discusses learning in terms of the growth and development of the self, recognizing that there is a tension between self-growth and human relationship, which he does not discuss in depth. However, he cites, with approval, Maslow's (1964) study of the lives of people who have achieved both the autonomy of the self and a deep relationship with a few people.

Though not present in Kidd's analysis, the Dadaist form of authenticity is to be found in Rogers's writings, which have also been influential in adult education, especially among groups emphasizing human growth and development in their own variety of experiential education. Recognizing that learning does not have to be restricted to education, Rogers (1969, p. 295) describes his ideal model of the person who emerges as a result of learning or therapy as follows: "Here then is my theoretical model of . . . the individual who has experienced optimal psychological growth — the person functioning freely in all the fullness of his organismic potentialities; a person who is dependable in being realistic, self-enhancing, socialized, and appropriate in his behavior; a creative person, whose specific formings of behavior are not easily predictable; a person who is ever changing, ever developing, always discovering himself and the newness in himself in each succeeding moment in time." This is the Dadaist position: authenticity lies in changing constantly and acting freely and unpredictably. For Rogers, the ideal person is totally free.

However, it is questionable whether this is ever actually achieved in society. Even if it were, the question remains whether this is a desirable aim. If the main end of this form of authenticity is for the actors to discover themselves at each moment in time, the end product is one that is completely self-centered. Indeed, elsewhere, Rogers (1961, pp. 163–182) can claim that the end of life is to be the self that one truly is. It might be asked whether this is really what characterizes an authentic human being. Does the authentic person really act in this self-centered manner? The self is to some extent a product of the social world and constrained by it. People learn in interaction. Don't these types of persons acquire anything from the richness of the people around them? We might ask whether Rogers's ideal person is the type of person we would like to see emerge from the process of living, let alone from education. But while important aspects of his position are considered unacceptable here, Rogers does raise important issues about the normative nature of being.

Peters comes closer to the thinking of Kidd and to the ideals of Buber and Marcel than he does to Rogers's analysis. He suggests (1966, p. 212) that "consciousness of being a person reaches its zenith, perhaps, in the experience of entering into and sustaining a personal relationship, which is based on reciprocal agreement, where the bonds that bind people together derive from their own appraisals and choice, not from any status or institutional position. They create their own world by voluntarily sharing together and mingling their own individual perspectives. . . . The obligations . . . which sustain their relationship are felt to be more binding than most duties simply because they are explicitly undertaken."

For Peters, then, a person is a conscious acting being, the highest achievement of which is in coming to terms with the constraints of the world and sustaining personal relationships voluntarily. For him, respect for persons is based in the exercise of practical reason. Respect for persons is both social and ethical, and only in relationships can values really emerge in everyday living. However, the person is the learned product of social processes, and Peters argues that educators are responsible for ensuring that the educational process is directed toward worthwhile ends.

Developing a Person in the World

In adult education, there has been a tendency to treat adulthood as a plateau, a separate status in social life that is achieved at a given age or state of maturity. Some of the research in this area has degenerated into disputes about whether adulthood is achieved at the age of eighteen or twenty-one, and so on. More substantial studies—for example, of adult cognitive development (see Allman, 1984, pp. 74–81 for a summary)—have examined the stages of the life cycle. Few, however, have explored the concept of personhood. Paterson's work represents an exception. He writes (1979, p. 17) that "education is the development of persons as independent centres of value whose development is seen to be an intrinsically worthwhile undertaking. It might be thought that this account of education is excessively individualistic." Paterson's focus is on adult education. If he had been writing about learning, he might not have had to rebut the idea that education is individualistic, as he does later in the chapter from which this quotation is taken. Elsewhere, Paterson (1979,

p. 70) extends his ideas about persons by suggesting that "the development of persons is essentially the enlargement of awareness and . . . this culminates in increasingly richer structures of knowledge and understanding." This reflects his assumption that people are centers of consciousness and that this conscious awareness has to be increased as personhood emerges. However, in line with his understanding of liberal adult education, Paterson regards the process of educating individuals as synonymous with producing an educated society. Consequently, he might be accused of overemphasis on the cognitive and the individualistic, since society is more than the sum of its individuals.

Philosophers of initial education have tended to emphasize the future: children are being educated in order to become adult human beings and play their part in the world. Thus development has been a consistent theme in many thinkers' understanding of education and psychology (Piaget and Kohlberg are obvious examples). In his *Democracy and Education* (1916), Dewey includes a whole chapter on "Education as Growth," in which he recognizes the helplessness of early childhood, the need to learn, and the gradual growth of the human infant. Like Paterson, he concentrates on education. He seems to use the term *education* ambiguously. He sometimes employs it the way *learning* is used in this study, whereas elsewhere (1916, p. 51), he relates it to schooling. He also regards education as a system for transmitting a society's culture (1916, p. 72). His emphasis on learning is especially evident when he claims (1916, pp. 49–50) that "our net conclusion is that life is development, and that developing, growing is life. Translated into its educational equivalents, that means (i) that the educational process has no end beyond itself; and that (ii) the educational process is one of continual reorganizing, restructuring, transforming." Education obviously has ends, although learning might not have. It does appear that in this instance Dewey is treating education as if it is the same thing as learning.

Naturally, many educational philosophers have examined the aims of education. One of them is Peters (1972, 1977), who sees one of its aims as developing persons, which was discussed earlier. He has also written a great deal about the educated person. Achieving this status is an objective of education, according to Peters. He describes the educated person as follows:

> (a) The educated man is not one who merely possesses specialized skills. He may possess such specific know-how but he certainly also possesses a considerable body of knowledge together with understanding. He has a developed capacity to reason, to justify his beliefs and conduct. He knows the reason why of things as well as certain things are the case [sic]. This is not a matter of just being knowledgeable; for the understanding of the educated person transforms how he sees things. It makes a difference in the level of life which he enjoys; for he has a backing for his beliefs and conduct and organizes his experience in terms of systematic conceptual schemes. (b) There is a suggestion, too, that his understanding is not narrowly specialized. He not only has breadth of understanding but is also capable of connecting up these different ways of interpreting his experience so that he achieves some kind of cognitive perspective [1977, p. 87].

To be a person fully is to be educated and rational, although Peters (1966, p. 178) does not restrict the concept of the quality of life to an intellectual elite. He also argues (1972) that it is difficult, if not impossible, to formulate a general theory of development in relation to education, since individuals can be advanced in some areas but not in others. At the same time, Peters has been accused of overemphasizing the cognitive dimension of his ideal type of person, although he claims (1972) that the mind is fundamentally a cognitive process, and it must also be emphasized that he was writing about the educational process rather than about life itself. He regards education as having a transformative capacity, meaning that educated people may continually develop different perspectives on their experiences. Yet for him, as for Dewey, organized learning leads to the development of autonomous persons, able to think and act for themselves. This has led Peters, at various times, to consider the concept of rationality and rational behavior as being crucial to developed human beings. Only through rational thought can autonomy arise, Peters would claim. Dearden (1972, pp. 58–72) also concentrates on autonomy, but he recognizes that since people live in society, autonomy cannot be absolute — a point that is accepted here since authenticity can only be fully achieved in relationships in which some aspects of autonomy are voluntarily given up in order for the relationships to be developed and sustained.

In a sense, educators and child psychologists have concentrated more on the becoming than on the being, since so much of a child's life is still to come, and in any case every organized educational process should have its own aims. But being and becoming cannot really be separated in this way; childhood is still a time of being and acting as well as becoming. The concept of being perhaps plays a more obvious role in adult education, where adulthood seems to be treated as a state of being rather than as one of being and becoming, although there is a growing literature on life-span development (see Tennant, 1990).

But education is only one institution in social living; children and adults experience others as they live in the wider society. One institution, above all, appears to emphasize development: the world of work. *Staff development, human resource development,* and the like are common phrases within the vocabulary of this form of adult education. Nadler and Wiggs (1986, pp. 4–5) suggest that human resource development "might best be viewed as a comprehensive learning system for the release of the organization's human potentials — a system that includes both vicarious (classroom, mediated, simulated) learning experiences *and* experiential, on-the-job experiences that are keyed to the organization's reason for existence (profit, survival, service, product, and so on)." They claim that the organization must provide learning and growing experiences for both individuals and groups, to assist their work within the organization and achieve performance change. Nadler and Wiggs suggest that a synthesis of personal and occupational growth occurs. While this synthesis may often exist, the organization often controls the direction of the developmental process. By contrast, Brinkerhoff (1987, p. 6) is unequivocal in his claim that the importance of this process does not lie in personal growth but in the extent to which it "produces value to the organization at a reasonable cost." From this standpoint, the direction of the growth and development is controlled, the person has subordinate value, and the learning is circumscribed in quite specific ways by the interests of the organization.

People are exposed to many more opportunities to learn than just those provided by the educational institution, but all of these are socially constrained. Both being and becoming involve the whole of life rather than just one part of it, and for some people the educational institution is by no means the one through which they experience those potential learning experiences that enable them to be and to become. Indeed, for some individuals the educational institution may inhibit development, despite the dedicated efforts of educators, since they do not regard this institution as relevant to their life or their world.

Before this discussion can proceed further, we need to explore the relationship between authenticity and growth and development.

Authenticity and Growth

Three formulations of authenticity were discussed above: the Polonian; the Dadaist; and the interactive position favored by Marcel and Buber, where people discover themselves in a relationship with others in which they also endeavor to assist the others to be themselves. The third position is similar to that of Gadamer (1976, p. 17), who sees language as the mechanism that binds people into a "linguistic circle." It also resembles Habermas's approach. Habermas's theory of communicative action has of course been very influential in recent years. He describes (1984, p. 286) communicative action as follows: "In communicative action participants are not primarily oriented to their own individual successes; they pursue their individual goals under the condition that they can harmonize their plans of action on the basis of common situation definitions." All three of the positions just cited acknowledge the need to break away from individuality and think about the person in society. But the third approach is favored here, because it is the only one that recognizes the fundamental significance of interactive relationships to individuality.

Lifelong learning is not the same thing as lifelong education, adult education, and so on. Lifelong learning is a reality of everyday life; the constraints on it are socially determined. It is possible within any social context for people to be and to behave in such a way as to help others be, and there is a certain rationality in this, because only in reciprocal relationships can being and becoming be maximized for everybody. This form of human relationship is possible even in extreme social situations, and then society usually both recognizes and rewards it. It is similar to Max Weber's (1978) concept of value rationality, which Weber contrasts with purposive rationality—calculating and trying to achieve one's own ends. But purposive rationality is not neutral; it too is rooted in certain values.

Scholars and others also disagree about the aims of education. Some believe that the goal is to create the educated person, one who acquires a certain body of academic knowledge and who has learned to use reason and plan actions accordingly. But human resource developers might claim that it is to learn the knowledge and skills necessary to fit into the organization and to work more efficiently. When stated as baldly as this, it is clear that the aims of the type of education that emphasizes the person are different from those that stress the person's place in the social milieu. While it is important to make this distinction, its elaboration lies beyond the scope of this study. Suffice it to say that where the person is the center of attention, the aim of education is focused on the development of the learners as persons, and being and authenticity coincide. But where the "product" is more important, the direction of the growth is tightly controlled and the personhood of the learners is neglected. This leads to inauthenticity.

Having explored some of the basic ideas about the person, we can see that there is an affinity between authenticity and reflective learning on the one hand and between inauthenticity and nonreflective learning on the other. The remainder of this chapter will be subdivided accordingly.

The Authentic Person and Reflective Learning

Authentic action is to be found when individuals freely act in such a way that they try to foster the growth and development of each other's being. This is a form of experimental/creative action, in which people plan and monitor their actions in order to achieve these aims. They need to develop as autonomous and rational persons within the context of social living, able to employ their reason (Peters, 1972) to plan their actions and to achieve the desired results. Since the development of another person's humanity is unique and idiosyncratic, the actors have to consider as many contingencies as possible. In Kelly's words, they are like scientists experimenting with their actions in order to achieve worthwhile ends.

Thus it may be seen that the actors have to be able to conform or to innovate, to criticize or to create, to act independently or in tandem with others, depending on the situation — but always with the end in mind of helping others develop their own humanity. An emphasis on critical thinking has become quite central to some approaches to education. In school and higher education, Meyers's (1986) work has been quite influential in this respect, while in adult education, Brookfield's (1987) efforts have been widely acclaimed. Brookfield has popularized the idea of developing critical thinking, highlighting how this can and should occur throughout the whole of life, although naturally he tends to emphasize adult life in his deliberations. (Of course, we might ask whether the idea of "critical" in this context is redundant, since all thought ought to have a critical element in it.)

For Brookfield (1987, pp. 114–116), the idea of creativity implies critical thought, although this is perhaps rather illogical since the latter implies an appraisal of something that already exists whereas the former suggests planning, the erection of something new and not yet in existence. Creativity may actually be a more fundamental faculty than critical thinking, though. But both entail the ability to think independently, to experiment, and then to draw independent conclusions — to learn reflectively. The ideas of rationality, autonomy, and independence, all discussed earlier in the chapter, surface at this point. Additionally, both creativity and criticality imply that nothing should be beyond the scope of reflective thought and nobody should stand above or beyond the possibility of contradiction. Fear that something cannot sustain critical appraisal may be one reason for not encouraging such approaches, and another is undoubtedly the desire of some people to exercise power over others, since these faculties often jeopardize the status quo.

There are many examples, however, of teachers who do not seek to exercise their authority over the learners, of managers who seek to enhance the humanity of their workers, and of situations where individuals work for the benefit of their peers. In adult education, in particular, educators recognize that they are not beyond contradiction and in fact that they should create situations where problems are posed and students and teachers engage in dialogue. Freire (1972a, p. 53) demonstrates that teachers and students can only learn together in dialogue:

> Through dialogue, the teacher-of-the-students and the students-of-the-teacher cease to exist and a new term emerges: teacher-student with students-teacher. The teacher is no longer merely the-one-who-teaches, but one who is himself taught in dialogue with the students, who in their turn while being taught also teach. They become jointly responsible for a process in which all grow. In this process, arguments based on "authority" are no longer valid; in order to function, authority must be *on the side of* freedom, not *against* it. Here, no one teaches another, nor is anyone self-taught. Men teach each other, mediated by the world, by the cognizable objects which in banking education are "owned" by the teacher.

Teachers' authentic actions have an unexpected result: the teachers learn and grow together with their students. But instructors who merely expound their knowledge in an authoritative manner are in no position to learn from their students.

Human resource developers might argue that much of their work entails similar authentic action. Certainly many occupational systems are changing, since there is growing recognition that human capital is not being fully exploited by denying people their humanity. Some work situations are gradually de-emphasizing repetition in favor of problem solving and even problem posing, and some workers are beginning to discover some autonomy in their work. But ultimately, the workers are still human capital and within the work situation and the ethics of such situations demand consideration by educators and others.

However, experimental action is clearly associated with rational thought and reflective learning, for both during the action and after it, actors might begin to reflect on the situation and learn from it. Significantly, in seeking to achieve another's development, individuals are themselves engaged in the highest forms of reflective learning, and they themselves grow and develop. Paradoxically, in not seeking to be themselves, they continue to learn to be and to become. In authentic action, human essence always emerges from existence and individuals grow and develop as persons.

It is perhaps worth noting that the Polonian form of authenticity often results in nonlearning, since it can take the form of bigotry, self-righteousness, or merely self-centeredness, whereby the actors insist on imposing their own definition on a situation and perform actions that are repetitive or ritualistic. Thus they are less likely to reflect and to learn and grow. Their potential is inhibited by their desire to be true only to themselves, and so they fail to develop. By contrast, the Dadaist approach implies an openness to every eventuality and consequently a willingness to learn from situations and grow. But this position is of dubious moral merit, since it places so much emphasis on individualism.

The Inauthentic Person and Nonreflective Learning

Inauthenticity occurs when individuals are unable to interact in order to help other people achieve their own personhood or when people's actions are controlled by others and their performance is repetitive and ritualistic. In this case, people reproduce the social situation and act within the organization's boundaries in a conformist manner. It occurs in education and industry, as well as in any other bureaucracy. A typical example is where the teacher, however well intentioned, tells the learners that they must learn their mathematical tables, that a procedure or skill must be performed in a certain manner, and so on, and where the learners are expected to learn in an unreflective manner and reproduce what they have memorized and practiced. They may reproduce the social situation and reproduce themselves, but their human essence is stymied. They are, but the process of becoming is inhibited.

In these situations, language also assists those in authoritative positions. Instructors do not always say to a group of recruits to an occupation, "This is how I undertake the procedure," but rather there is a tendency to claim that "this is the way it is done." Language has objectified the procedure; the subjectivity implied in the first approach is lost in the second. But the former allows for the possibility of dialogue, while the latter conveys the expectation of conformity. The former allows for experimental action and mutual reflective learning, but the latter demands repetitive action and nonreflective learning. Moreover, in the second case, those in authority are in no position to learn from those they are subordinating, and so through their own inauthenticity they fail to learn and to develop. Unfortunately, through their own inauthenticity, they also prevent others from doing so.

In situations like this, the personhood of the learners is denied; they are merely reflections of society and cogs in the machine. Society is allowed to function smoothly, new entrants to a social group can fit in without disturbing its norms, and so on. This is often what education does despite its claim that it produces change agents, because as each generation of new recruits to an occupation or profession go through the educational system and then enter their chosen field, they rarely disturb the practices of the group. The group predominates. The rhetoric of change and growth may be there, but in fact, much of the learning is nonreflective.

According to Heller (1984), the concept of person demands particularity and individuality, but in situations like the ones just described, these characteristics appear nonexistent. The personhood of the learners is denied and they are treated as if they are malleable objects—like clay in the potter's hands.

If the institutions of society function most efficiently when individuals learn in a nonreflective manner and act repetitively and presumptively, then we should consider the idea of non-reflective learning in greater detail. Are all the ideas about producing change agents (London, 1988) merely rhetoric to maintain the morale of educators? Perhaps educators have to come to terms with their role in producing people who fit in and play their part. Social systems are always normative in character, even though they are frequently presented as if they were neutral; efficiency is a normative concept, as is political expediency, and so on. Social systems that inhibit authenticity need to be justified, and so do those who might encourage this inhibiting process.

We can pose an intriguing question at this point: if every-one tried to be an authentic person, to learn reflectively and interact in such a way as to encourage the growth and development of other people, would society exist? Some thinkers have postulated the need for a new alternative on the assumption that society in its current form would be inconceivable. This has led to both religious and secular proposals—for the New Jerusalem, the classless society, and so forth. But this solution might be beyond the realm of possibility (see Levitas, 1990, for instance). In any case, this points up a paradox: reflective learning is considered the highest form of learning and the achievement of personhood, however it is phrased, is deemed an end of education and even of life itself—but the achievement of these goals in the present form of society is curtailed.

Conclusion

Having contrasted reflective and nonreflective learning, we should add that the picture is not as straightforward as it might seem; naturally, there are times when people can maximize their reflective learning and others when they need to learn in a non-reflective manner. This would be true whatever type of society people live in, provided that there was social interaction and concern for the humanity of others. Social interaction is essential to being a person, so that the type of society people live in is important in these considerations. Without moving too far into the realm of political theory, it would be possible to make out a strong case for a minimal state (Hayek, 1944; Nozick, 1974), where the governing elite stands back and arbitrates disputes and allocates resources according to need and interest rather than intervening constantly in the affairs of the populace. However, a minimal state would have certain drawbacks, such as the difficulty of redistributing wealth.

The paradox remains, but while people seek to exercise power over others, however well intentioned they are, the possibility of achieving a society in which everyone is able to be a person and achieve some form of authenticity remains a distant ideal. We might recall Buber's (1961) argument that neither individuality nor collectivity provides a definitive answer but that it is only in an open relationship with other people that reflective learning and authenticity can be fostered. People can only learn to be persons in interaction.

8

Authenticity, Autonomy, and Self-Directed Learning

We saw in Chapter Seven that the authentic person has to be free. All existentialist philosophers claim that human beings are free to act in any way they wish. Indeed, freedom is a condition of authentic humanity, whatever the moral constraints imposed on it, such as those suggested by Buber (1961) and Marcel (1976). However, according to Macquarrie (1973, p. 177), when it comes to deciding precisely what freedom is, existentialist writings are evasive. The same charge could be leveled at adult educators, who frequently employ the term *self-directedness* imprecisely, as many of them recognize (Brookfield, 1988; Caffarella and O'Donnell, 1988; Long, 1988).

The adult education literature has also assumed that adults are free, although a rigorous analysis of self-direction is lacking and the type of freedom implied is unclear. When discussing the point at which adults define themselves as adults, Knowles, (1980, pp. 45–46), for instance, comments that "adults acquire a new status in their own eyes and in the eyes of others, from [their] non-educational responsibilities. The self concept becomes that of a self-directing personality. They see themselves as being able to make their own decisions and face the consequences, to manage their own lives. In fact, the psychological definition of adulthood is the point where individuals perceive themselves to be essentially self-directing. And at this point people also develop a deep psychological need to be seen by others to be self-directing."

Knowles's claim, repeated in his more recent writings (Knowles, 1989, pp. 91–94), is perhaps more ideological than empirical, since the possibility for self-direction actually occurs much earlier, in childhood. Conversely, it will be recalled that Riesman (1950) discovered many adults to be "other-directed" and Fromm (1984) suggests that a fear of freedom exists, so that not all adults appear to have this deep psychological need to be self-directing. Both of these contradictions point to some of the conceptual problems surrounding the idea of autonomy and also to the lack of a single uniform psychological definition of adulthood. Indeed, many existentialist writers seem elitist when they suggest that the mass of people do not value freedom (Macquarrie, 1973, p. 181). The reason for this might lie in the difference between free will and freedom to act.

In contrast to other theorists, Chené does explore the idea of autonomy, which she interprets as meaning "self-directing" (Chené, 1983, p. 39). She returns to the Greek roots of the word and points out that it refers to situations where individuals set their own rules, although it is possible to conceive of autonomous people being free to act within the limits of preexisting rules. She suggests (1983, p. 40) that autonomous learning involves three elements: independence in the learner, the learner's creation of norms, and the learner's ability to foresee and choose. Placing her discussion within an adult education framework, she relates it to the pedagogical context, the teacher-learner relationship, and the learning activity.

Long (1989, pp. 8–10) also brings the dimension of pedagogical control into his discussion. He realizes, however, that low degrees of pedagogical control are essential to self-directed learning. Tough (1979, pp. 18–19) notes that less than 1 percent of all the self-directed learning projects he has investigated were done for credit. Thus, since so much self-directed learning occurs outside formal educational settings, it may be wise to exclude education from the initial consideration of self-directed learning. But pedagogical context will play an important role later in this discussion.

We begin the chapter by examining the concept of free will. Then we consider the freedom to act. Finally, we explore self-directed learning in relation to these concepts.

Free Will

Since individuals grow and develop within a social context and internalize much of the surrounding culture, two possibilities for freedom exist — interior and exterior freedom — and self-directed learning must combine both. We will concentrate here on interior freedom. We could view this as a type of freedom in which a person could have reached decisions to act other than those that were reached. At first glance, this approach might be regarded as self-evident, but if this were the case, philosophers would not have spent so much time considering free will. The decision to act in one way and not another is the essence of planning. It is now necessary, therefore, to investigate whether planning is really free and rational, or whether it is in some way predetermined.

As the human essence emerges from existence, it is continually affected by previous experiences. Hence, we could claim that those previous experiences embedded in individuals' biographies determine future decisions to act and as a result inhibit free will. Consequently, it could be claimed that individual plans occur as a result of a very sophisticated program like a computer program in the mind, and that any decision has, therefore, been predetermined by prior biographical experiences. This would mean that people do not really have free will. Their thought processes are habitualized as a result of their learning and socialization, making them no more than computer programs in operation. The apparently planned behaviors are the logical and predetermined outcome.

On the surface, this position appears to be quite straightforward, even if it is not very attractive when expressed in these terms. People have learned to cope with situations in specific ways, so that they do not have to give them much thought. They can decide to act almost unconsciously and monitor their actions at a very low level of consciousness. Their decisions are determined by their social situation, and their actions follow. Such a position can account for the fact that individuals' decisions to act in similar circumstances might diverge greatly, since their biographies are unique. Because their biographical programs are their own, the outcome of their operation is individuality but not freedom. This approach does not appear to account for the fact, though, that at different times, many people appear to act out of character. For instance, individuals who have had unfortunate experiences in school as children may decide to return to school to further their learning, even without the incentive of credit. They study for the enjoyment of learning (Houle, 1988, pp. 24–30). The fact that people do not always act in accordance with their apparent biographical programs suggests that some degree of freedom exists, even if people do not seem to exercise it on all occasions. Indeed, this can be developed further, since, as has been pointed out, throughout life people are confronted with alternatives. They have to choose, because this is the nature of pluralist society. As the human essence emerges from existence, it is itself continually confronted with choice and decision, and so the human biography is itself full of conflicting possibilities. However, it might be argued that this merely means that the computer program is much more sophisticated. But it still does not account for people acting out of character, unless the argument runs that when they do so, it is because the biographical program in the mind has utilized conflicting possibilities from the past experiences, evaluated the decisions that were made then, and decided quite rationally that a new approach is required. This raises the following questions: Is this apparent acting out of character still determined by previous experiences? Or is it the result of rationality? Or is rationality merely a more sophisticated "computer program" learned throughout life?

The parallels between rationality and computer programs is acknowledged through the use of terms such as *computer logic*. In addition, different cultures at different times in history have obviously disagreed on what self-evident truth is. Hence, rationality might be regarded as relative and culturally specific, and there are many anthropological research reports that suggest this to be the case (Evans-Pritchard, 1936). Moreover, it is clear from the previous discussion of learning that every learning experience is added to the human biography; this process might result in an increasingly sophisticated program that determines future planning. At the very least, any one choice, if such exists, is likely to affect the available choices in any subsequent planning situation, so that a degree of predetermination seems to influence every choice. This would only appear to be true if a restricted number of possibilities existed as a result of any previous choice, though. But this does not occur, for while any one choice closes some future doors, it can also open others to a multitude of new possibilities. The computer analogy might therefore be flawed at this point. However, the outcome of new choices might still be viewed as the result of predetermined dispositions, whether they are rational or not. In short, we have still not demonstrated the existence of free will.

The logic of the foregoing argument is that either rational or irrational planning can be related to the sophistication of the biographical program, and therefore people are not totally free from their previous experiences. This appears to be an inevitable result of learning: whatever people learn is bound to affect their future choices. Hence, a paradox emerges, at least on the surface — that every learning situation seems to restrict future choices — since people often do reach decisions that are in accord with their own character or biography. Thus, freedom does appear to be restricted, and we could claim that people only think they are free, because they are not sufficiently introspective to be aware of the processes through which they have gone.

But such a position is contrary to that held by most people, including many scholars. Dennis Wrong (1977), for example, attacks it in his well-known paper on the conception of oversocialized individuals. People claim to know that they are free and, more significantly, that the plans that they make are not predetermined. They know that they could have reached a decision to act otherwise, and even though their decisions may be predictable, they are still responsible for them. Hence, once again the computer analogy appears to be a weak one, since the computer cannot think or reflect on its processes, even though it might be programmed to monitor them. Indeed, human beings would hardly be capable of authenticity if they were nothing more than sophisticated computers. But still, the argument for autonomy of will appears unproven, despite these assertions that people do have free will.

The fact that people claim to know that they could have reached a different decision when confronted with a choice has to be taken seriously. Either those who make such claims are continually deluding themselves, or there is a conspiracy by people to delude the human race that it does not have the free will that it thinks it has, or else they are actually free in some situations.

People can delude themselves some of the time, but it is inconceivable that human beings should go through life seeking to deceive themselves all the time, claiming that they are free when they know that they are not. Likewise, it is total nonsense to think that there should be a plot by humanity to deceive itself into believing that it is free. Consequently, some situations where freedom of choice is possible must exist. If this is true, then is the whole of the preceding argument false? Clearly, this is not so. Previous experience often guides the decision-making process, and many decisions do not have to be thought about a great deal because experience allows for presumption to occur. By contrast, people sometimes cull from the depths of their experience in order to make conscious decisions based on past experiences. In other cases, those past experiences obviously affect the present situation unconsciously as a result of suppressed or unrecalled memories. There are also times when specific situations leave people in some doubt and any decision they make is not self-evident; times when the moral duty to do something may be contrasted with the desire to act in a different manner; times when what was learned in one situation has to be rejected in another; and times when the desire to conform to previous learning experiences conflicts with the possibility of introducing change and experimenting. There are times when people make decisions knowing that there are other alternatives, even when their decision is deliberately out of character. There are also times when people deliberately loosen the reins of constraint and try to create totally new situations rather than follow the apparent rules of rationality. These choices, and the actors' claims that they feel free to make whatever decisions they want, have to be taken seriously.

In fact, the person who always acts in accord with the rules and regulations, who can always be relied on to act "rationally" in keeping with previous learning experiences, is often regarded as rigid and inflexible. Often no emotion and no affection, and even a restricted form of morality, underlies this form of behavior. It is rather like the animal programmed to respond to stimuli but unable to learn from situations where decisions are not self-evident. The analogy of the computer program breaks down here, for while this analogy makes sense in many circumstances, in others, people seem to exercise discretion and act independently. Freedom appears at the points where decisions have to be made and where it is possible to arrive at decisions other than the ones that are made, where the outcome of a decision is not necessarily known, and where the human being is like the scientist experimenting with life (Kelly, 1963).

Many philosophers have not been overly concerned about the decision-making process, since they have claimed that it should be based on rational thought. To some extent, they have taken the nature of that rationality for granted; they have focused on the relationship between the will and the act. In discussing autonomy, Lindley (1986) summarizes three classic positions, those of Kant, Hume, and Mill. Kant bases his entire argument on the idea that acts of free will are performed by means of pure rational thought, but this argument fails at the points where rational ideas conflict with emotion, affection, and morality. Additionally, there is no obvious reason why an apparently rational decision should be acted on. Hume, by contrast, argues that a combination of rationality and affect underlies autonomous acts. (A problem arises, however, when desires appear to be irrational.) Mill argues that autonomy is a vital aspect of human life but must be combined with respect for persons. This view is consistent with that of Buber and Marcel, discussed in Chapter Seven, though for them, respect for persons emerges as a result of being autonomous. All of the preceding considerations suggest that humankind has free will. While it cannot be proven beyond any doubt that people are autonomous, a great deal of circumstantial evidence supports this contention.

Free will makes it possible for new learning to occur; otherwise, established patterns would just be reinforced. This is part of the paradox of learning: if people act only as a result of previous learning rather than with the context of present situations, their growth is stifled and they become less able to respond reflectively in future situations. If, on the other hand, they decide to act adventurously, looking forward rather than backward and not necessarily knowing what the outcomes will be, they can acquire new knowledge, skills, and attitudes. In other words, through creativity people develop, because new learning opportunities keep on presenting themselves. But, paradoxically, new forms of behavior are not always acceptable within organized society, and so the next section of this chapter examines the idea of freedom to act. Much of the following analysis has been influenced by Habermas (1989, pp. 27–56).

Freedom to Act

Implicit in the idea of planned action is the notion that the actor not only has free will but also has some freedom to act. But another feature of planning is that it recognizes the contingencies of the situation and even the wisdom of restricting free action in order to achieve future ends. Hence, it is important to elaborate on the concept of freedom of action here.

Everybody acts in space, often space over which they have little or no control or ownership. Thus, their freedom to act may be curtailed by those in power, and — as the existentialist philosophers claim — these restrictions can prevent them from becoming authentic persons. Traditionally, analyses of space have started from the distinction between private and public space. But while this is a useful point of departure, it is necessary to extend the analysis as a result of the structural changes in contemporary society.

Public space has a long and significant history: it is the space in which the state exercises power through law and regulation. People are expected to obey the law and conform; if they fail to do so, they risk formal or informal punishment, either by the state or by the people with whom they interact. As a result, individuals tend to conform to what is expected of them. Likewise, the state ensures that its system of law is preserved through a number of mechanisms that reinforce its legitimacy. The existence of law and the power to ensure conformity means that although people have the free will to think that the law is wrong, illogical, and so on, for the most part they are constrained by external forces to conform, to act repetitively, and to recognize that their freedom to act is limited.

However, in recent centuries, mechanisms emerged for critical public debate about the nature of society. The coffee houses in England and the *salons* in France allowed private persons to create a public sphere where they tried to subject the law to reason. This was an early self-directed learning process where people taught and learned through public debate in a democratic environment. Public debate became a significant feature in the development of contemporary society, for while the emerging bourgeoisie could not exercise power, it was in a position to reason about it. But the public sphere in this sense has ceased to be of significance in present-day society. Public space is controlled by the state and the large public institutions, some of which may themselves be state controlled, and individual freedom to act is limited.

Many actions are performed in the private sphere, though, where liberty of action has always resided. But society has undergone tremendous changes in recent years. Now private property is hardly the basis of freedom of action, despite claims to the contrary, for much action is carried out in space not owned by the actors. For instance, the large industrial and commercial organizations are private, inasmuch as they are technically owned by private individuals. Those who control that private space may be free to act within certain limits specified by, or may act on behalf of, those who actually own the space. This is the age of managerialism. But those who have no control over the private space of their work are less free. This brings us to the point made by some existentialists about the masses not being concerned about freedom: they may know that they have free will, but they also know that they do not control a great deal of the space in which they act. Thus, they decide that discretion is the better part of valor and conform to the expectations of those who do control it. In contemporary managerial society, people who control private space have the freedom to act in it, but those who do not control it have only the freedom granted to them by those who exercise power. This, then, is a matter of managerial style, with authoritarianism inhibiting the authenticity of the workers and facilitation enhancing it.

Since people appear to have free will and the ability to think and to plan, they do not always succumb to the exercise of power meekly or unquestioningly; there are many examples of negotiation between those who have power and those who do not. Individuals and groups negotiate for the opportunity to put their own ideas into action. Indeed, in education, for instance, the idea of the negotiated curriculum reflects the fact that learners often know what they want to learn, even if their knowledge is not as full or as sophisticated as their teachers'. Naturally, people may also rebel; knowing that they have free will, they demand the freedom to exercise that will. Disobedience and revolution are signs that there is free will without the freedom to act. Paradoxically, they are positive signals about the nature of humankind.

Educational space is controlled by the teachers, not the learners, although the learners may be granted certain control by those who have the power. Some of the discussion of self-directed learning hinges on this point, which we will return to in the final section of this chapter. The same argument may be made about human resource developers who work in corporations: they may be in a position to grant learners control over learning space or to take other steps that allow learners to be self-directed for a while. By contrast, they may have fewer opportunities to ensure that such freedom to act occurs in the workplace itself.

However, most people own some space — private, or privatized, space. This has traditionally been the intimate sphere of the family. The structure of some types of private homes reflects the demise of public space within family life: the more lavish homes had a great public hall at one time, but now the hall has been reduced to a small entranceway leading to the family's private rooms. The family itself has undergone even more transformation. One result is that the home no longer has many family rooms; rooms for individual members of the family have become more important. Here in privatized space, people are freer to act. However, the internal constraints discussed in the first section of this chapter still exercise some power over the actors, and so they are far from being totally free. And in addition, even within the family, freedom is still constrained for some members. Male "heads of the household" may try to control that space, thus limiting the freedom of women and children.

Not only does freedom exist in the privatized space; it also exists in time, when people are free of the constraints of their work and so can exercise the ownership of private space in leisure time. But the fact that people have this freedom does not necessarily mean that they are going to take advantage of it. Many people act repetitively or presumptuously on their world or build up obligations that restrict their freedom. In these instances, when a life crisis — even a small one — occurs, some of these obligations may be destroyed, and people are free again to act in new ways (Aslanian and Brickell, 1980). Others may simply not wish to avail themselves of the freedom. Privatized space is never totally free of the influence of those who control either the state or the large corporations. The media can penetrate even this privatized world, and individuals are open to its insidious influence. Moreover, people are exposed to social pressures to conform even in the most privatized space in contemporary society. Indeed, it could be claimed that from childhood onward there are always pressures to conform — not to the world of nature but to the created social and cultural world. People are only sometimes aware that they are free and that they have the space to exercise that freedom in. However, they do not necessarily feel any sense of loss, for as Fromm (1984) argues, a fear of freedom is common, and conformity helps produce a sense of security for many people. In other words, not everyone feels a deep-seated need to be free. Many probably do not consider this to be a significant issue, since their actions are of a presumptive nature.

From this analysis, we can conclude that while people do have free will, if they wish to exercise it, the freedom to act is disproportionately distributed in the population, with those who have more control of private space having more opportunity to be free. Many, especially from the working classes, have few opportunities to act freely, even though they may have free will. However, the psychological constraints on freedom are considerable, so that many people appear to have a propensity to conform to the prevailing social pressures. But sometimes conformity creates problems for the conformist, since it goes against the individual's conscience. Hence, while Freud has demonstrated the significance of conscience, it is sometimes through conformity that people feel that they have betrayed their own biography. We now have to apply these conclusions to an analysis of self-directed learning.

Self-Directed Learning

As noted earlier, *self-directed learning* is one of those amorphous terms that occurs in adult education literature but that lacks precise definition. Knowles (1975, p. 18) describes self-directed learning as "a process in which individuals take the initiative, with or without the help of others, in diagnosing their learning needs, formulating learning goals, identifying human and other resources for learning, choosing and implementing learning strategies, and evaluating learning outcomes."

Knowles criticizes some of the other labels to describe this process for implying that the learning occurs in isolation, whereas he maintains (1975, p. 18) that "self directed learning usually takes place in association with various helpers, such as teachers, tutors, mentors, resource people, and peers." This statement indicates that he is not concerned with self-direction in itself, but with a nonformal approach to learning that approximates his formulation of andragogy. At the same time, Knowles's ideological position is consistent with many of the points argued in this study, since he emphasizes the mutuality of human beings.

Nevertheless, he does not really use the term *self-directed* with sufficient conceptual rigor, as an analysis of the above definition suggests, since it is so broad as to be almost meaningless. Indeed, Long (1988, p. 2) points out that "conceptualization about what adult self-directed learning is, or is not, varies from weak to non-existent."

In this section, we refine the notion of self-directed learning by applying our previous analysis of free will and freedom to act to learning itself. We take two different approaches. The first uses the model of learning that was discussed earlier and applies our conclusions about free will and the freedom to act to it. The second examines a hypothetical learning sequence and shows that while self-directed learning is possible, people have a greater propensity toward other-directed learning.

Learning and Freedom

Different forms of learning are possible in different situations. For example, it does not matter whether actors control space if their learning does not involve any action. Hence, memorization and contemplation can occur wherever free will is exercised. But paradoxically, nonlearning can also occur wherever free will is exercised because, by definition, free individuals have the freedom not to consider or to reject the opportunity to learn. Additionally, if people do not wish to exercise their free will, they can be other-directed or tradition-directed—that is, doing what others tell them or doing what they have always done. In these situations, they may find it difficult to be creative or innovative; indeed, they probably find it difficult to exercise any aspect of critical thought.

Action is an intrinsic part of certain forms of learning. In these instances, the control of the space does affect the learning that occurs. People can practice skills they have learned if they control the space, though they can experiment if they have sufficient freedom. Teachers of adults, for instance, do control educational space, and the style by which they manage that space may be more significant than the teaching method they use. The more they try to control the space, the more they will determine the forms of learning that can occur.

It follows from this that self-directed learning, in forms other than memorization and contemplation, occurs when people feel that they have some control over the space in which they act, be it delegated or owned. Figure 8.1 summarizes this position. Self-directed learning is only possible in three of the six boxes (3, 4, and 5). However, since the nature of the control of space differs, it is very unlikely that the forms of self-direction will be the same, a point that is pursued below. By contrast, incidental learning may occur in almost all situations, but especially in those that fit into boxes 1, 3, 4, and 6. Incidental learning refers to unintended learning, often occurring in tacit and unintended situations (Marsick and Watkins, 1990, p. 127), so that when actors are in positions where they are unable to act presumptively, they are forced to think and learn from the experience. Incidental learning and self-directed learning can occur simultaneously, but they are at different ends of the spectrum: one is planned and intended, whereas the other is tacit and unintended. Unintentional learning is reactive and reflective, but self-directed learning is proactive and covers all aspects of learning — it can be creative or critical, cognitive or psychomotor.

The different ways that space is controlled in the three situations in which self-direction is possible means that we cannot regard these situations as similar. Candy (1990, 1991) makes

Figure 8.1. Freedom and the Control of Space.

Control of space	Free will	
	Desire to exercise free will	No desire to exercise free will
Controlled by others	Alienating (1)	Other/tradition (2)
Control is delegated to actor	Limited autonomy (3)	Tradition (4)
Actor controls space	Autonomy (5)	Anomic (6)

this point clearly when he distinguishes between learner-controlled instruction and autodidaxy: the former occurring in situations where teachers delegate control to learners and the latter where the learners have absolute control of the space where the learning occurs. Candy's term *autodidaxy* epitomizes the position of learners who want to utilize their free will as well as to control their own space. In fact, he makes the point (1991, p. 18) that in the autodidactic domain, learners are often not even conscious that they are learners, whereas in the other domains, they possess varying degrees of control. A teacher or a manager, for instance, may grant almost total control to a student or an employee to pursue a learning project, but they may have to urge those who do not wish to exercise their free will to become even the least bit self-directed. Even in the former situation, however, vestiges of control remain that subtly influence the learners' choices and "even the criteria used to make those choices" (Candy, 1990, p. 18). In the latter situation, paradoxically, control has to be exercised to help people become more self-directed. Candy (1990, p. 14) correctly suggests that "an indiscriminate application of the term self-direction to both phenomena has done much to blur the distinction between the two." His argument is similar to the position assumed here that delegated control is not the same as absolute control, for in the case of the former, learners have a responsibility for learning to those who have delegated control, whereas in the latter case, they are responsible to themselves alone. This distinction recognizes the reality of the control of public and private space. Sometimes those who exercise that control may not fully recognize it, since they genuinely want to encourage the learners to be totally self-directing. This may be especially true in an educational setting. Consequently, it is clear that where control is delegated, self-directed learning is a teaching technique rather than a learning strategy.

A Learning Sequence

To examine the propensity to be other-directed in learning, a learning sequence is suggested here that includes the possibility of enrolling in an educational course. In this sequence, nine major elements are isolated: disjuncture, decision to learn, type of participation, aims and objectives, content, method, thought/language, assessment, and action/outcome. These do not always occur in precisely the same order in each type of learning, but this does not raise difficulties for the following analysis. Figure 8.2 depicts a variety of sequences that might occur. The arrows indicate the possible directions that can be taken at each point in the decision process, with the dotted lines indicating the direction of the weaker propensity to act. Many arrows flow directly downward, although those on the self-directed side are interrupted at the point of thought/language, which indicates that no person is an island and that certain internal constraints always exist. We now address each of the major elements in turn.

Disjuncture. Disjuncture has been discussed in a number of places in this book. It can occur in the context of either the primary or the secondary mode of experience. The potential for learning exists wherever there is disjuncture between the learner's biography and experience; it provides a catalyst to the questioning process that results in learning. Disjuncture can be either self-induced or other-induced. For example, people can have an experience and realize that they need to learn more before they can cope with the situation. Or workers might be informed by their supervisor that they need to master some new technique to perform their job more efficiently.

We noted previously that disjuncture is wider than either need or interest. Individuals can look into the future and decide they should have a specific form of knowledge or be able to perform a certain skill that they think might be useful at some point. Thus another form of disjuncture is created—between anticipated experience and biography. This might be called a want. Wants, in this case, relate closely to interests, and they can certainly be other-induced. The whole idea underlying advertising, for instance, is to create wants.

If the disjuncture, whether it is a need or a want, is other-induced, then can the learning that follows be self-directed? It could be argued that the creation of the disjuncture is not actually

Figure 8.2. A Model of Self-Directed Learning.

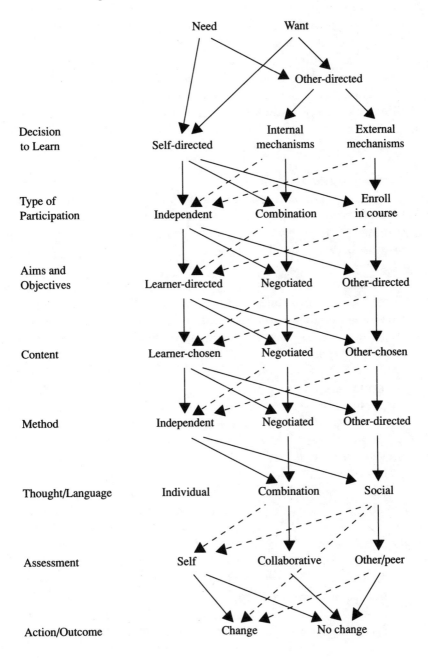

part of the learning process and consequently that it is superfluous to this discussion, regardless of whether it is self-induced or other-induced. Alternatively, it might be argued that it is highly relevant since it is the start of the learning process, but that it does not impinge greatly on the type of learning that follows. If this is the case, if the disjuncture is created by the teacher in a teaching and learning situation, we might argue that self-directed learning could actually be initiated by the teacher, even though it was suggested earlier that when the teacher delegates control, self-directed learning is a teaching technique.

Decision to Learn. Experiencing a need or a want to learn does not necessarily result in learning. Nonlearning is a fairly common phenomenon, as was suggested earlier, even when disjuncture has been experienced. Hence, there is no automatic connection between the first stage and the beginning of learning, since experience does not determine ensuing action, if the earlier discussion on free will is valid. This is why the issue of motivation becomes important at this point (see Wlodkowski, 1985). The reaction to disjuncture might involve enrollment in an educational course or it might involve trying to obtain resources for other types of learning.

If the need or want has been other-induced in an unequal situation, such as the workplace, the learners might lose their autonomy and be forced to enroll in a course of instruction. But if the learners do not have anyone else compelling them to learn, at least not overtly, it might be claimed that self-directedness emerges here. Knowles (1975, p. 18) suggests that self-direction occurs in this situation, since the learners diagnose their own learning needs and take the initiative in implementing their learning strategies. But this may represent an oversimplification. Riesman (1950) shows that while some people are inner-directed, others are other-directed. This raises a key problem about the concept of self-direction, because some people who might appear to act independently have actually responded because of their reference group. Thus it becomes difficult to claim that they are actually self-directed. Though there is considerable research on why people participate in adult education, there is less that relates these psychological types to the learning process itself.

However, at the very least it can be shown that there are three possible responses at the point of the decision to learn: other-directed overtly, other-directed as a result of internal mechanisms, and self-directed. Houle's (1988) three types of learners might all fall into the third of these categories — self-directed learners.

Type of Participation. The term *participation* is usually restricted to taking part in an educational class, and this is how it is used here. Two possibilities arise at this point in the learning process: either the learners decide to participate in an educational course or they decide to learn independently. *Independent learning* was a term that Brookfield first used when he started studying this phenomenon, and like many others it seems to have been lost as the present term has gained popularity. Independent learning might, however, also be conceptually false. This is because, as Brookfield (1985, pp. 7–8) himself has shown, all self-directed learning occurs within a social context. Hence, he was right to stop using the term because of its implication that learning is an isolated process, but it is employed here to indicate a learning process that occurs independently of the educational institution. This highlights an important distinction between education and learning: education is the institutionalization of learning, but learning is, at least in one sense, individual. Learning is broader than education and can occur outside of the educational institution, in all other institutions, and even beyond all of them.

Those learners who were classified as self-directed earlier are, at this second stage, now able to decide to learn independently or to enroll in a course to satisfy their learning needs or wants, or they can decide to combine the two. It is less likely for those who were classified as other-directed to decide, or even wish, to learn independently or through a combination of the two. But since there is a chance that they may do so, any understanding of self-direction at this stage must allow for these eventualities.

Aims and Objectives. This is one of the two elements that Mocker
and Spear (1982) utilize in their analysis of self-directed learning, but they cite only two alternatives — control by the learners
or by others. Conceptually these two terms are distinct, and they
are used with different meanings in curriculum theory, but they
are discussed together here since the distinction does not appear to add anything to the discussion. Even so, since their work
was published, the concept of negotiation has become common-
place in education, and so this becomes a third possibility. Where
the learners remain outside of the educational institution, they
are more likely to choose their own aims and objectives, but
those who have decided to participate in a course of study are
less likely to do so. The learners may have aims that conflict
with the teacher's objectives for the course, so that having enrolled, they may lose some of their autonomy. In other cases,
those who have entered the educational institution might be
given a chance to negotiate their aims and objectives.

　　The relationship between teacher and learners is not a
simple relationship, and it has to be carefully examined (Chené,
1983). Research on teaching styles is still in its infancy, but the
leadership study of Lippitt and White (1958) will suffice to make
the point. Lippitt and White isolate three forms of leadership:
democratic, authoritarian, and laissez-faire. Interestingly, the
democratic teacher does not necessarily encourage either self-
direction or negotiation; sometimes this teacher determines that
there will be self-direction or negotiation in an authoritarian
manner. (This may be called facilitation.) Obviously there is
nonauthoritarian facilitation too, as Hiemstra (1988) shows, but
the conceptual problem lies with the more authoritarian approach by the teacher. Is it self-directed, at the level of aims
and objectives, content, or method, when the teacher has determined in an authoritarian manner that one or more of these
aspects will be self-directed or negotiated? We might claim that
while the process appears to be self-directed, this is not really
the case.

　　We could extend this argument a little, because if the
learners have great respect for a teacher, they might be influenced by this sense of respect and do what they think the teacher
considers best for them. In such instances, to what extent do

the learners have genuine autonomy? These considerations show how difficult it is for genuinely self-directed learning to occur in an educational institution, however democratic the conditions might seem to be.

From a different standpoint, we could argue that the self-direction is actually a teaching method. We might recall that as children are encouraged to undertake projects and other forms of learning exercises in the school situation, self-direction is employed as a teaching method — one that is not specifically adult. Some research, such as that of Lewin (1952), suggests that active participation is more likely to result in behavioral change, and the Lippitt and White (1958) study also shows the advantages of democratic approaches in working with children. Thus, we will treat self-directed learning as an educational technique, one that is not unique to adult education.

Content. The next stage in the process is the selection of content. Again there are three possibilities: self-selection, other-selection, and negotiation. Self-selection is possible when the learner has remained outside of the educational institution and is learning for learning's sake. It will become clear now that this type of person is close to Houle's (1988, p. 16) learning-oriented person.

By contrast, those who are enrolled in a course may be required to complete the set curriculum or the examination syllabus. It does not matter how much apparent autonomy they have; ultimately they are expected to learn the material outlined on the syllabus. This regimentation has given rise to part of the radical criticism of education. Critics contend that there is no choice and that ultimately, education is a socially and culturally reproductive mechanism. (See, among others, Bowles and Gintis, 1976; Freire, 1972b.)

In cases where the educational process has high status, such as some forms of university education, the teacher — or university professor — actually determines the shape of the course each academic year. In these instances, the possibility of genuine negotiation emerges, provided that the learners wish to enter into such a situation. If it is forced on them, the same types of arguments emerge as have already been presented.

Method. Method is the second element included in Mocker and Spear's (1982) analysis. Much of the preceding discussion applies to this section also. We have noted cases where teachers might have decided that it is good for the students to learn independently, or by negotiation, so that they encourage contract learning and projects and so on. While these approaches do contain elements of independence, they are ultimately teaching methods. The extent to which a teaching method may be equated with self-directed learning is debatable, but it is obvious that if teachers are making decisions, the process entails more than an element of other-direction. Gibbs's (1981) excellent book on teaching students how to learn makes this clear.

Thought/Language. This is deliberately left here as a rather broad category, because there is a tremendous amount of debate possible at this point, especially if linguistic communicative interaction is taken into consideration. For instance, we could discuss this from the perspective of the use of language in thinking, from the perspective of rationality in thought, and from the perspective of intuitive thinking and similar concepts. We can only make a few general points here; see Jarvis (1987, pp. 86–112) for further discussion.

In beginning to develop his sociology of knowledge, Mannheim (1936, p. 2) wrote that "only in a quite limited sense does the single individual create for himself the mode of speech and of thought we attribute to him. He speaks the language of his group; he thinks in the manner in which his group thinks. These not only determine to a large extent the avenues of approach to the surrounding world, but they also show at the same time from which angle and in which context of activity objects have hitherto been perceptible and accessible to the group or the individual." No person is an island. Each person utilizes the language of the group, which also directs the thought processes to some extent. Hence, it will be noted that in Figure 8.2, there is no totally independent person.

We might extend this argument to suggest that in most cases, people adopt the same lines of thought as those who have gone before them. Thus critical theory becomes significant at this point. Brookfield (1985, p. 14) argues that the learners need to experience an internal change in consciousness, since if they suffer from false consciousness, they will not know what is in their best interest. But he is not totally in agreement with the critical theorists, because he is concerned with relating this change of consciousness to adulthood rather than with the issue of emancipating people from false consciousness or repressed knowledge. In general, the debates about self-directed learning appear to have omitted a great deal of relevant analysis.

Assessment. Often during and almost always at the end of the learning process, a form of assessment takes place. In the case of learners who remain outside of the educational institution, it is relatively easy to assess how much they have learned, whether their needs or wants have been satisfied, and whether they have achieved their aims and objectives. However, for those within the educational institution, those following set syllabi, and so on, this is a harder process. They may be given the opportunity to engage in a collaborative form of assessment in some situations, but normally the assessment will be other-directed, even if it appears as a form of peer assessment. In these instances, the question is usually whether criteria other than those set by the learner have been satisfied. However, we could argue that this and the following element lie beyond the actual learning process. It is also conceivable that even if the assessment were other-directed and the learners were found not to have met the expectations others had for them, they could decide to begin learning all over again, and this still might be perceived as a form of self-direction.

Action/Outcome. The outcome of any learning is either innovation or some form of conformity. We have already discussed these alternatives.

Conclusion

This chapter has demonstrated yet another paradox, that while the ideology of society is that people are free and autonomous,

9

Being and Having

The fact that human beings have both essence and existence, or mind/self within the body, has a major implication: they have the need both to be and to have. This chapter focuses on learning as a specific and basic example of this dichotomy. The first section explores the distinction between being and having, the second concentrates on being, having, and learning, and the third illustrates the discussion with special reference to education.

The Distinction Between Being and Having

The body is born into the world as a physical phenomenon, a biological mechanism, and as such has its own needs. As infants begin to develop, they reach out for things, and these attempts to possess actually occur before they have a self. Maslow (1968) places these needs in the lower strata of his hierarchy. Once the distinction between body and mind is drawn in this way, though, it is difficult to sustain the idea that a hierarchy exists at all, since his five levels of need fall into two distinct categories. The lower ones are *having* needs, whereas the needs for self-esteem and self-actualization might be conceived of as *being* needs. However, the having needs are biological ones, and unless they are initially satisfied there could be no body within which the mind and self emerge and through which they are sustained. Thus certain having needs are essential to human existence. In later life, unless these needs continue to be satisfied, the human being could become dehumanized.

It is important, therefore, to differentiate between being and having. Perhaps the clearest way to do this is to cite Fromm's (1981, p. 12) summary:

> In the having mode of existence my relationship to the world is one of possessing and owning, one in which I want to make everybody and everything, including myself, my property. . . .
>
> In the being mode of existence, we must identify two forms of being. One is in contrast to *having* . . . and means aliveness and authentic relatedness to the world. The other form of being is in contrast to *appearing* and refers to the true nature, the true reality of a person or a thing in contrast to deceptive appearances.

Not surprisingly, throughout history the being mode has been regarded as of a higher order than having. Since human beings are situated in a body that has physical needs, the satisfaction of which are necessary in order to exist, though, the being and having modes are not totally opposed to each other. There is a complex interdependency between them. But during most of the following discussion, we will treat the two modes as antithetical to illustrate their differences.

The having mode is self-explanatory in many ways, but a number of important points need to be made about it. We consider four briefly.

First, for the mind and the self to begin to emerge from the body, communicative relationships must exist between the young child and other human beings. The relationships themselves and the secondary experiences of communicative interaction are of crucial importance to the growth and development of the human essence. The significance of human relationship has already been discussed in relation to socialization and to human being and becoming. People are more important to people than are things. Objects possessed, such as beautiful works of art, can become the focus for contemplation and reflective learning can occur as a result, but the learning occurs as a result of the meditative response of the learner rather than through the possession as such; a live, dynamic relationship is never possible with things.

Second, the having mode attaches significance to things that have existence but not being, or if the phenomena actually have being, they are treated as if they are objects. Hence, to treat persons as slaves or as other kinds of possessions is to dehumanize them and treat them as if they merely have existence, which destroys the potential of the dynamic relationship. The same is true when people in the labor force are treated as cogs in a machine or as implements in the process of production. The possibility of relationship is eliminated, and the potential rewards from human interaction are lost.

Third, as Marcel (1976) points out, having always implies some act that was already over when the thing came into the possession of the person who possesses it, but being is an ever-present phenomenon.

Fourth, possession lies at the heart of contemporary Western civilization and is a fundamental assumption of capitalist economics. A person who possesses many things is often given high status. Advertising encourages people to purchase commodities they do not need, and conspicuous consumption has become a major feature of the system. This way of life has become deeply ingrained. Any other set of values has come to be regarded as deviant, if not wrong. There is a certain irony in the fact that capitalism will not function unless there is a flow of money and a continual purchasing of new commodities, since its whole philosophy is grounded in the having mode.

One of the social and political ideologies of contemporary society that has apparently not encouraged possession has been communism; in such countries private property was disallowed and public ownership lauded. (See Ryan, 1987, for a clear discussion of some of the recent thought on this topic.) However, that system still rewarded social position with the control, if not the ownership, of property — with successful party officials having their villas in the countryside and so forth — and thus it still encouraged possession. It was neither true to its own communist ideology nor did it actually embrace a system of property rights, so that it gained the advantages of neither system. It clearly failed to achieve the egalitarian outcome it espoused and also failed to gain the type of respect that the great religious thinkers and practitioners have gained through their own condemnation of possession.

Possession inevitably affects the possessor in some ways. Macquarrie (1973, pp. 87–88), summarizing Marcel's work, writes:

> To have something is not just to stand in an external relationship to it. The very having of something affects the person who has it. He becomes anxious about it and instead of having it, it begins, so to speak, to have him. There is a real danger to our humanity as the world becomes increasingly industrialized, computerized, automated. . . . Rising affluence brings new dangers. It leads to the acquisitive society, the rat race, the infinite desire to possess. In its relation to the world, as in so many other aspects, human existence finds itself at the centre of a tension and must survive in the face of opposing pressures.

The body does have needs, and these must be satisfied. The having mode is important for human existence, but contemporary Western society has overemphasized its importance. The tension indicated in the preceding quotation between the human being and the values of the contemporary world perhaps indicates that there should be a critical relationship between the two and that the taken-for-granted, presumptive response to the world may not always be in the best interest of humanity. It will be recalled that the culture into which individuals are socialized is biased in favor of those who exercise power and consequently toward those who support the current system. Hence, reflective, critical learning is necessary in people's relationship with the world, though the paradox is that people seek to exist in harmony with their world.

Having or possessing can therefore be detrimental to being in some respects. But, by contrast, being refers to experience—something that cannot be possessed and retained since it occurs in a particular period of time and then survives as a memory. Though people sometimes try to capture an experience, they inevitably fail since they are attempting to ensnare being within having. All experiences offer the possibility of learning and growing, and it is through these experiences that the mind and the self emerge in the first place. Being, then, is about active involvement in experience through which the human essence emerges and is nourished. In this sense, Maslow's higher-order needs reflect reality—for they are about being involved in a loving relationship, about being self-confident without being arrogant, and about self-actualization. However, the way Maslow uses these terms seems to suggest that everything revolves around the self, rather than being oriented toward active relationships that encourage mutual growth. Being is about being alive, and in that sense being is always becoming. There is always more potential to be realized, since growth need not end as long as being remains.

Being and having are, in sum, two very different approaches to life, and their emphases diverge in many ways. Because of the nature of contemporary society, having often seems to predominate. This is true even with respect to language, as will become apparent in the following section. Since the learning process is at the heart of being, it will be useful to examine it within a society that emphasizes having.

Being, Having, and Learning

Mind and self are learned phenomena, and so learning is at the center of the process of growth. As was pointed out above, the learning that is involved in being is active, participative, and reflective. Gadamer (1976, p. 50) suggests that "understanding . . .

cannot be grasped as a simple activity of the consciousness that understands, but is itself a mode of the event of being." Learners engage in relationships with the world and with their teachers in both primary and secondary experiences and in informal, nonformal, and formal situations. They bring their own biographies to the teaching and learning situation and enter a participative dialogue; in the learning process, the learners' knowledge, skills, and attitudes become fused with the knowledge, skills, and attitudes of the teacher. The same considerations apply outside the formal classroom situation. In seeking knowledge from books, people are actively engaged in the learning process and thus are gaining insight and growing. In discussions with others, they are trying to establish an active constructive relationship in which everyone participates and from which everyone benefits. If they specialize in specific areas of knowledge, that knowledge becomes part of their being and their experience, and others will acknowledge that they are authorities, giving them credit where it is due. Authorities do not need to demonstrate their expertise to impress others; the goal is to engage in a reflective, collaborative learning process so as to enrich oneself and other people.

There is a profound difference between knowing and having knowledge. It is the difference between actively participating in the process of creating knowledge, on the one hand, and on the other hand digesting whatever others transmit. In simplest terms, it is the difference between being and having. Having knowledge can mean having a certificate in such and such a field. Or students take notes in lecture sessions instead of engaging in active participation; they have books and seek confirmation from authorities that they are correct, not different or wrong; they demonstrate that they have attended certain classes. If they are then going to learn, they often do so through memorizing, internalizing the course material in a nonreflective manner. *Knowing* can also be used in another sense — that of having knowledge as if it were a commodity. It is this that Marcel (1976, p. 83) condemns when he suggests that having is always about assimilation. He notes (1976, p. 145) that "knowing is a mode of having. The possession of a secret. Keeping it, disposing of it — and here we get back to . . . the 'shewable.'

The absolute possession of a secret or a mystery — mystery being that which by its very essence I cannot dispose of. Knowledge as a mode of having is essentially communicable." Students expect to take possession of what the teacher expounds or the author has written and communicate it back on an examination. Teachers often encourage this approach; they see themselves as the fount of wisdom and demand that the learners listen and memorize. But in exercising the authority of their position, they *have* authority rather than *are* the authority.

Adult educators are frequently confronted with the results of this process. Students want handouts and other supplements so that they can go away happy because they have the something tangible from the learning experience. They can then inwardly digest it — that is, learn it in a nonreflective manner. This is not to suggest that teachers should not produce handouts. Handouts can be usefully employed to get the students away from the fear of not gaining knowledge as a result of a teaching and learning session, by telling them that there will be a handout at the end and so they should feel free to engage in the debate with the teacher and not worry about trying to capture the knowledge.

Education as Having or Being?

Since education is a social institution, we would expect it to reflect the values of the society of which it is a part. But education involves the institutionalization of learning; from this standpoint, we might expect it to encourage the being mode. It is, in short, trapped in a dilemma: will it emphasize the having or the being mode? It is argued here that it tends to adopt the rhetoric of being but the practices of having, and that this is inevitable because of its institutional status.

Some writers clearly distinguish between two types of education — one oriented toward being and the other toward having (Jarvis, 1985). With respect to the latter approach, Freire (1972b, pp. 45–46) offers these disparaging remarks:

> Narration (with the teacher as narrator) leads the
> students to memorize mechanically the narrated
> content. Worse still, it turns them into "containers,"

into receptacles to be filled by the teacher. The more
completely he fills the receptacles, the better a teacher
he is. The more meekly the receptacles permit themselves to be filled, the better students they are.

Education thus becomes an act of depositing,
in which the students are the depositories and the
teacher the depositor. Instead of communicating,
the teacher issues communiqués and "makes depos-
its" which the students patiently receive, memorize,
and repeat.

As "depositories," the students are then assessed to discover if
they have actually retained the material. If they can repeat it
nonreflectively but correctly, they are judged successful.

The final step is the awarding of credit and certificates.
Modern society demands that courses culminate in credentials
that demonstrate to the world that the learners have acquired
specific knowledge or skills. Without the proper certificates, students cannot continue to the next level of education — becoming
imprisoned in a global classroom (Illich and Verne, 1976) —
and cannot obtain certain jobs. Because of the enormous importance of certification, a market has grown up around it, and
education sells its wares (certificated courses) in the marketplace.
Fake institutions are also cashing in; there is a market for bogus
certificates and fake qualifications, often purchased at exorbi-
tant prices from pseudoeducational institutions. Even respec-
table universities have to award certificates for the shortest of
courses so that, through the mechanism of credit transfer, students can construct a portfolio of awards to demonstrate to a
skeptical world the amount of knowledge they have. Even if they
no longer possess the knowledge because they might have forgotten it or have rarely used it, it does not matter — all that counts
is that they have the certificate.

The one form of education that has traditionally avoided
the certification process is liberal adult education, whose goal
has been to help adults pursue an enjoyable pastime, learning
what they wished without examination or certification. Over
the past few years, however, a growing consensus has emerged

that even liberal adult education should be like the other forms of education. Institutions are increasingly offering modules for credit, and liberal adult education is being threatened by the values of a having society. The danger is that it will end up emphasizing the certificates to the detriment of the teaching and learning experience. The problem for education is that it is expected to conform to the having ethos of contemporary society, even though its philosophy might be closer to the being mode.

This is not a diatribe against certification; it is a criticism of the abuse of what is a necessary system in education. Learning occurs in the private sphere, and society is anonymous and to some extent depersonalized. People move between locations and occupations. How can applicants for a place in a course or for a job be assessed when they are not known? References can be written about the person, but they may not tell the whole story. How can potential students determine the value of courses they want to take, unless there is a reputable certificate at the end? Public certification is a guarantee of something — even if only that the learners attended a reputable educational institution, or that they once possessed the knowledge or the skills, or that they were given the opportunity to gain them by taking specific courses. Certification, then, might be important for education in the being mode as well, because the privatization of learning and the anonymity of the public world provide almost no other way of recording and communicating experience.

Freire (1972b, pp. 56–57) has this to say about education in the being mode: "Problem-posing education affirms men as beings in the process of *becoming* — as unfinished, uncompleted beings in and with a likewise unfinished reality. Indeed, in contrast to other animals who are unfinished but not historical, men know themselves to be unfinished; they are aware of their incompleteness. In this incompleteness and this awareness lie the very roots of education as an exclusively human manifestation. The unfinished character of men and the transformational character of reality necessitate that education be an on-going reality."

Education involves a dialogical relationship in which human beings communicate and share experiences, so that their human essence might stand out more fully through their learning. This is to be found in many, but by no means all, forms of adult education. In some cases, this sharing occurs between the learners working in groups, where all the participants are regarded as equal members. This equal relationship is extended to the teacher, when one is present. It is not necessary for anyone to claim special authority; people's expertise is recognized in the ordinary course of things. In groups of this kind, all the participants are encouraged to give of themselves in communicative interrelationship. Here there is no nonreflective acquisition of facts, no perennial endeavor to hold onto a body of knowledge, but a consistent attempt to become more conscious of people and the world and of their richness.

In a well-known passage, Peters (1965, p. 110) offers a similar view of education: "Education . . . can have no ends beyond itself. Its value derives from principles and standards implicit in it. To be educated is not to have arrived at a destination; it is to travel with a different view. What is required is not feverish preparation for something that lies ahead, but to work with precision, passion, and taste at worthwhile things that lie to hand." Peters goes on to relate this to the quality of life. For him, this is about being rather than having—about education providing "that touch of eternity under which endurance can pass into dignified, wry acceptance, and animal enjoyment into a quality of living" (p. 110).

These approaches are much closer to the frequently expressed humanistic philosophy of adult education than to the practices involved in educating children (although Peters's philosophy of education concentrates on early education). There are reasons for this: for instance, the system of schooling through which children pass emphasizes the having mode rather than the being one; society expects the having mode to be emphasized; adult teachers find it harder to enter a communicative relationship with a class of children than with a small group of adults, and they also find it easier and sometimes very necessary to be in authority rather than to be recognized by the class as an authority and a person. (See Kohl, 1971, for a superb example of what happens when a teacher succeeds in the being mode with thirty-six children.) Does this mean that adult education actually has a different philosophy from school education, or that andragogy is different from pedagogy?

Certainly teaching and learning in the being mode are entirely different from teaching and learning in the having one. But this does not mean that the two modes occur in different forms of education, with school education occurring in the having mode and adult education in the being mode. Education as a whole — that is, lifelong education — can take both forms; the being mode often occurs in the creation of the relationships between teacher and learners and among the learners, and the having mode when education is regarded merely as a means to an end. Hence, Knowles's (1970) original approach was clearly wrong when he separated andragogy from pedagogy on the grounds of the age of the learners, as he recognized in later situations of his books (for example, Knowles, 1980). Whether the learning occurs in the being or the having mode is not intrinsically related to the age of the learner but is determined by the situation in which it occurs. The differences between the modes tend to stem from the nature of the educational activity and from the types of relationships that are forged between teacher and learners and learners and learners and also from the forms of learning and teaching that are emphasized. If the learners are encouraged to be active participants in an exciting relationship with the teacher, the being mode comes to the fore, but if the teacher presents the material for mechanical consumption by the students, the having mode takes precedence. Obviously, this form of relationship is more feasible with small groups of adult students, which helps explain why the distinction between adult and children's education has been drawn. But, as noted, this is an artificial distinction.

Conclusion

Education is, therefore, faced with an unresolvable dilemma, and this is especially true for adult education. Education is frequently regarded as a humanistic process (Jarvis, 1983c) in which individual students learn and grow and develop. It is regarded as a major element of being — as a process through which the human essence emerges from existence in active participative relationship with others, some of whom might be experts. Yet the very nature of the society in which education occurs emphasizes the having mode and expects repetitive action and nonreflective learning so that it can produce people who can rehearse what they have acquired. As a result, education has been forced to adopt the characteristics of contemporary society. In many ways, this market approach to education is acclaimed as the most efficient and beneficial to the society as a whole. But the paradox is that it seeks to implement the lower levels of learning and to reward the having of knowledge rather than being and the higher levels of learning and human development. The higher ones remain and people still manage to grow, even though the forms of learning that influence this process most sometimes lie outside the educational institution.

The paradoxes of learning in society are quite profound, as this chapter demonstrates. The following chapter pursues this by relating learning to meaning and truth.

10

Meaning and Truth

The problem of meaning has hovered around the edges of learning theory without having been fully incorporated into it, despite its obvious relevance. Not all scholars have neglected this topic. For example, Mezirow (1988, p. 223) defines meaning as "a process of construing or appropriating a new or revised interpretation of the meaning of one's experience as a guide to decision and action" (also see Mezirow, 1991, pp. 12–13). Likewise, according to Dahlgren (1984, pp. 23–24), to "learn is to strive for meaning, to have learned something is to have grasped its meaning." Both of these definitions relate learning to the hermeneutical process. But both imply (although this is probably not the authors' intention) that experience has a meaning, which is open to debate.

It is appropriate to turn to the subject of experience. Primary experience is meaningless until it has meaning imposed on it either by the actors in the situation or by observers and interpreters — and then it is likely to have two sets of meaning: participative and nonparticipative ones. The meaning given to the participative experience need not assume verbal form until it is communicated to others. At this point, people say, for instance, "It is hard to put into words, but . . . " It is also in situations like this that it is possible to see the process of transforming experience into knowledge — the learning process. The nonparticipative meaning is, in fact, about secondary experience. When people give or are given an interpretation (or meaning) of someone else's experiences, they are communicating information, and this is a secondary experience. Meaning is then communicated linguistically between people. If there are different interpretations of events, a negotiation of meanings in communicative interaction often has to occur, and when mutual understanding has been reached, the information experience has been transformed by reflection into knowledge.

Now that we have made these opening points, we are still left with the fact that the problem of meaning has not been fully incorporated into the vocabulary of education. Therefore, this chapter starts with a brief philosophical discussion of existence and knowledge. We then go on to explore the concept of meaning. Next we relate the search for meaning to learning, to understanding, and to truth and knowledge, respectively. Then we link meaning, truth, and nonlearning to demonstrate some of the paradoxes of the human condition. Finally, we discuss meaning and legitimation crises.

Existence and Knowledge

Philosophy has traditionally examined a number of basic problems, two being the problem of being and the problem of knowledge. Not surprisingly, educational philosophy has started from the epistemological problem — that of knowledge — so that it has been concerned with ideas such as rationality, forms of knowledge, and so forth. The history of rationalism in Western philosophy can be traced back to Descartes, who reached the conclusion, "I think; therefore I am." For him, the ability to think and therefore to know enabled him to conclude that he existed. Existentialism, however, starts with the problem of being (ontology). Macquarrie (1973, p. 125) turns the Cartesian formulation around nicely and suggests that "I am, therefore I think." Life's experiences, then, are the basis of thought and learning, and so existentialists explore the meaning of being rather than that of knowledge. Hence, the affective domain constitutes a legitimate arena from which to learn.

Individuals are born into the world and they exist. From the outset, they have experiences, and these experiences tend to be patterned and repetitive. Thus young children learn to associate experiences and consequences — that is, they tend to give meaning to their experiences — and these interpretations of experiences are stored in the brain. Gradually, they construct a whole body of memories of both experiences and their outcomes. They must also internalize their culture. As Luckmann (1967, p. 51) writes, "Empirically, human organisms do not construct 'objective' and moral universes of meaning from scratch — they are born into them. This means that human organisms normally transcend their biological nature by internalizing a historically given universe of meaning, rather than constructing universes of meaning."

For Luckmann, the human organism only becomes a self when it has acquired an independent universe of meaning — when it has learned nonreflectively the encompassing configuration of meaning — and incorporated into it its own early strivings for meaning. The self, then, is a universe of meaning trying to live in harmony with the sociocultural world. When this is not achieved and disjuncture occurs, it seeks new meaning in order to reestablish this harmony. New meaning is continually unfolding with every new experience of life (Bohm, 1985), and the self gradually changes and develops with new learning experiences. But having been internalized and memorized, meaning develops independently, and individuals construct their own subjective and individual meaning systems that both relate to the social world into which they were born and reflect their own history and biography. Constructing meaning is part of the inner human experience, and yet through interaction with others, meaning systems become objectified. It is objectified meaning that is transmitted across the generations and between contemporaries, after it has been learned through early socialization and through subsequent life experiences.

Both modes of experience are important to this process. Primary experience is direct action experience, so that the knowledge gained from this form of experience may be practical in its application — that is, it is "knowledge how" (Ryle, 1963) knowledge. People can frequently explain what it means to them to have a particular kind of knowledge or skill. This is a very personal kind of meaning that comes from participation. Therefore, two forms of knowledge emerge by learning from primary experience: the knowledge how and individual hermeneutical knowledge. By contrast, secondary experience is a form of communicative interaction; it comes close to Ryle's (1963) "knowledge that." This communication is linguistic information, which is transformed into knowledge through the learning process. It can be knowledge about phenomena and thus might also be empirical or pragmatic, or it could be logical-rational knowledge or hermeneutic information. Individuals are not compelled to accept uncritically the information they are given, and they can question the information, whether it be empirical, pragmatic, or hermeneutic. It is at this point that critical thought and negotiation of meaning come together and learning becomes reflective. In every instance, therefore, knowledge occurs as a result of experience, and the learning process is always transformative — something that happens at the intersection of people and their social world.

The Concept of Meaning

But what is the meaning of meaning? Thus far the term *meaning* has been used without definition. Since it is ambiguous, it is necessary to explore some of its many meanings; however, we should not lose sight of the fact that this discussion, like any other, is conducted within the framework of a biased culture and language, so that the conclusions we reach may themselves be socially constructed. We consider four usages. First, the word *meaning* can have a metaphysical meaning; in this case, it denotes the meaning of existence itself. Second, it has a sociocultural meaning, in the sense that Luckmann uses it, which is to equate it with cultural knowledge that is learned during the process of socialization. Third, it is used as a noun in this objectified sense (that is, things appear to have meanings). Fourth, *to mean* is used as a verb, and then it conveys individual understanding or intention.

Metaphysical Meaning

The quest for human authenticity implies that human being has a problem of meaning. Fromm (1949, pp. 44–45; original italics) summarizes this nicely:

> Man can react to historical contradictions by annulling them through his own action; but he cannot annul existential dichotomies, although he can react to them in different ways. He can appease his mind by soothing and harmonizing ideologies. He can try to escape from his inner restlessness by ceaseless activity in pleasure or in business. He can try to abrogate his freedom and to turn himself into an instrument of powers outside himself, submerging his self in them. But he remains dissatisfied, anxious, and restless. There is only one solution to his problem: to face the truth, to acknowledge his fundamental aloneness and solitude in a universe indifferent to his fate, to recognize that there is no power transcending him which can solve his problem for him. Man must accept responsibility for himself and the fact that only by using his own powers can he give meaning to life. But meaning does not imply certainty. Uncertainty is the very condition to impel man to unfold his powers. If he faces the truth without panic he will recognize that *there is no meaning to life except the meaning that man gives his life by the unfolding of his powers, by living productively;* and that only constant vigilance, activity, and effort can keep us from failing in the one task that matters — the full development of our powers within the limitations set by the laws of our existence. Man will never cease to be perplexed, to wonder, and to raise new questions. Only if he recognizes the human situation, the dichotomies inherent in his existence, and his capacity to unfold his powers will he be able to succeed in his task: to be himself and for himself and to achieve happiness by the full reali-

zation of those faculties which are peculiarly his — of reason, love, and productive work.

There is much in this quotation that reflects the discussion in the previous chapters. Here in Fromm the Polonian authenticity emerges, the self-centeredness that demands that human beings should concentrate on themselves and the fundamental aloneness of individuality. Yet there is also love and creativity. It is only in interaction that the self is born. Learning through interaction leads to the birth of a self that is continually seeking meaning — but continually being frustrated in that quest. Fromm claims that there is no meaning to life, except the meaning humankind gives it. Not everyone would accept this position, because humankind has constructed complex theologies and idealistic ideologies that provide a meaning to existence (Hanfling, 1987a, 1987b) — but they are constructed, even socially constructed! (Here it would be possible to enter a debate about revelation, but that lies beyond the scope of this study.) The endless quest for meaning, to make sense of existence, however, is something that everyone understands.

Sociocultural Meaning

Luckmann writes of a universe of meaning into which individuals are born. He emphasizes (1967, p. 44) the connections between the metaphysical and the nontranscendental and regards them as a total system: "Symbolic universes are objectivated meaning systems that relate the experiences of everyday life to a 'transcendental' layer of reality. Other systems of meaning do not point beyond the world of everyday life; that is, they do not contain a 'transcendental' reference." People are born into these universes of meaning and acquire them through the socialization process.

Mezirow describes systems of meaning in a similar way and distinguishes between meaning perspectives and meaning schemes. He defines the term *meaning perspective* — which is based on Freire's use of conscientization in his discussion of perspective transformation — as "the structure of psycho-cultural assumptions within which new experience is assimilated and transformed by one's past experience" (1981, p. 6; Mezirow and Associates, 1990, p. 2) and as "a form of consciousness involving a particular constellation of beliefs, attitudes, dispositions, etc." (1985, p. 145). While there are slight differences in these two definitions, Mezirow is focusing on the structures of thought through which individuals make sense of their own experiences. These are the rules for interpreting experience (Mezirow and Associates, 1990, p. 2).

He defines (1988, p. 223; Mezirow and Associates, 1990, p. 2) *meaning schemes* as "sets of related and habitual expectations governing if-then, cause-effect, and category relationships as well as event sequences, goal orientations, and prototypes." He claims (Mezirow and Associates, 1990, p. 3) that these are mostly acquired uncritically in childhood and tend to be reinforced by subsequent experiences. He thinks that they change much more frequently than meaning perspectives do; changes in meaning perspectives are more momentous in the life of the learner. (Mezirow sees them as being similar to a religious conversion or a "Eureka experience.") By contrast, the transformation of meaning schemes is closer to everyday learning (Mezirow, 1988, p. 224). The point that this kind of transformation is an everyday occurrence — that is, a normal learning experience — is a key point in this chapter.

Mezirow's central concern appears to be with the transformation of meaning perspectives, which he regards (Mezirow and Associates, p. 13) as a feature of adulthood. (However, there is considerable evidence in the sociology of religion to suggest that adolescence is the time when commitment to, or changes in, specific meaning perspectives occur.) Since he has concentrated on this aspect of learning so far, he has not offered a complete theory of learning as such; although his most recent study (Mezirow, 1991) approaches this, it is still concerned with learning from secondary experiences rather than with learning in general. However, he does specify that changes in meaning perspectives require more of a critical approach to understanding, so that critical thinking lies at the heart of his theory. Perspective transformation is, for Mezirow (1981), an emancipation from cognitive distortions through a process of critical reflection. The outcome is the discovery of a new conceptual frame of reference that enables the learner to view the world in a different light; this is sustained through a process of dialogue and consensus.

Mezirow's distinction between meaning perspectives and meaning schemes is unfortunately not presented very clearly, since both his perspectives and schemes are necessary in the hermeneutical process of making sense of experience. In addition, though he claims (Mezirow and Associates, 1990) that meaning schemes are rules for interpreting experience and meaning perspectives are principles for doing the same thing, the difference between rule and principle is not straightforward. There is at least one other point of confusion: "habitual expectations" and "cause and effect beliefs," which are meaning schemes in his formulation, are theoretical, but according to his own definition, theories are contained within perspectives. Some differences are clear, however. His meaning schemes appear to relate closely to the concept of the lifeworld—that implicit construction of reality necessary for the functioning of everyday life—whereas his perspectives seem to involve a more conscious level of awareness.

Meaning *as a Noun*

Though we have been talking about systems of meaning, it is possible to use the term *meaning* much more specifically: words have meanings, situations have meanings, experiences have meanings, and so on. But words do not have meanings in themselves, nor do situations. Language is a system of arbitrary symbols. Nothing has intrinsic meaning; things only appear meaningful later in life because individuals grow up to take their universes of meaning for granted. These meaning systems reflect the subcultures into which they were born, and they are learned unreflectively and memorized. It is these early experiences that give rise to the birth of the conscious self, which finds its place in a specific social structure and social situation. Within this specific situation, using a subculturally specific language, individuals emerge.

Meaning systems are socially constructed, but they are also situation specific. Individuals have their own socially constructed and yet individualistic universes of meaning, and these are contained within their individual biographies. Hence different people may have different interpretations of a situation, and interpretations reflect something of both the interpreters and their social situation. Indeed, it follows from Bernstein's (1971) work that language might be used differently by different social groups. A simple example is that in American English the word *elevator* means the same as the word *lift* in English English—in the latter an elevator is a mechanical hoist. Understanding how others use language and the meaning that they are trying to convey is part of the hermeneutic exercise. Achieving understanding is an outcome of the learning process. This understanding enables people to place their own meaning on a word, a situation, and so on. Meaning is, therefore, an outcome of learning and has to be linked conceptually to knowledge. People's individuality is reflected in the different meaning they attach to objects, events, and so forth—for understanding is being. But frequently, the understanding is objectified and the word or the situation has meaning—and being becomes having.

To Mean

When people say that they mean something, they are trying to convey an understanding or express an opinion to other people. It is here in the verb *to mean* that the subjectivity of meaning is to be found—communicating is seeking to share understandings, opinions, and attitudes with other people. Even when the word is used in the sense "They meant to do it but they forgot," the speaker's intention is still to make others understand the experience.

Meaning, then, is a complex concept, and it is difficult to provide a single definition. It contains elements of interpretation and of understanding—both aspects of the learning process. Initially, however, meaning refers to interpretations of human experience, and therefore the study of hermeneutics lies at the heart of understanding both the process of interpretation and also of learning. Once these understandings are objectified, meaning tends to be treated as something beyond individuals and as an objective phenomenon, but it is actually objectified since there is no empirical meaning.

People can place meaning on a phenomenon, but they can also create it as a result of reflecting on an experience or can share it through interaction, which is primarily a linguistic exercise. The fact that meaning can be shared sometimes makes it seem objective, since this commonality allows people to assume that an object or a situation has a definite nature. Hence, meaning is regarded here as an objectification of a subjective understanding of any aspect of human experience.

Meaning and Learning

Luckmann (1967, p. 50) suggests that an organism becomes a "self" by constructing with others an "objective and moral universe of meaning." As such a universe of meaning is constructed, many questions of meaning are posed. This process of focusing on the "unknowns" of human experience begins in early childhood (Piaget, 1929) and appears to be fundamental to humanity. As the child's universe expands, its questions of meaning change. For most people, trying to understand the meaning of their existence is an intermittent but lifelong quest. Mezirow (1988, p. 104) argues that people move through a maturity gradient during adulthood that involves a sequential restructuring of frames of reference that enable them to construct meanings; change occurs as the meaning perspectives of others are adopted. Three points need to be highlighted here. The first is Mezirow's notion that there is a sequence, as if people are moving in a linear manner through time. This idea of sequential maturation is open to questioning, since ultimately it almost presupposes some form of predestination. Second, the only way that people can acquire new perspectives, according to Mezirow, is through adopting those held by others. This position contains an implicit denial of creativity. Third, he suggests that this process occurs only in childhood and before the development of an individuated self.

This brief analysis (which is expanded in far greater depth

in Jarvis, 1983b) demonstrates that even though children are born into a universe of meaning, they are still faced with questions, for which they do not have ready answers. They learn answers, but these are less definitive than they might have been in an earlier period. Since many of the systems of religious meaning no longer appear to satisfy people as easily as they did in the past, questions of meaning have gained new importance in the contemporary world. As Fromm points out, people have become increasingly aware that absolute meaning does not exist, although the quest for certainty still seems to be a basic human impulse.

The mechanism of this quest is significant for this analysis of learning. When people are in harmony with the world, when their meaning system is sufficient to cope with the daily process of living, they are not faced with "unknowns." But if they are suddenly confronted with a situation with which their meaning system cannot cope, they are forced to ask questions, and disjuncture — the need to seek meaning, to learn — arises. It does not matter whether the unknown demands a major theological exposition or merely a brief explanation from everyday experience. Paradoxically, an awareness of ignorance is the beginning of wisdom. Plato (1956, p. 135) makes this point in the passage where Socrates asks Meno about the slave boy: "Do you suppose then that he would have attempted to look for, or learn, what he thought he knew (though he did not), before he was thrown into perplexity, became aware of his ignorance, and felt a desire to know?"

The desire to discover meaning is fundamental to humanity. This assertion raises some important questions about motivation theory in education; some studies suggest that human beings do not want to learn. Perhaps motivation provides the impetus to enrolling in a course or devoting time to learning certain subjects — but not to learning as such. If the philosophy of education had started from an existentialist foundation, some of the questions raised would have been rather different.

Meaning and Understanding

It is perhaps not surprising that hermeneutics finds many of its origins in interpretations of religious writings, so that their meaning can be clarified and mediated to the present (Gadamer, 1976, p. xvi). But the search for meaning is not only a religious quest; it is a quest to understand all aspects of experience. What is the meaning of that word or this experience? Words appear to have meanings, actions have meanings, situations have meanings, and experiences have meanings. It is this objectified interpretation of reality that people are born into and learn, initially unreflectively, through the process of living.

Only in communicative interaction can interpretations be shared and a meaning agreed on, when one person's understanding meets with another's and the two are fused. Interpretation is an interactive process, for "to understand means primarily for two people to understand one another" (Gadamer, 1975, p. 158). This process also has an openness that encourages critical thought and reflection. It is this openness to dialogue that is at the heart of human authenticity—openness to the understanding that one person is willing to share with another. Gadamer (1976, p. xvi) makes the point that understanding is not merely a reconstruction of a past event but a mediation of its meaning into the present. But people only share meanings that they or others have imposed on phenomena. Meaning is shared or created through communication with the spoken and written word and through nonverbal gesture. In being shared, it becomes objectified and treated as if it were objective knowledge—that is, as if the meaning resided in the word or the situation rather than in the person. However, Gadamer (Warnke, 1987, p. 9) emphasizes that two forms of understanding in any sharing may be distinguished: the truth content and the intention of the communicator. In this study, we are concerned with the former rather than the latter. The significant factor about personal communicative interaction is that the primary experience—the direct action meeting of two or more persons—is one where there is harmony, or else the secondary experience will be distorted.

Gadamer (1976, p. 15) also recognizes that "understanding is language-bound" and that people live "wholly within a language," although it might have been more accurate to claim that individuals live wholly within their own language or dialect. Hence the meanings that are imputed to words will themselves affect the understandings individuals gain, either in dialogue or in reading and studying. It becomes essential to understand the meaning that a speaker or writer gives a word to understand what is being communicated.

From this discussion, it may be seen that understanding is a subjective outcome of the learning process. Of course, the term *knowledge* conveys a sense of objectivity, unless speakers or writers specify that this is their interpretation. It will be necessary in the next section to discuss the relationship between meaning and knowledge, but before we do this, we should examine one other aspect of this process of meaning and understanding.

Because the process of understanding involves a fusing of two meaning systems, individuals do project their own meaning quite actively in an open dialogue or in reflective reading, and so the other's meaning is not automatically understood; indeed, it can frequently be misunderstood. Individuals can block the learning experience or distort their interpretation of the situation in a variety of ways, and this will obviously affect their learning and understanding. Hence it is possible to debate whether an interpretation is correct or a learning outcome acceptable — this is part of the sharing that enables learning to occur. Learning is the combining of what is already contained within the self with that which is understood through the experience.

The process of learning is private and individualistic, but it is still possible to distinguish patterns in people's actions and in their learning. These patterns were outlined earlier in this study: some individuals might be in situations that are meaningless to them — anomic situations from which they can learn very little; others might be in situations that are meaningful and from which they can learn, although they do not understand everything about them; others can be in situations that they consider to be totally meaningful but in which they act presumptively and are therefore unable to learn; still others may impose their own meaning on situations, so that they, too, cannot learn from them. But we should mention that not all learning is necessarily good, and, as Dewey (1938) points out, there are occasions when miseducation occurs.

Meaning, Truth, and Knowledge

The question "What is truth?" has haunted Western civilization for more than two millennia. Is there absolute truth? Can indisputable meaning be discovered? Can there be a single interpretation that is always acceptable to everyone? Or is meaning merely relative to a situation? Is there no objective truth at all? Can someone *have* the truth? The philosophical questions underlying this section cannot be resolved in a satisfactory manner in this study, although it will be clear that if meaning does not reside in phenomena but in people's understanding of the world, it is difficult to accept the idea of an objective truth being verifiable. This does not rule out the logic of holding a reasoned position of faith (Ward, 1990), but it does negate the idea that such a position can be proven.

The same dichotomy is apparent here as in the previous section: does objective truth exist, or are there phenomena that have unchanging and self-evident meaning? If objective truth exists, can people break through the cultural relativity to discover what is true beyond the confines of culture? If not, is everything relative? This seems to be one of the paradoxes of human existence — from the earliest days of language, humankind has revealed its basic quest for meaning. Children's "why?" for every experience that they do not understand (Piaget, 1929) reveals the origin of this quest, and adults' "why" indicates that it continues throughout life. But are the answers that are discovered true? Can they be regarded as indisputable? Can they be verified? People want to treat their interpretations as if they are true; they want to regard the meanings that they impose on words and actions as if they are unchangeable. People appear to be conservative in seeking security in meaningful answers and unchanging truths, but that was one of the messages of that myth of the Garden with which this study opened — humankind cannot get back into the Garden, into that timeless eternal existence — for there were guards at its entrance. It is also one of the realities of modernity: in pluralistic societies, single unchanging interpretations of phenomena are always open to question and debate, and so experiences throughout life provide people with the opportunity to learn, to change their minds, and to adapt their systems of meaning to relate to novel situations. Lifelong learning is a symbol of the way meaning unfolds with new experiences throughout life; it shows that people can keep seeking and finding meaning, but always there is new or deeper meaning that lies beyond it.

Meaning seems to be relative, but it is often translated as if it were objective and unchanging; sometimes it is as if people collude in a delusion to feel secure. As Luckmann points out, everybody is born into a universe of meaning, and so it appears objective because this is their experience of it and it reflects the traditions of the culture into which they were born. But to fit into society, it is almost a prerequisite that people accept some of its preexisting universe of meaning, even though this universe is socially constructed and might not always function in their best interest. Skeptics are sometimes treated as outcasts because they throw doubt on what is generally accepted. But there is more than a good chance that in many situations the cultural answer will satisfy the questioners, and they may believe that they have acquired a meaningful answer. The apparent objectivity of the answer becomes a criterion for accepting it as true, or its functionality in the everyday world reinforces the idea that it is valid.

Two similar ideas emerge here: truth and unchanging meaning. While not quite the same, they function similarly in human life. If people think that they have discovered the truth or that a word has a certain meaning, they tend to treat this meaning as being unquestionable and act accordingly. Indeed, assumptions of truth, or at least of unchanging meaning, are prerequisites for social life, since people can only interact on the assumption that their words and actions are going to be understood by others. However, these prerequisites remain cultural constructs, and what is true for one person may not be so for another.

Being is about understanding, which in turn is about knowing rather than having knowledge. Individuals are knowing persons—that is, they have a subjective understanding gained through reflecting on their observations of the world, on actions and experiences, or in the encountering and sharing process discussed earlier. As a result of their interpretations, they learn and reach understandings, and they can then claim that they know, believe, and think. Sometimes, however, one person may claim that other people have the necessary knowledge. And then the subjective dimension becomes objective, being becomes having, and understanding becomes having knowledge.

Individuals hold beliefs, ideologies, an understanding of the world, a familiarity with culture and language that enable them to function meaningfully in their world. These beliefs and understandings become part of their biographies. Sometimes people recognize them as being relative and subjective, but others may regard them as objective and true. Within their experience, individuals have degrees of certainty about elements of their understanding; in some instances they are highly certain, but in others less so. They sometimes know something to be true, in other cases they believe it to be so, and at still other times they think that it might be. In some situations, they are open to having their understanding changed, but in others, they may be less prepared to have their perspectives transformed. Such is the complexity of the human biography; its very structure reflects both the social background and the past experiences of every individual. People are their biography, and as they enter potential learning experiences throughout life, they seek to interpret them and respond to them, so that it might be claimed that all meaningful knowledge results from interpretation of experience, or that learning is the process of transforming experience into knowing or understanding. Through this process, individuals acquire understanding that they may regard as objective knowledge that is "true." This is what guides their actions, although they often realize that their beliefs are only relative and that they can learn and change their minds if they discover anything more satisfying. But sometimes they are convinced that they have actually discovered truth, and nothing will change their minds. It is this dilemma that now has to be examined.

Meaning, Truth, and Nonlearning

There are many people who believe that they have discovered truth; they may be adherents of a religious faith, exponents of a political ideology, or merely self-confident people. There are others who believe that they have discovered the truth about certain aspects of life, so that they proclaim their beliefs and values and exhort others to join them. Heretics are excommunicated, banished because they cast doubt on the truth. Many who claim to have the truth are regarded as bigoted. Yet everybody approaches certain experiences in life thinking that they understand them and that they can act presumptively on them. They are prepared to impose their certainties on situations. Others bring their uncertainties, their openness, and even their misunderstandings and seek to learn from the situation.

There is a certain paradox in the claim that people spend much of their lives searching for the truth, but when they believe they have found it, they can no longer seek it. Once people know, then they may not be able to learn, because they impose their certainty on a situation and act accordingly. In fact, they may not even consider potential learning experiences (nonconsideration was one of the forms of nonlearning discussed earlier). People project their meaning systems on a situation and assume that they understand it, and so they act presumptively and nonlearning occurs. Sometimes individuals think that they have the authority to impose their understanding on a situation, and so those with whom they interact may be prohibited from acting or may be expected to learn nonreflectively. People with deep convictions — fundamentalists, political zealots, authoritarian personalities, people with beliefs that they cannot or will not change, individuals with life-styles that they do not want to change — all can enter a situation and have a potential learning experience but fail to learn anything from it. The paradox is that those who could learn from such experiences are often banished from the communities of those who believe that they have the truth.

Contemporary society rewards people who can present themselves with confidence, who can cling to their own meanings and have the apparent leadership qualities to convince others that these interpretations are correct. People who can function well within a bureaucratic framework are also most acceptable, because chameleonlike, they can adapt to different regimes. Yet these are all potential nonlearning situations or, at most, nonreflective learning ones. Many people find it hard to relate to those who keep asking questions; teachers are taught that if they try to produce reflective, critical thinkers, they should be prepared for a difficult time (Passmore, 1967, p. 209, highlights this problem). Nonlearning, or at least nonreflective learning, seems to be the general expectation.

But it might be claimed that the implication of this position is that people should not be confident, should not believe that they are correct, and should never be in authority. Another implication is that everything is relative and always changing, so that people should always be expected to change their minds. Four points, at least, need to be made in response to these possible criticisms: people can be confident without being arrogant; people can be in authority without being authoritarian; people who seek the truth can never be sure they have found it; in open relationships, it might be possible to discover unchanging understandings about life. Each point will now be discussed briefly.

Arrogance is the state of mind whereby actors have an exaggerated opinion of their own importance and their own understanding, so that they ensure that others are aware of their knowledge: they impose their meaning system on a situation without considering other people. They are not open to the situation, and so they cannot share the understandings and insights of other participants. Confidence should be a matter of having faith in one's understanding but being quite prepared to be open to others and indeed willing to adopt new perspectives if these seem desirable. Confidence, then, does not preclude openness, whereas arrogance does.

Authoritarians have been thoroughly researched in the social sciences; these people are inflexible and are unwilling to change their minds. They accept what they are told in an unreflective manner and expect the same to happen when they try to impose their meaning on others. Authoritarians are not neces-

sarily in the highest places of authority, although in dictator-
ships they often are. There are two types of legitimate authorities: the officeholder and the expert. The officeholder has the
authority of office and thus has the responsibility to ensure that
the organization functions smoothly. Having responsibility does
not preclude openness to others or to a wide range of situations
and does not prevent learning from occurring, although those
who hold office are often experienced persons who have reason
to believe that their understanding is correct. This belief can
be beguiling, and the officeholder's responsibility can become
an exercise of power or authority; then there is usually little openness. Bureaucratic organizations try to overcome any possibility of change in this way because they lay down rules and procedures that the officeholders must follow, whoever they are. This
ensures continuity and stability but inhibits learning possibilities. The experts (the professionals) rely on the acceptance of
others that their expertise is valid; they should always be open
to the views of others, for their authority depends only on the
others' recognition of their expertise. Gadamer (1975, p. 248)
notes that "the authority of persons is based ultimately, not on
the subjection and abdication of reason, but on recognition and
knowledge — knowledge, namely, that the other is superior to
oneself in judgment and insight and for this reason his judgment takes precedence, i.e., it has priority over one's own."
Gadamer maintains that authority must be acquired rather than
bestowed, although he is a little idealistic at this point, since
bureaucratic organizations tend to expect officeholders to exercise authority as well as responsibility. However, even in the
exercise of authority, people can be open to others, and they
perhaps learn more as a result.

If there is truth, it is by definition unchanging and should
be proven in every situation. Teachers who will not allow students to question or doubt but assert that what they teach is
the truth show that they have scant confidence in their claims —
since if what they teach were true, it would stand the test of
human questioning and learning. If knowledge is relative and
changes over time, then for teachers to claim otherwise is itself
an untruth. This provides an interesting clue — to claim other-

wise might *always* be untrue, and so there might be some phenomena, such as human values, that do not change over time. Values experienced in human relationships, such as love and trust, seem to be constant, and it is because people can experience them in relationships that they can learn and grow through interaction. Teaching, then, becomes interaction and relationship — a mutual search for truth — rather than imposition and instruction. This is a paradox, for in the relationship there lies the possibility of something constant, but the knowledge outcome of a teaching and learning transaction is relative.

People do have to impose their interpretations on others at times, but this should certainly happen less often than contemporary management-oriented society expects. Some people have an almost pathological desire to demonstrate that their understanding is correct, or that they are in control of a situation, or that other people should agree with them. This is unfortunate, because those who insist that they hold the correct interpretation project that interpretation on potential learning situations and so are unaware of any disjuncture between their biography and their experience. The result is that they cannot learn from such situations.

Meaning and Legitimation Crises

People's meaning systems are legitimated by the fact that they are continually reinforced in social interaction and because the institutions of society also tend to support them. When people enter a discussion, they generally find it easy to reach a situation in which they can communicate; when they are exposed to the media, they frequently find support for their views; and when they expect disagreement, they find it. This is the process of legitimation, which was discussed more fully earlier.

Habermas (1976, p. 118) points out that the function of systems of meaning is to maintain social stability and avoid social chaos. These systems can present a semblance of order even in periods of instability. But sometimes meaning systems break down. On other occasions, crises in the life cycle occur, and people find it difficult to impose a meaning on their new, sometimes tragic situation. A not-infrequent question to the counselor or the priest is, Why has this happened to me? People's social situations also change; they change jobs and residences and lose their reference groups, thus removing the support mechanism that they had previously relied on for their meaning systems. Aslanian and Brickell (1980) discovered, for instance, that *Americans in transition* are more likely to enroll in adult education classes (hence the title of their book, *Americans in Transition: Life Changes as Reasons for Adults Learning*). Sociologists of religion have found that adolescents going through the status change from childhood to adulthood are more likely to become committed to a religious faith through conversion than almost any other age group, as they seek meaning systems and reference groups to reinforce their ideas about life.

Meaning systems and people's beliefs about the truth are contingent on the support of the legitimation systems in society. If those systems are removed, people begin to doubt, and this doubt encourages them to enter potential learning situations with a real possibility of disjuncture between their biography and their experience, so that once again they are open to learning. However, it does need to be noted that there are both moralities and immoralities in this situation; for legitimation is as much the process of brainwashing and indoctrination as it is of the experiences of everyday life and even the techniques of the clever teacher. In life situations, the morality may be public rather than private, a matter of social (in)justice or political debate, or a contingency of complex society that might be perceived as amoral. However, if legitimation or legitimation crises are brought about by other than a concern for the authenticity of all the participants, it might be considered to be immoral.

The point about legitimation crises, however, is that even belief in the truth is rarely, if ever, so strong as not to require the social support of the legitimating institutions or persons. The possibility of learning emerges, paradoxically, when that support is weakened or withdrawn, or when someone perceives inconsistencies, distortions, or inadequacies in the socially constructed meaning system.

Conclusion

The process of discovering meaning usually teaches those who learn that meaning exists beyond it. The very fact that still more meanings can be discovered indicates that the quest for meaning might not be meaningless. Meanings, however, are only relative and may in some way point to yet more sophisticated questions being asked and more sophisticated answers being given in this human quest that Fromm (1949) suggests has no ultimate answer. Bohm (1985, p. 75) writes that "in physics, reflection on the meanings of a wide range of experimental facts and theoretical problems and paradoxes eventually led Einstein to new insights concerning the meaning of space, time, and matter, which are at the foundation of the theory of relativity. Meanings are thus seen to be capable of being organized into ever more subtle and comprehensive over-all structures that imply, contain, and enfold each other in ways that are capable of indefinite extension — that is, one meaning enfolds another, and so on."

Meaning, then, is capable of greater levels of interpretation and learning — and so for those who have not reached the end of the inquiry, for whom there is still another level of meaning, there is still further opportunity to learn. But those who have the truth are both unable to learn and may expect others to learn unreflectively in order to reproduce their knowledge. Where power is exercised, this expectation is common, because power and a belief in correctness or truth often go together. We turn in the next chapter to the way some of these considerations apply in the workplace.

11

 Learning, Personhood, and the Workplace

While existentialists have been very concerned about the dehumanization of work, they have not concentrated a great deal on other aspects of it. Thus it is now important to investigate the relationship between learning and the workplace. Our concern is not merely with vocational education (or human resource development, which is rapidly becoming an institutionalized vocational training system), nor are we confining ourselves to continuing professional education. This chapter focuses on the learners and the way they learn in the workplace. It is not only about their jobs but about them as well: it is about all of the experiences from which they learn rather than just those from which they are intended to learn. It is about the way that they are and are continually becoming persons in the workplace.

The modern world of work has two major facets, technological and bureaucratic. It is important to explore these in some detail in the first section of this chapter to understand something of the way the modern mind is shaped by society. Simmel (1971, p. 85) observes: "Modern mind has become more and more calculating. The calculative exactness of practical life which the money economy has brought about corresponds to the ideal of natural science: to transform the world into an arithmetic problem, to fix every part of the world by mathematical formulas. Only money economy has filled the days of so many people with weighing, calculating, with numerical determinations, with a reduction of qualitative values to quantitative ones."

Simmel looked at the rationality of the modern mind with a degree of regret for he clearly considered it not to be a great improvement upon what was in the process of disappearing. Society has become more rational and more bureaucratic, so that the behavior most often prized is that of conformity to those procedures laid down by the bureaucratic organization. The second section of this chapter explores the kinds of learning that occur within this type of society. The final section returns to the question of the rationality of contemporary society and indicates why there is a need for a critical consciousness.

The Modern World of Work

The workplace, for most people, lies in other-controlled private space; they do not own it, nor do they often control it. Individual private space — that is, leisure time for the most part — is separated from the controlled private space of the world of work by the fact that the former is controlled and often owned by the individual.

In contemporary society, different workplaces tend to be similar, since they all reflect the ethos of the modern order: they are technological and bureaucratic. Bureaucracy implies that there is a hierarchy of management, with the workers (the managed) being in the lower strata and the managers (the organizers and administrators) being in the higher strata. The higher up the organizational ladder people move, the farther they are from the actual workplace and the more they assume executive decision-making functions and control the space in which they work. Apart from the managers and the managed, a third group of working people exist in some organizations: the professionals. However, they are slowly being forced into the management hierarchy and are finding themselves either managers or managed, albeit in a slightly different way from other workers; they are being moved away from the actual sphere of work for which they were initially prepared.

The other major institution of contemporary organizational society is technological production. Berger, Berger, and Kellner (1974, pp. 31–32) specify a number of features of this mode of production, including mechanisticity, reproducibility, working within a sequence of production, and measurability in terms of output — usually in quantifiable terms. The work performance of individuals is regarded as a component of the whole process. Because of the nature and structure of work in modern society, the workers are replaceable in the production process — a fact that they are well aware of, as they show when they insist that "the process can get along without me." Managers also recognize that this applies to them. As individuals, managers are no longer important to the process, but as functionaries they are. Berger, Berger, and Kellner (1974, pp. 37–38) describe the modern self in this way: "A specific kind of double consciousness develops. In this case the dichotomy is between concrete identity and anonymous identity. The individual now becomes capable of experiencing *himself* in a double way: as a unique individual rich in concrete qualities *and* as an anonymous functionary."

Hence, the self-identity is subdivided into two distinct forms: the work identity and the nonwork one. This is part of the process of developing in the modern world, learning to become a person and a nonperson — at the same time in some cases — in the different spheres of life.

It is a truism to point out that any type of large-scale technological production requires bureaucratic organizational frameworks to achieve the organization's ends. Weber first recognized the inevitability of bureaucracy for the rational organization. According to him (1947, pp. 329–330), in bureaucratic situations the norms of authority are based either on rationality, expediency, or both; these norms are abstract and impersonal and are applicable to all the members of the organization; and people obey authority as members of the corporate group and respect the office rather than the officeholder. The officeholder is considered to be competent in the office and is expected to administer the stipulated procedures to everyone in the organization. Hence, the officeholder, as officeholder, must be inflexible, and the worker affected by the bureaucratic procedures should be passive and powerless. Berger, Berger, and Kellner (1974, p. 59) make a useful distinction between work and bureaucracy: "In his work the individual is always *actively involved*. As a client of bureaucracy he is always *passively involved*. In encountering bureaucracy, the individual does not basically do things; rather things are done to him."

In this organizational and technological world of work, individuals learn to become divided selves and to cope with life. Bureaucrats learn to behave in repetitive ways and memorize procedures; clients learn to cope with the procedures. Learning how to fit in is a nonreflective learning process. As the world has grown more complex, the concept of the adult has actually changed: "While undoubtedly there are certain features of the individual that are more or less stabilized at the conclusion of primary socialization, the modern individual is nevertheless peculiarly 'unfinished' as he enters adult life. Not only does there seem to be a great objective capacity for transformation of identity in later life, but there is also a subjective awareness and even readiness for such transformation" (Berger, Berger, and Kellner, 1974, p. 73).

Berger, Berger, and Kellner regard the modern identity as open, differentiated, reflective, and individuated. The preceding quotation suggests that the individual self continues to grow and be transformed throughout life. This begins in a secondary process of socialization in which people learn to adapt to the world outside of their family of origin; they learn to become workers, managers, professionals, and even unemployed. We now turn to this process of learning in the workplace.

Learning in the Workplace

Since all learning begins with experience, people's workplace learning begins with the type of work they are employed to perform and with their position within the bureaucratic hierarchy. However, it must also be recalled that there are two basic forms of experience: primary and secondary experience. The former involves the actual experience people have in a given situation; this type of experience molds their self-identity to a great extent.

The latter involves experiences in which interaction or teaching occurs over and above the primary experience. Hence, in the workplace there can be two simultaneous experiences: that which the workers are experiencing and that skill that they are being taught in a human resource development or continuing professional education program. A great deal of the learning from primary experience that occurs in the workplace is either incidental or unintended (Marsick and Watkins, 1990).

Marsick and Watkins (1990, p. 12) suggest that "formal learning is typically institutionally sponsored, classroom-based, and highly structured. Informal learning, a category that includes incidental learning, may occur in institutions, but is not typically classroom-based or highly structured, and control of the learning rests primarily in the hands of the learner. Incidental learning [is] a byproduct of some activity, such as task accomplishment, interpersonal interaction, sensing the organizational culture, trial-and-error experimentation, or even formal learning." Neither of these definitions, however, is sufficiently precise to include all the situations that are envisaged here. For instance, in anomic situations, where little or no action is possible, some learning might occur — but it is incidental to the situation and to the intention underlying the original situation itself. Similarly, informal learning might take place in situations where the learners have little freedom simply because they are in informal groups. Informal learning, then, occurs in social situations in which there are norms of social interaction, but no prespecified formal procedures of bureaucratic organization. By contrast, incidental learning is learning that occurs almost coincidentally with action or nonaction; it is something for which there can be no preplanning and that must be reactive to, and reflective on, an unintended experience.

Through all forms of learning, but especially those of a primary nature, the individual's self is molded and develops. However, primary experiences in the workplace are also bound to be affected by the individuals' positions within the bureaucratic hierarchy, so that workers will have different learning experiences from managers, and so on. The context of the experience is crucial to understanding the ensuing learning. For the sake of convenience, three types of worker are discussed here: manual workers (often referred to as *blue-collar workers*); managers or nonmanual workers, sometimes regarded as white-collar salaried staff; and professionals and semiprofessionals, who have specialist preparation and qualifications. We could have used a more elaborate typology, such as the one employed by Carnevale, Gainer, and Villet (1990, pp. 44–85), but a three-way distinction is sufficient to illustrate some of the main features of learning in the workplace.

Manual Workers

Manual workers control very little of their own work space. Their actions are controlled or managed by others, and for the sake of efficiency, the division of labor results in their undertaking even more detailed and repetitive action. The theory underlying this form of work behavior is that if the workers can act almost unthinkingly, they will perform a task more efficiently and will therefore contribute to greater profits for the organization. The following description of assembly-line work reflects this philosophy: "Try putting 13 little pins in 13 little holes 60 times an hour, eight hours a day. Spot weld 67 steelplates an hour and then find yourself one day facing a new assembly-line needing 110 an hour. Fit 100 coils into 100 cars an hour; tighten seven bolts three times a minute. Do your work in a noise 'at the safety limit,' in a fine mist of oil, solvent, and metal dust. . . . Speed up to gain time to blow your nose or get a bit of grit out of your eye" (Bosquet, 1972, p. 23).

This might be considered an extreme form of production; tasks of this nature are increasingly being replaced by automation, and where this is not possible, boredom is sometimes lessened by job rotation introduced by a more enlightened management. However, the point is that the actions are performed in a space that the workers cannot control. This does not mean that they do not learn coincidentally from the experience. On the contrary, they learn that rapid, repetitive work is boring. As a worker from the Ford Motor Company is reported as saying, "It's the most boring job in the world. It's the same over and over again. There's no change in it. It wears you out. It makes you awful tired. It slows your thinking right down. There's no need to think. It's just a formality. You just carry on" (Beynon, 1975, p. 118).

The fact that the workers in these situations do not control their work space or their behavior does not prevent them from reflecting on their experiences. They know that while they are involved in a productive enterprise, it is not a creative one for them. The production process may be meaningful to the organization, but it is not very meaningful to them as human beings. They soon learn that the company has invested vast sums of money in the production process and that they are almost powerless to change it. They also learn that the companies will call in trainers with expert solutions to their problems rather than consult the workers themselves (Robinson and Robinson, 1989). They learn that there is "no need to think," and so they turn their minds off and do not try to learn creatively about how best to perform the job. They might just as well think about other things.

The examples we have just considered show how workers' lack of opportunity to think creatively about their work in an oppressive situation might lead to a dehumanizing process rather than the frequently illustrated optimistic one of growth and development. In environments such as these, there is no way that human beings can achieve authenticity; these situations produce its antithesis, and the human essence becomes a means for individual existence (Fromm, 1966, p. 54) rather than the essence of humanity developing from existence. This is the condition that Hegel first termed *alienation* and that Marx subsequently popularized. Fromm (1966, p. 53) describes it as follows: "The alienated man is not only alienated from other men; he is alienated from the essence of humanity, from his 'species-being,' both in his natural and spiritual qualities. The alienation from the human essence leads to an existential egotism, described by Marx as man's human essence becoming 'a means for his *individual existence*. It [alienated labor] alienates from man his own body, external nature, his mental life and his *human life*.'"

Of course, less extreme situations exist where the workers control some of their work space and where the informal learning between workers that occurs as a result of their social interaction can result in enriching experiences. Such informal interaction can take place because the work behavior is presumptive and repetitive, but the conditions under which it is performed are not oppressive. An enjoyable social environment may emerge in which unintended learning results.

In some of these situations, such as office work, there is a lack of formal training (Carnevale, Gainer, and Villet, 1990). Some people consider skills learning or memorization to be the very essence of training. This is what Freire (1972b) has called "banking education" and what I have described as "education from above" (Jarvis, 1985, pp. 45–55). The fact that such training does not exist means that the work situation can become one of experimental learning. But if the workers have not been taught the necessary skills for adequate job performance — for example, computer skills — stress is probably inevitable.

Because of the often-repressive nature of the working environment, a feature of modern society is a differentiated self-identity. The self-identity of the workers that is created as a result of learning in the workplace can be totally different from that learned through their leisure-time experiences. But this depends to a great extent on how individuals use the time and space that they own and control.

Managers

Many more educational studies have been conducted of management training than of the training of blue-collar workers, because management training more closely resembles general education. Even though managers rarely own their own work space, they certainly control much of it, and since their jobs are not so clearly defined as those of the workers, they are usually freer to experiment with the way they perform them. Indeed, Argyris (1982) points out that many managers are expected to design their own jobs and undertake them in whatever manner they consider to be the most effective. In other words, their work is about being creative, reflecting on action, and learning. Often the workplace offers a potential learning situation for managers because they have to plan, monitor, and retrospect on actions. They are engaged in problem solving and interacting with other workers—from whom they can also constantly learn. Work provides a situation of experiential learning, and managers are free to alter their behavior to demonstrate their current state of learning. For them, the workplace can provide all forms of learning through which they can grow and develop, so that there are clearly times when occupational growth and personal growth can occur simultaneously through the learning that is going on.

Professionals

Most of the research into professional practice has not concerned itself with learning on the job, even though some early research (Rogers, 1962) suggested that most professionals learned innovations fairly rapidly, and Tough (1979) also indicated that many professionals engaged in continuing learning for their own professional ends. Traditionally, professionals have been regarded as independent practitioners who control and frequently own their own work space. Recently, however, there has been a decline in independent professionals, as more have been employed in large organizations. But even then they are given a certain degree of freedom to control their own work space. However, it was not really until Schön's (1983) publication that it was demonstrated that professionals were actually engaged in all forms of learning, especially the higher forms such as reflective skills and experimental learning, in the actual performance of their work. Schön argues that because professionals control their own work space, they are free to reflect in action and to learn from the process. He records (1983, p. 64) the claim of an opthalmologist who stated that "in 80 or 85 percent of the cases, the patient's complaints or symptoms do not fall into familiar categories of diagnosis and treatment" and points out that the physician must try to make sense of new situations and invent experiments to test out hypotheses about the patient's condition. Professionals, in other words, learn in the course of their work. Schön (1983, p. 50) makes the point as follows:

Both ordinary people and professional practitioners often think about what they are doing, sometimes even while doing it. Stimulated by surprise, they turn thought back on action and on the knowing which is implicit in action. . . . Usually reflection on knowing-in-action goes together with reflection on the stuff at hand. There is some puzzling, or troubling, or interesting phenomenon with which the individual is trying to deal. As he tries to make sense of it, he also reflects on the understandings which have been implicit in his action, understandings which he surfaces, criticizes, restructures, and embodies in further action.

Throughout Schön's work, it is clear that professionals are learning in practice, even though they may not regard it as such. Their work is in itself a stimulus through which they may learn and develop as persons. Like the managers, they have a certain degree of control over their work situation and their work is not routinized, so that they can experiment and learn. Professional growth may, under certain circumstances, also be synonymous with personal development.

In the situation of the manual workers, growth and development are inhibited, while in the case of the managers and professionals, there is opportunity to learn and grow, provided the persons concerned are open to the potential learning opportunities their work offers. It is clear that the control over the space is crucial to the way people learn in the workplace. The workers, if they are expected to think and learn, are required to be mechanistic in what they do. Managers working in bureaucracies have certain restrictions placed on them by virtue of their positions, but overall they have sufficient freedom to learn in the process of their practice, while professionals have traditionally had the most freedom and perhaps the most opportunity to learn in and from their practice. However, there has been a tendency in recent years to treat professionals as employees rather than independent practitioners, so that some of their freedom to learn and practice has been removed—which reflects something of the crisis of professionalism experienced in the 1970s. Additionally, fear of litigation has curtailed much of the freedom of the professionals, especially in the caring professions, since only conformity to standardized practice might appear safe in a court of law. These situations inhibit the freedom of professional practice and have changed the basis of much of the learning that occurs in practice to conformity and memorization of correct procedures. Clearly, this has not actually changed these professionals' situations into those of the workers, although many of them are aware that they are being moved in this direction. The movement toward competencies in practice, and therefore in continuing professional and managerial education, is another development in modern rational society that is limiting freedom by trying to make everything safe.

The fact that both the manager and the professional learn in practice, usually after having been prepared for their occupation in universities, means that they develop a body of knowledge that revolves around practice—what Ryle (1963) calls "knowledge how" as opposed to "knowledge that." This is also the knowledge that the manual workers have. Nyiri (1988, pp. 20–21) suggests that it is learned in the following manner:

> One becomes an expert not simply by absorbing explicit knowledge of the type found in text-books, but through experience, that is through repeated trials, "failing, succeeding, wasting time and effort . . . getting a feel for a problem, learning when to go by the book and when to break the rules." Human experts thereby gradually absorb "a repertory of working rules of thumb, or 'heuristics,' that, combined with book knowledge, make them expert practitioners." This practical heuristic knowledge, as attempts to simulate it on the machine have shown, is "hardest to get at because experts—or any one else—rarely has the self-awareness to recognize what it is. So it has to be mined out of their heads painstakingly, one jewel at a time.

Practical knowledge is learned after classroom knowledge, because the practitioners bring to the practice situation their own biographical store of knowledge, including that learned in the classroom, and they use that knowledge as one of the constituent elements in learning from the new situation. However, every practical work situation provides a potentially new experience from which to learn, and provided that the actions do not become habitualized, the workers may keep on learning and their expertise might be enhanced. Expertise grows out of experience and the learning that ensues from it — for the expert is one who has learned from experience and who knows both how a performance is undertaken and that it will produce specific results. Expertise continues to be enhanced with practice and should continue to be enhanced with every new learning experience, but often actions become habitualized and performance becomes presumptive, so that new learning opportunities are curtailed. Another threat to the learning process is the increasing introduction of technology into production, because it has made much practical expertise redundant.

Practical knowledge is similar in many ways to everyday knowledge, discussed in the next chapter. The significant point here is that workers create their own practical knowledge as a result of the practical experience, and this is profoundly different from trying to use and apply the knowledge that they have learned in the classroom mechanically to reproduce a standardized and measurable procedure. The latter approach underlies the rationality of modernism. If this rational approach is apparently reshaping professional and perhaps managerial functions in the direction of the dehumanizing practices of the workers rather than enriching the workers' practices, it should not be accepted without question. Thus it is now important to return to the idea of rationality to examine it in greater depths.

Rationality

Weber believes that society is becoming more rational through the process of social evolution. He illustrates this process in a number of ways — for example, by demonstrating how leadership changes from being charismatic to being rational-legal, by show-ing the way movements become institutionalized and bureaucra-tized, and so on. Above all, he addresses the concept of ration-ality itself. As was pointed out earlier, he suggests (1947, p. 115) that there are four types of social action: *Zweckrationalität, Wert-rationalität,* affectual action, and traditional action. *Zweckration-alität* is a "rational orientation to a system of discrete individual ends" that are not absolute (p. 115). *Wertrationalität* is a "rational orientation to absolute value" (p. 115), whereas affectual action is emotional action and traditional action involves long-established practice. This last form is a manifestation of con-servatism, but significantly, it is the rationality underlying prac-tical knowledge. For the purposes of this analysis, *Zweckration-alität,* or purposive rationality, refers to the "expert realization of the given objective without questioning the values, wisdom, or morality of the objective" and *Wertrationalität,* or value ra-tionality, denotes action "directed by a system of values" (Ala-nen, 1988, p. 3).

It is not always recognized how pervasive purposive ra-tionality is, particularly in the field of education. Kerr, Dun-lop, Harbison, and Myers (1973, p. 47) take this ideal for granted: "industrialization requires an educational system func-tionally related to the skills and professions imperative to its tech-nology. Such an educational system is not primarily concerned with conserving traditional values or perpetuating the classics: it does not adopt a static view of society, and it does not place great emphasis on training in traditional law. The higher edu-cation system of the industrial society stresses the natural sci-ences, engineering, medicine, managerial training . . . and ad-ministrative law."

This quotation reflects something of the debate between education and training that has already been implicit in this chapter, because according to these authors, the purpose of edu-cation is to produce people appropriate to the workforce, peo-ple who have the necessary knowledge and skills to undertake the tasks that contemporary technological society demands. They do not question the values that pervade this society. As one ex-pression of these values, education has begun to be offered as a market commodity that educational institutions have to sell to prospective clients. Educational courses are written in the language of behavioral objectives, with the end result of the process being the fulfillment of these objectives, and the form of evaluation is impact evaluation — that is, impact on the efficiency of the work situation. The cost-effectiveness of the education is assessed, and it is generally argued that those who have more education will earn more money. A recent study in Sweden has concluded that "adult recurrent education constitutes a factor of importance in explaining differences in occupational achievement between workers with similar qualifications, because adult education is found to exert direct effects on occupational status and significant total effect on earnings" (Tuijnman, 1989, p. 196).

In the language of contemporary society, this appears to be logical — for it reflects the rationality of purposive action. It seems natural that education should be used in this manner and also natural that those who are successful in the educational process should receive greater rewards, for after all, that is the way this world functions. The system benefits, and those who participate in the system benefit as well.

Before we criticize this approach further, we should examine another approach to education — one that seems less instrumental because it is based on the idea that education can be a life-enriching experience. Among the most prevalent concepts in the education of adults, especially in the more humanistic forms of adult education, is Maslow's hierarchy of needs. This hierarchy moves from the satisfaction of basic physiological needs to needs of belonging and esteem and ultimately to self-actualization. Many adult educators cite this hierarchy with approval, and clearly it makes sense to do so. It is reasonable to argue that students who follow the educational process should be enriched and should learn to self-actualize. Educational success is judged by the extent to which students claim to have achieved a degree of self-actualization, and courses are offered with this as an educational aim.

On the surface, the two forms of education being discussed do not seem to have a great deal in common — the first is preparing the learner for a place in the workforce and guaranteeing efficiency in the capitalist technological world, and the second is about achieving self-actualization through the educational process. While they appear to be different, however, both are products of the same cultural system; both have been shaped by purposive rationality. Indeed, both are attractive in contemporary society partly because they appeal to the purposive rationality of the modern mind.

It would be easy at this point to offer a criticism of one or other of these approaches and to try to demonstrate that the first is not really education at all, as Paterson (1979) does in his criticism of vocational education in general. He claims that only the liberal education of the individual is truly educational and that all other forms of education fall short of the highest educational ideals. For Paterson, the farthest removed from true education is training, or the purposeful educational form of seeking to prepare manual workers for their occupational role. It would also be easy to assert that the other form of self-actualizing education approaches a form of therapy that helps people mature and achieve a more adult and enriched state, in which they feel that they are able to "do their own thing."

The question we are concerned with is this: to what extent are these forms of education actually rational? Consider the following example. A person attends vocational education to learn how to be a successful manager in a large technological capitalist company during the day but in the evening attends a course to learn how to self-actualize, thinking that both courses would be useful preparation for the management role. On the surface that might well be true, and this would appear to be a logical course of action.

But what happens when that person learns in the first course that in order to succeed in the company, it is necessary to comply with company policy regardless of whether it is consistent with the manager's own ideals? In other words, if the day-time course is to achieve its ends, the individual must learn that self-actualization is not always the best thing — or that the apparent purposive activity of both courses calls for one set of purposeful activities to displace the other. The aspiring manager is confronted with a choice: which approach should be adopted? The choice is no longer purposive rationality, for both alternatives involve purposive rationality. It is an ideological choice; which should predominate, the company or the individual? This is always the choice, even though it might not be presented quite so starkly when only one course is offered. In other words, the ideology of the age—even in education—is presented as purposive rationality. Practice, then, is merely a form of the dominant ideology, presented as if it were rational and value free.

This discussion implies that a conflict of interest could exist. Such a conflict would have to be resolved by other means than purposive rational choice. It might be claimed that to choose to be the manager is still a purposive rational choice, because as a result of the training, the individual gets more financial reward and more opportunity to exercise power and influence in society. Hence, the choice is logical. But others might claim that to reject this form of training and job and to seek another that encourages the participants to achieve their potential and self-actualize also makes sense. It is also purposive. Both choices are possible, and so the potential conflict of interest might have to be resolved by another form of rationality: value rationality.

Thus far the meaning of the term *rationality* has not been discussed explicitly. Weber (1947, p. 115) suggests that this term implies the most appropriate means to achieve the actor's rationally chosen ends. But this is tautological. Dictionary definitions emphasize that *rational* means using logic or reason or acting in accordance with the principles of logic or reason. This is significant, because the purposive rationality discussed above fits these definitions perfectly—but so does value rationality! The only difference is that the criteria employed to assess rational action differ.

This conclusion is very different from the interpretation by Schluchter, cited by Habermas (1984, pp. 281–282), that holds that purposive rationality is more rational than value rationality. Schluchter appears to offer no reason for considering one to be more rational than the other, except the instrumentalism of purposive rationality. While Habermas does not concur in this conclusion, he proceeds to employ the terms *high* and *low rationality* as if he feels that the idea does have some merit. But I reject the use of *high* and *low*. Either purposive or value rationality can appear more rational, depending on which set of criteria one uses to judge; both are valid.

However, this ethical approach is part of the problem, since the apparently "scientific" nature of purposeful rationality makes it seem more rational than value rationality. This is because the scientific approach reflects the values of the age. Pursuing our previous example of the two courses a little further may reveal something of the underlying ethical assumptions. The person could attend the management course to become more effective as a manager, to gain promotion to a better job, and so on. From this standpoint, the vocational education course could be seen in a positive light. But there is another way of looking at the management course: the manager is sent by the employing organization to learn how to be a more effective manager because, after all, the manager is merely a cog in the enterprise and has to learn to play a more effective role so that the enterprise can become more profitable. The manager is a means to an end. But was it not one of Kant's categorical imperatives that people should never be treated as means, only as ends?

What of the self-actualization course? If people attend courses like this so that they can learn to self-actualize, they are emphasizing individualism and exhibiting the same self-centered approach to educational activity that they might have taken in the management course. Both forms of education appeal either to selfish or to capitalist values. (This is not to claim that Maslow's hierarchy of needs is necessarily a selfish statement, only that an individual seeking to self-actualize might have egotistical motives.) And both forms of education involve value rationality.

Conclusion

As the human essence emerges from existence, it is molded by modern society into a technological and bureaucratic person. This process splits the self-identity into the person and the nonperson, and yet the world of work appears to be rational and value free. People judge themselves and their performances, and are assessed by others, as if society were free of values. But the foundations of this society are in fact based on values, values that become apparent when the types of learning encouraged are of the lower forms and the type of person required lacks wholeness. It is the very claim to rationality that needs to be questioned, even the understanding of what passes as rational in modern society, and so it is necessary that people should all have the opportunity to learn reflectively and to be critically aware of the social processes that pass for rational. Unfortunately, the hierarchical nature of society, and particularly of the workplace, inhibits this. Some people are expected to learn non-reflectively, while others are expected to learn in a reflective manner, and so their human essence emerges in slightly different forms.

People are always in the process of becoming different individuals because society provides different experiences from which they can learn. As they age, they learn and perhaps eventually acquire wisdom. This is the focus of Chapter Twelve.

12

Aging and Wisdom

Life is a flow of experience, frequently moving between public and private space, between space that is controlled and that over which there is little or no control. Sometimes that flow of experience appears continuous, actions are performed presumptively, and actors presume on the world, confident that they can cope with the situation. At other times the flow seems to stop, and an action is planned or another reflected on. These are the moments when new knowledge might be learned, new skills and different attitudes acquired, and new perspectives gained. There are times when an actor observes the performance of another with admiration or appreciation and later seeks to imitate it. This is the way that everyday knowledge is learned and everyday beliefs are acquired.

From childhood to old age, the paradoxes of learning in society are the same. This book started by examining the former, and as it draws to a close, it analyzes the latter. We have observed that human becoming is a learning process—but that this process is paradoxical. These paradoxes have been seen in public and private space, in freedom and control, and in leisure, work, and education. The emphasis on having has been criticized from the perspective of being, and learning has been demonstrated to be a social process. Learning begins, paradoxically, when the learners do not know and when they cannot act unthinkingly in the world.

Thus it may be seen that as long as individuals respond to the disjunctures between the experiences they have and the stock of knowledge, skills, and attitudes that constitute their biography, the more they can learn. Learning transcends all forms and institutions of society and may be lifelong. But since people have the freedom to respond to a potential learning situation or not to consider it, as the case may be, lifelong learning is not inevitable. Yet the longer people live, the more significant their stock of knowledge, skills, and attitudes is likely to be. The ancients referred to this as the wisdom of the elders, but in modern society, where "scientific" knowledge is the most highly prized, these rich biographies are retired and often treated as insignificant and outdated. They may be outdated in scientific terms, although this is not always true, and they may have difficulty adjusting to social change. But still, the elderly have a rich repertoire of experience.

This chapter discusses the relationship between aging and wisdom. The first section considers the connection between aging and learning in everyday life. In the second section, we relate wisdom to practical knowledge. The third section sketches several possible responses of older people to learning experiences.

Aging and Learning in Everyday Life

Aging is usually associated with old age, and educational gerontology is certainly one of the most rapidly advancing areas of study within education. However, the verb *to age* means to grow older or even to make older. Consequently, a two-year-old child ages every day as much as a seventy-two-year-old person does. But just because the duration of the day is the same for both the child and the older person, this does not mean they experience them in the same manner. Indeed, there are obviously many differences. Apart from the biological connotations of aging, other differences include the fact that the child may change more rapidly as a result of experiences, but the child has also had fewer experiences with which to respond to the new ones and may also have different perspectives on those experiences. While time is not changing any more rapidly for one person than for the other, it might be consciously experienced differently — the child might experience time as moving slowly, whereas for the older person, it seems to move much faster. For the child, there might be many more new experiences to explore, while the older person might detect more similarities between different experiences, and this will inevitably affect the types of learning that occur. Because the child's experiences are more likely to be new, its actions might be more experimental, so that any subsequent learning will bring a lot of new knowledge; the older person might presume on the world much more and consequently appear to learn less. However, this is not an inevitable conclusion. The point being made here is simply that while time is objectively a constant, experience is not.

On one level, aging is the process in which a biological organism, such as the human body, exists in time and changes physically. On another level, however, it is the process in which the existent utilizes the subjective experiences it has undergone during the period through which the biological body passes. Obviously these two processes occur simultaneously, and they are also interrelated, since any physical aging might have repercussions for the mental process and vice versa. There is a third major dimension that has to be incorporated into this discussion: the social. Any experience is shaped by the social situation in which people find themselves. An elderly white male is bound to have different experiences from a young black female. Experience, then, is bounded by time, space, society, and subjectivity.

Time is experienced in two different ways, as Bergson makes clear in his studies of time, duration, and freedom. The first is *durée,* or duration, when a whole sequence of events is experienced as a simultaneous whole. This sequence of events may either be familiar or totally incomprehensible to the people experiencing them. In the former situation, the persons having the experience can presume on the world and monitor it with a fairly low level of consciousness, but in the latter, the individuals having the experience distance themselves from it and observe it without really participating in it. In neither situation is a great deal of learning possible, and so while the physical body is aging during this sequence of events, the mind is hardly being affected by them and the human being is not maturing as a result of the process.

Time may also be experienced as a series of discrete moments or events. Commenting on Bergson's philosophy at this point, Lacey (1989, p. 27) says that "in order to think about the world, still more to talk about it, as opposed to simply experiencing it, we have to 'freeze' it, i.e. apply concepts to it which can be applied repeatedly, whence they can be called universals. If language is to serve its purpose in fixing our thought and communicating it to others it must abstract and words must denote the same things for different speakers and for the same speaker at different times, and some words must be applicable to more than one thing." In this form of experience, time is frozen; an event is conceptualized within the framework of time and then thought about in a socially constructed language. Obviously, a duration could also be conceptualized as an event, as a single experience to be thought about. Bergson uses the illustration of a melody — a number of musical notes flowing together to make a whole. It is possible to consider either single notes or the whole melody, but "duration implies consciousness. Its essence is to flow without ceasing, and consequently not to exist except for a consciousness and a memory" (Lacey, 1989, p. 29).

It will be recalled that at least three different processes occur in the human consciousness in relation to acting and learning: looking forward (planning), monitoring the present, and retrospecting. Significantly, it is only when individuals plan or retrospect that they can actually learn from experience and grow, and only through retrospection are all the forms of learning possible. It is as if humankind has to stop time in order to take time to learn and grow — a reflective need of modernity. Perhaps this is one of the major functions adult education can perform for people caught up in the hustle and bustle of modern life. Being too busy is one of the major reasons for nonlearning, and so adult education can provide an opportunity for people to get off the merry-go-round of busy-ness and to reflect on their world. Here, indeed, lies the concept of the sabbatical. In Hebrew, the word from which *sabbath* is derived means "to rest," and stopping, resting, and thinking are essential if humankind is to develop.

Every experience about which individuals retrospect is perceived through all the learning embedded in their biographies as a result of previous experiences. No experience, then, is free of previous ones, and this affects the way they perceive and respond to other situations.

Thus it may be seen that aging raises philosophical questions that have to do with the mind and body and their inter-relationship (Ryle, 1963). Biologically, the body ages as a result of natural processes. The biological aspects of aging are beyond the scope of this book for the most part, though we should note that chemicals can influence the biological processes in such a way as to affect learning. For instance, drugs can alter perception and therefore subjective experience, and this in turn must have an impact on the learning that occurs. Our focus, however, is on the development of the mind. Clearly this occurs through learning — learning from the experience of everyday life.

Surprisingly, everyday life has not been widely studied, although Heller's (1984, pp. 165–215) work is important here since she examines the relationship between knowledge and everyday life. She recognizes (1984, p. 199) that all learning begins with action and experience: "Action is often followed by review of that action: a reflection or recapitulation of the action, and distanced from it in time or in time and space. (Whether I approve in retrospect of what I have done or not — I think about it.) We all know what it feels like to realize after the event what we ought to have said or done in the first place — in other words, to have hindsight. But inadequacy of preparatory thought is not necessarily to blame here: often, action itself produces the feeling that we ought to have acted or spoken differently."

Here Heller points to planning, monitoring, and then reflecting on action. The processes interrelating thought and action are all here, and they show how learning occurs from everyday experiences. Heller goes on to suggest that this everyday knowledge is always opinion and never scientific knowledge: opinion is inseparable from practical activity and taken-for-granted knowledge, but scientific knowledge begins where taken-for-granted knowledge becomes questionable. This is a problematic claim, inasmuch as everyday experience might well give rise to the realization that new knowledge is required to cope with a new situation. Heller (1984, p. 166) acknowledges this when she says that "the best example of this [adopting a theoretical attitude toward the world] in relation to the world of things is provided by cases of failure, lack of success; when a method I have used over and over again fails to work, the pragmatic attitude itself, the desire for efficiency, makes me stop and ask 'Why?' 'What has gone wrong?' — and at once I am thinking along theoretical lines."

The significance of this claim is twofold. First, as has been argued throughout this study, learning begins when there is a disjuncture between biography and experience that leads to a questioning attitude. Second, everyday knowledge is pragmatic in nature. Learning from primary experience results in pragmatic knowledge, and this is true whether the situation involves professional practice or everyday experience.

As long as actions produce the desired end results, the actors have no need to think — they can presume on the world and monitor their actions. There is, in these situations, a degree of near certainty that the desired ends will be produced the next time, so that actions are determined by a degree of probability. This is where rational planning occurs, the probable outcomes of actions are considered, and choices are made accordingly. Often these choices are made in the light of the norms and customs that prevail at the time. Individuals imitate the prevailing forms of behavior, and the actors do not need to be taught by their role models; observation and appreciation are sufficient motivation. Not only do actors learn from the expertise of others, they also learn from their mistakes: "'It's a wise man who learns from the misfortunes of others.' Subsequent reflection is not confined to my own actions: in exactly the same way, I can reflect on those of others as well, and observe the results. Indeed, this is one of the main channels whereby we acquire experience of everyday life. In the final report, however, this kind of thinking (acquisition of experience) is directed towards my own praxis" (Heller, 1984, p. 199).

People seek to generate behavior that is identical to the behavior they observe and on other occasions to correct what they consider to be wrong behavior on the part of others. Heller regards this as analogous thinking. Often people perform rituals because of analogous ideas, and the basis of a great deal of superstitious behavior is analogy (Jarvis, 1980), which reflects an underlying belief in efficacy. Thus, it might be seen how reproductive forms of behavior appear and are justified.

Learning from everyday experience is a process that occurs all the time. People develop and mature from all of these experiences — for learning is fundamental to the process of human development. Not all learning produces the "correct" solution, however. Consider the following illustration. Through a self-directed learning exercise, a person acquires the skills to repair a problem in an old car. However, the fault keeps recurring, and the second time the fault is repaired it becomes easier, because the lessons learned on the previous occasion are put to use. This is just as Knowles suggests it should be — experience is a useful reservoir for future learning. The next time the fault occurs, it seems even easier to repair than the previous time, because of the experiences gained on the previous two occasions. This is consistent with Knowles's formulation, and it makes sense. A pattern for the repair emerges, and each time the fault occurs, it gets easier to repair it. The only trouble is that the fault keeps recurring because the self-directed learning exercise did not completely solve the problem in the first place, and the pattern that evolved to repair the fault became habitualized. As Berger and Luckmann (1966, p. 71) write, "Habitualization carries with it the important psychological gain that choices are narrowed. While in theory there may be hundreds of ways to go about the project . . . , habitualization narrows these down to one."

The point about this rather natural process is that it relieves people of having to make decisions and having to learn new things; it enables activity to occur with economy of effort and a minimum of choice. Indeed, once an action has been habitualized, it inhibits further lessons from being learned because people tend to take recurring situations for granted. This is both a paradox of existence and a paradox of experience and learning. Having learned something that works, people presume that it will always do so, and as Heller (1984, pp. 175–182) asserts, this is either a case of overgeneralization or one of generalizing from a particular situation. She shows (1984, p. 178) that once individuals have overgeneralized, there is a tendency for their prejudgments to turn into prejudices: "In such circumstances, my pre-judgments turn into prejudices, which my experience does nothing to correct or over-rule, since they are bound up with my interests: that is, I am affectively interested in retaining these prejudices (though not only affectively)." This reflects the previous argument, stemming from the idea that for some people, authenticity occurs only when they feel that they are being true to themselves — that is, they have the truth, are certain of it, and do not want to learn anything more about it.

As individuals mature, they have a wide variety of experiences; from some they learn, but from others they are unable to do so. Even so, with the passing of years, people do acquire a rich reservoir of knowledge based on their experiences. Here Knowles's formulation of andragogy is obviously correct, for much of this knowledge can be used as a basis for further learning and can be useful to others, and so it is no wonder that it was called the wisdom of the elders.

Wisdom and Practical Knowledge

Wisdom is not an educational concept, but it is closely related to learning. *Collins Dictionary of the English Language* defines it as "the ability or result of an ability to think and act utilizing knowledge, experience, understanding, common sense, and insight" and as "accumulated knowledge, erudition, or enlightenment." Wisdom is in some way the store of knowledge, opinions, and insights gained, often through long years of life.

Wisdom often implies being able to provide reasons for why things are the way they are, and in this sense it is metaphysical and presociological. It explains the "thus-ness" (Heller, 1984, p. 214) of this world. Heller (1984, p. 212) suggests that it stems from a form of contemplative learning that could occur only after humankind had conquered the physical hardships of survival: "The emergence of contemplation as an independent mental attitude depends on man's having attained a state of existence beyond the struggle for mere survival. . . . The world in which he lives and moves awakens man's interest and curiosity. And whenever there is neither need for, nor possibility of a pragmatic attitude, man's [interest and] curiosity become ends in themselves. Anything which is of pragmatic interest in one co-ordinate system can become an object of contemplation in another."

While the emergence of a separate priesthood had to wait for the division of labor in society, there is no evidence to suggest that humankind had not begun to contemplate long before then. Having the ability to explain the way that the world works and also to explain its "thus-ness" lies at the heart of wisdom. Indeed, this is the basis of philosophy—the love of wisdom. The possession of wisdom was much treasured in the ancient world, because the sage had contemplated the nature of existence and taught and learned. Wise people were nearly always old, since they had accumulated the experiences and knowledge and incorporated them into their own lives. But this was, of course, less true of the Greek philosophers, who developed the art of philosophical contemplation and made it a way of life.

In the modern world, many of the explanations once sought from older people are explained by science. The retired are consigned to the scrapheap and their accumulated learning treated as obsolete—like so many other things in this "throwaway" world, where obsolescence is now designed into the system. But the experience of the elderly is still their own reality, and they can continue to learn and develop: "In the later years, the imposed expectations for changes in work/retirement and the innate drive to re-focus induces reintegration of cognitive and social repertoires. Havighurst . . . described this as a refocusing of one's past into the present in order to derive *meaning of life* for the present: the act of reviewing one's 'biography' and, potentially, the emergence of wisdom" (Thornton, 1986, p. 74).

Perhaps only in the later stages of life, when people are freed from many of the constraints of contemporary society and when they own their own space, are they able to stop and contemplate and to come to terms with life. Certainly there is something metaphysical in this idea, although it is as much a psychological process as a metaphysical one. It might be a manifestation of spirituality or religiosity, but it is not necessarily something that could be called Christian or Muslim or Buddhist.

Moody (1986, p. 127) also highlights this process: "Those older people commonly judged 'wise' are those who respond to genuinely novel situations by applying the lessons of experience in an entirely new context. They do not abandon past experience, but they apply their learning analogically." He notes that there is a return to story telling to assist people in their search for meaning in this rapidly changing, technological world. At the same time, he recognizes that there are some older people whose learning and actions have become habitualized, so that their reactions to new experiences are rigid. They are unable to respond to change, and so they take refuge in not learning from their experiences, or in learning that they can no longer respond with equanimity to the altered circumstances. They may, therefore, have to create an environment in which they can live and act in confidence.

Wisdom, then, is learned from experiences throughout life. Older people synthesize it, which enables them to cope with a rapidly changing world and pass on to others the fruits of that wisdom. They are potential mentors (Daloz, 1986) for any who wish to seek advice and support. It is unfortunate that, unlike the experts in the world of work, they are often not called on to share their expertise — even in that industrial world in which many of them functioned for so long.

Like wisdom, practical knowledge is gained through experience, by trial-and-error and through learning over sustained periods. It will be recalled that Nyiri (1988, p. 20) maintains that individuals become experts not by acquiring textbook knowledge but by primary experience, trial-and-error experimentation, breaking the rules, and so forth. The experts in the world of work are rather like sages — people who have learned from their primary experience in a creative manner and are able to act in a repetitive, almost ritualistic, way simply because of the experiences they have had. They are also potential mentors for new recruits to an occupation or profession. They are not seeking to pass on textbook knowledge, although they possess it, but are endeavoring to help the new recruits learn by experience, using their own experiences as guidelines. The wise are experts in living, and the occupational experts are wise in the ways of the world. Both are experts in practical knowledge. While the textbook and the classroom are important in education, education is beginning to rediscover the practical knowledge and wisdom of the experienced practitioner, and the mentor has become a significant person in preparing new recruits to practice their occupation. Perhaps as the world discovers that everything does not necessarily become obsolescent with age, the wisdom of the elders will once again play a more significant place in the learning of the young. But not all elderly people can cope with the modern world, nor are they all potential mentors, as the final section of this chapter illustrates.

Older People's Responses to Learning Experiences: A Typology

Throughout this study, it has been argued that learning is a lifelong process (see also Thornton, 1986, pp. 62–92), but not all the experience is an aid to learning, as both Dewey (1938, p. 25) and Moody (1986, p. 33) point out. Past experiences should have helped prepare people for their present situation: "Every experience should do something to prepare a person for later experiences of a deeper and more expansive quality. That is the meaning of growth, continuity, reconstruction of experience" (Dewey, 1938, p. 47). Experience, then, helps to mold the self, which struggles in a constant effort to understand the changing world. This insoluble dichotomy of human existence asserts itself in old age, for older people have established patterns of behavior and also systems of meaning that have helped them through the long years of their lives. Thus they have reached a stage in their development when perhaps it is natural to assume that they can take much for granted, act presumptively, and live in harmony with their world. This might well have been the case when the world changed slowly and people valued the accumulated wisdom of the elders. They had reached that stage where they were in harmony with their world — but that is a world that has since been lost. Now the world changes rapidly, and not only is it not the world into which many of the elderly were born; for some, it is hardly the world into which they retired. There is constant disjuncture between their experience and their biography, and this is both encouraging and disconcerting. A great many experiences in the modern world are potential learning experiences, but most of the past experiences of the elderly may be of little avail in this rapidly changing world.

Of course the elderly can still learn — but when time seems limited and future experiences appear curtailed by the exigencies of age, why should they? If they are happy in space that they both own and control, some may not wish to learn. But others may still see the world as a challenge and seek to respond to the disjuncture between their biography and their experience. A number of types of responses may be detected; three common ones are discussed here: those of the harmony seeker, the sage, and the doer.

The Harmony Seeker

The elderly have spent their lifetimes seeking to construct a self and a system of meaning that would enable them to be at peace with the world and end their days in harmony with it. But the world that they have known has passed them by, and they express their amazement and concern when they ask, "What is this world coming to?" How do they respond to this potential learning experience? Do they just keep on learning, developing mind and a self, in a never-ending quest to achieve harmony with a world that is constantly changing, or do they recognize that it is a never-ending quest and that they have to find a harmony in the world they know? If they cannot presume on the world around them, they can reject the potential learning experience and even the alien world because they can presume on the world of their own homes and other familiar things in their lives. To some extent, they can shut the world out and live in a world they know. Indeed, they can look back on the world that has disappeared and can reminisce (Merriam, 1985) and reflect on experiences long gone but still alive in memory. They can contemplate the past, even learn from it, but for them, nonlearning is essential if they are to hold together all that has made them what they are. They have developed mind and the self and now seek harmony and peace. Learning still occurs, but selectively, and there are an increasing number of instances of presumption and others of rejection.

The Sage

But not everyone wants to be the harmony seeker, because for many older people, life is still an intellectual adventure. They are still engaged in the quest, still facing the inevitable and unavoidable disequilibrium. They are still content to live without patterns of existence that restrain them. Disjuncture, as always, lies at the start of new learning. But like everybody else in the world, they do not have sufficient interest or time to respond to every potential learning experience. In their old age, they do have more freedom to be selective, though. They may not be constrained by the demands of employers. They can choose the experiences that they will ignore and those that they will learn from. For this group, there is time to be a reflective learner, time to be critical, time to relate all the new information from the information society to their previous experiences (Moody, 1986, pp. 122-148). The young can gain much from these older learners. Yet in a world where the wisdom of the elders is devalued, the learning of this group is often neglected.

The Doer

Not all older people fall into the two previous categories, so that a third is suggested here. As a result of improved health care, people are enjoying good health well into old age. Many people can therefore enjoy activity in their retirement — sports, travel, church, societies and clubs, and entertainment. For them, life is still active, and they may not consider potential learning experiences because they do not have the time or the inclination. A great many of life's activities may still consist of presumed experiences; other learning experiences may be acquired, as with people of younger age groups, in the course of living a full life.

Other types of responses no doubt exist, since this classification is by no means exclusive, but it does reflect some common responses to being and learning among older people.

Conclusion

People acquire everyday knowledge through the experiences of daily living. These experiences mold them and help them develop, and they learn to respond to future experiences in their own ways. Whether in the everyday world or the world of work, living gives rise to the same type of learning experiences — learning from experience. Experimentation, trial and error, imitation, learning from success and failure, and so on all stimulate personal development. For some, the retirement years are the only time in their lives that they have actually owned and controlled the time and the space in which they live and act, and yet for others, this is not a time of freedom and self-development. Naturally, this is partly a matter of people's personality and their physical state. Yet, since retirement is a time of freedom and of learning for many, it is not surprising that educational gerontology and study tours, international travel, and so forth for the elderly have become more popular. The human essence continues to emerge and humanity is still molded until the physical body cannot sustain the spirit any longer.

In earlier days, when the elders had acquired wisdom, they were respected and their wisdom sought after. In contemporary society, wisdom is not knowledge, and the learning of older people is no longer valued. But society has begun to change, and the changes themselves are paradoxical in nature, as Chapter Thirteen demonstrates.

13

Learning and Change

Change is found in every area of life. There is, for instance, developmental change in people as they age, status change, geographical change, and a multitude of other forms of change. Indeed, change is endemic to social living, and any form of stasis is a rarity, if not an impossible occurrence, since societies and people exist in time. Nevertheless, people habitualize their actions and often appear to treat their external world as if it were static and unchanging. Since there is an indissoluble link between people and their sociocultural milieu, change in either the people or their surroundings is bound to upset any apparent harmony that has been established between them. Hence, disjuncture between people's biographies and their external sociocultural world is not an exception, but a rule.

But change is rarely revolutionary in character; it is most often evolutionary and gradual. The disjuncture between biography and experience is not likely to be anomic, so that potential conditions for learning are a common occurrence throughout life. Paradoxically, however, once people have learned, they have become more experienced and have therefore changed, so that learning is itself one of the social processes that helps create the conditions for yet more learning. Lifelong learning, then, is itself both a symbol and a reality of modern society. But if the change is too swift, individuals may have difficulty in adjusting to the new social conditions, and then they enter situations of nonaction and perhaps nonlearning. They may suffer some form of anomic response or feel that they are prevented from responding because they are too busy, and then the disjuncture experienced is stressful.

The focus of this chapter is on the relationship between learning and change. Paradoxes are inherent in this relationship: learning is a response to change, but it also creates it; learning is a mechanism of adaptation, but it also has the capacity to evoke it; people learn to be safe, but learning is also a risk-taking activity.

The chapter begins with an examination of the ways the social structures inhibit learning. Next it considers some of the possible outcomes of learning. It then addresses the issue of whether education produces change agents. Finally, it focuses on learning and risk.

The Inhibiting Features of the Social Structures

Like culture, social structures do not exist. They cannot be handled or produced for inspection, so that they are not external to the people who experience them, although the different roles people play and the varying degrees of influence they exercise on others are self-evident and beyond dispute. Hence, the differentiation of society is clear, and the structures of a social system are apparent only through the systems of interaction that occur between the members of a social group. Behavioral patterns are self-evident, since the process of interaction is habitualized in ways discussed earlier. Therefore people who form long-standing relationships create expected patterns of behavior that, in turn, create obligations for continuity and even reproduction. People who exercise power over others have certain expectations of how others with less power or influence will act in their presence, and those with less power might act in keeping with their understanding of the expectations of the power-holders. Analysis of this form of social interaction has been conducted most incisively in a number of studies by Goffman (for instance, 1959, 1968a, 1968b, 1971, 1972). Goffman's often brilliant analyses reveal that people ritualize their behavior; they create for themselves forms and patterns to which they expect to conform and that they expect others to understand and adhere to when appropriate. People tend to take for granted the patterns of behavior that they have evolved, so that they are often unaware of the ritual involved. This is a paradoxical situation, inasmuch as people know that they are free to act otherwise but feel constrained to conform, often by relationships that are of their own making.

It was argued earlier that ritualized behavior provides little opportunity to learn. As in the harmonious situation in the Garden of Eden, there may be no disjuncture between the external world and the inner biography. But patterned behavior is essential to the smooth functioning of diverse and diffuse modern society. Many institutions, such as bureaucratic organizations, have evolved so as to ensure that regardless of who the office-holders are, their functions will still be performed in the same manner. Many people appear to have both their public and private lives surrounded by such obligations, so that they have little freedom to do other than conform, even though they still feel that they could act otherwise. Society's structures, including structures of people's own making—norms and folkways that manifest themselves in social action and relationships—guarantee that people's actions are repetitive and ritualized. They may feel disjuncture between their biography and their world but because of their own expectations or those of others, they reject opportunities to do things differently and learn. There are other times when disjuncture turns into dissonance and people do feel compelled to resolve the dilemma in which they find themselves. Obviously, they may not be able to do so if they are subject to the authority of others. The instruments of the state are often used repressively, in some cases to convince people that it is in their best interest to conform and in others, to force them to do so. Some people are brave or foolhardy and risk the consequences of not conforming—they may be authentic persons, but they suffer for being so.

We can now see why existentialists view power as so problematic. Those who exercise power over others often create situations where inauthenticity is manifest, for inauthenticity occurs, according to the different existentialist positions discussed earlier, wherever people cannot be true to themselves or to their situation. The Polonians seek to be true to their biography, the Dadaists to the situation, and those who follow Buber's (1959) understanding of relationships seek to be true to the people involved in the situation with them. At the same time, it has to be recognized that those who hold power do not always employ it in a negative manner; some actually use it constructively to enable others to act in certain ways that may be in their best interest.

For whatever reasons, people frequently find themselves in situations that provide potential learning opportunities and they do experience disjuncture, but they sometimes still feel unable to act otherwise. They feel that the social structures inhibit their potential, and they become dispirited. By contrast, others appear to strive against the odds and transform their situations. This process frequently means that old obligations have been fulfilled and new opportunities occur. To some extent, this might depend on people's social skills or on their holding fast to their Polonian principles.

But change is endemic to modern society, so that social situations change. People grow older, change their status and their occupation, move from one neighborhood or city to another, and so on. In the same way, managers change, governments change, and dictators are removed, so that the power relationships change. Suddenly, some of these inhibiting relationships disappear. People are free to act or speak in a less inhibited fashion. Again, however, they do not always do so. Some people follow their habitualized patterns; Riesman (1950) calls them "tradition-directed" people. Fromm (1984) suggests that the lack of freedom provides a sense of security from which some people do not wish to be free, but rather they seek only to submerge themselves in the outside world. Some others are able to respond to their newfound freedom and act differently and learn from their new primary experiences. Perhaps the best-known research in adult education that documents this is by Aslanian and Brickell

(1980), who have shown how life transitions increase adult learning.

In these situations, the disjuncture they experience often causes people to plan experimental or creative behavior, monitoring it and then reflecting and learning from it. They acquire practical knowledge; they may have observed the experimental behavioral pattern in another's actions and copied or avoided it, and they may occasionally have even experimented without any observed precedent. Heller (1984) discusses many of the behavioral patterns of everyday life in detail; these patterns become the basis for learning from experience. However, the same pattern may be observed for secondary experiences: some people seek to hold on to what they already accept, almost afraid of being presented with new information in case it contradicts the information they already possess, while others are quite happy to be presented with new ideas to consider and discuss.

People may not respond to the same changes in the social conditions in the same way. Very rapid social change may mean that the disjuncture between some individuals' biographies and their sociocultural milieu is greater than they can bear. They know that they need to reestablish the equilibrium but are unable to do so, and this results in feelings of stress. Stress is another facet of modernity; it causes some people to opt out of the "rat race" of modern life and others to seek therapy or find other solutions. Consequently, the number of people undergoing therapy has increased, and many more educational or therapeutic courses are being offered.

Learning, then, can be disturbing for some but exciting for others — it is part of the paradox of the human condition. Even so, the human condition is one of human relationships, and in an apparently unstable world, those relationships may be threatened. This is the subject of the following section.

The Effects of Learning on the Learners

Perhaps one of the best-documented changes in society since industrialization has been the change that has accompanied the emergence of the division of labor. Durkheim (1964) calls it a change from mechanical to organic solidarity; Tönnies (1963) regards it as one from community to association. Society has become more differentiated and more organizationally oriented. Paradoxically, as society has become more organizational, people have become more individuated. The tendency for people to regularly meet together and form close-knit communities sharing common interests has diminished. People are certainly born into families, but even the stable relationship of parents is no longer as common as it used to be. Yet the ideals of friendship and marriage still exist.

Throughout this book, it has been pointed out that learning occurs throughout the life span, but obviously some people have more opportunities to learn than others. The more people learn, the more experienced they become and the more that they grow and change. However, this does pose problems for people who initially have close relationships, unless they each have similar opportunities to learn and develop. Consider the mutual interdependence of a dyadic relationship, for example; whether it is friendship or marriage is irrelevant. One member of the dyad is given the opportunity to experiment at work and to undertake new forms of action and learn from them, and also has a chance to meet new people and acquire new knowledge through secondary experience. In contrast, the other member of the dyad has a steady, satisfying job and does not do a great deal that is new. But the lack of new opportunities to learn from either primary or secondary experience means that the growth and development of that person is slower than that of the first member of the dyad. One member is learning all the time and changing rapidly, while the other is exposed to fewer opportunities to learn and so changes at a slower pace. One of the features of dyadic relationship can be its intensity; another might be the shared interests of the partners. But as a result of learning, people's interests change and they envision fresh horizons and determine new goals. The dyadic relationship might be stretched and even broken.

It is not only unequal opportunity to grow that is a problem; some members of dyads like their partners the way that they are and object to any change in them. A partner changes and develops new interests, and the original partnership is threatened by the process, even terminated. People returning to education often encounter these difficulties, because acquiring new knowledge changes their perspectives, and if their friends and partners are not supportive and aware, they may experience tension in their relationships. Many adult educators are aware that returning women students often face this problem. Thompson (1983) provides numerous examples; what amounts to liberation for the women represents a threat to some of the men in the partnerships.

Here, then, is a profound paradox about learning. People live in relationships; indeed, this book has emphasized that mind and the self are formed in relationships. Human relationships are fundamental to society's existence. It is only in these relationships that fundamental values such as love, truth, and justice can become manifest between people. Hence, Buber (1959, 1961) and others urge that wherever possible, relationships should be created and maintained, even though the process is sometimes painful, for it is only in encounter that community can develop and only in relationships that the fullness of humanity can be realized. Yet here again is a paradox of learning, since it is regarded as something that is life enriching but it is also individuating, threatening to some relationships, and can create its own unhappiness and destruction.

People become more experienced as a result of learning; learning is both individual and individuating, and it changes people. Unless relationships are strong enough to endure change, they are threatened — another feature of modern society. Not everyone grows; some prefer the stasis of nonlearning. But as a result of learning, others seek to become change agents within the social group.

Change Agents and the Problems of Structure

People learn to adapt to change, but another aspect of the paradox of social living is that learning also helps people evoke change. Freire (1972b, p. 41) discusses the concept of praxis — that is, where "true reflection . . . leads to action." For him, reflection should result in action. The results of reflection need to be in harmony, and the action is part of the process of humanizing the world. It is a symbol of liberation, and the creative process becomes the responsibility of liberated people. They are change agents in the social and political world, in the same way that educators often believe that they are producing change agents to return to organizations and change them. Learning does produce change in people, but the question is whether those people automatically put their learning into practice and change the organizations within which they function. Adherents of behaviorist theories of learning imply that the resulting action is automatic, but Argyris and Schön (1974) suggest that practitioners have espoused-theories and theories-in-use, and they suggest that harmony does not always exist between the two. We have seen that actions are often creative and experimental and that they are planned, considered, and monitored, but we have also emphasized that the structures, obligations, and power relationships sometimes inhibit behavioral change despite the fact that learning has occurred.

Throughout this study, the tension between learning that individuates and social relationships has been implicit. It has also been clear that learning does produce changed people whose relationships, however, are not automatically changed as a result of the changes they experience. Negotiation of change in the relationship may be easier in a dyad or small group than it is in a large bureaucratic organization or a town. If change in the relationship in a dyad or small group is not possible, those relationships can be terminated, even though this is sometimes painful. But in larger organizations, communities, and societies, it is less easy for individuals to terminate their relationships; they may be employed in an organization or live within a community or a society, so that they have to either accept the current situation and experience dissatisfaction or try to change the situation.

Hence, the community educator frequently works for change, and the change agent also seeks to alter the structures and procedures of the bureaucratic organization. Community educators are often regarded as radical or political because they adopt strategies aimed at changing society. Lovett, Clarke, and

Kilmurray (1983, pp. 36–40) propose four models of action in the community:

1. A community organization/education model in which individuals are encouraged to engage in education and develop personally so that they can "better" themselves and leave their community—hence, terminate their relationships and seek new ones
2. A community development/education model in which educators act as resource persons helping people in the community learn so that they can develop richer communities for themselves
3. A community action/education model in which adult educators commit themselves to deprived communities and work with them to change the situation
4. A model in which educators align themselves with people in deprived areas and provide education to illuminate the problems of an area

In the second and third models, the emphasis is on people who have learned remaining in the community and trying to change it as a result of their learning. This is not as a result of automatic action, but through carefully planned action that does not necessarily affect personal relationships but wider social ones. Through political and community action, individuals try to influence others, especially those who exercise power, to change certain aspects of social living, usually through a redistribution of resources. Their communication is at a level of secondary experience, so that direct relationships are not threatened; they try to communicate information to others to persuade them to change their actions. Collective action is often encouraged, rather than individual action, since it is sometimes dangerous for individuals to expose themselves as change agents, because people do not always welcome change. Hence, the structures of society appear to resist the pressures that the change agents exert, and those who hold the reins of power continue to use the social institutions to ensure that no change occurs.

Thus it is clear that the ability to effect change is related to the position people occupy in the social structures. Leaders and managers are obviously in the best position to produce organizational change, and many of the people London (1988) cites as change agents occupy such positions. Enlightened management can create change, although bureaucratic management with too many levels of hierarchy inhibits change and efficiency in a rapidly changing world. A bigger problem exists when the people who have learned and have been changed as a result of their learning experiences are not in positions of power or influence in organizations. This is often true of those who have been sent by their organizations to continuing professional education courses. Employees may return to their employing organizations full of new ideas and changes as a result of their learning experiences, only to be confronted with a management that does not want to change or even to learn. Organizational structures and procedures appear inflexible because the management does not want to initiate change. In these situations, employees either have to become activists to try to get management to change, often being seen as "troublemakers" as a result, or else their two alternatives are to quit their job or conform — the latter often resulting in declining job satisfaction.

It is therefore easy for educators to believe, without ever seeking to understand the impact of new learning on both the learner and the organization, that their courses are producing change agents. It is not uncommon to hear educators or educational policy makers claim that their courses are producing change agents, though in fact the employing organization often do not want change and fail to change with the advent of new employees. Indeed, it is here that the practitioners on the shop floor often deride the theoretical perspectives of the training school, and talk of the "real world" is to be found in the practice setting. One element, but by no means a major one, in the distinction between theory and practice is located at this point: people prefer habitualized action, but learning often involves change.

People, then, grow and change as a result of learning; this is a continuous process throughout life; organizations, though, have a tendency toward inertia. People prefer harmony rather than the tension of change and new ideas, so that some managers prefer to train employees to "fit in" rather than enabling them to grow and perhaps become change agents. Here, then, the paradox of learning is revealed yet again — reflective learning can produce change and growth and good management often tries to see to it that staff have this opportunity, but stability or even apparent stasis is comfortable, and change can be frightening. Training is often regarded not as an opportunity to learn reflectively and grow, but to learn unreflectively and conform.

However, organizations are not impersonal structures. They consist of people in patterned relationships performing specified roles, so that change becomes possible when those relationships are restructured as a result of learning. Argyris and Schön (1978, p. 29) maintain that "organizational learning occurs when members of the organization act as learning agents for the organization, responding to changes in the internal and external environments of the organization by detecting errors in organizational theory-in-use, and embedding the results of their inquiry in private images and shared maps of the organization." This is possible if the agents are in powerful positions in the organization or if those who exercise power favor change. But even then, if "private images" and "shared maps" are to be changed, the change agents themselves have a major teaching role to play, which is only possible when the organizational climate is conducive to change. If such a climate does not exist, the agent is as political as the radical community educator is.

Learning and Risk

People live in an organizational world: it is a world of bureaucracies. Not only are all the organizations bureaucratic, but so is the state. Bureaucracies have their procedures and expect conformity, so that it is safe for individuals, having learned how to function in a bureaucracy, to follow the established customs and to conform. It becomes a nonlearning situation, where people live in harmony with their sociocultural world and act ritualistically. However, to initiate change, or even to be proactive in learning, individuals have to choose to be different. Proactive learning demands that people be prepared to act contrary to the expected procedures and create new situations and new experiences from which they can learn. Underlying proactivity, therefore, is an element of risk. This is the risk of just breaking away from the established procedures and consequently of being less certain of the outcome of the action than would normally be the case in bureaucratic society. It is also the risk, paradoxically, of offending those with whom relationships have already been established.

Open society, society that seeks to break the inertia of bureaucracy, is inevitably a risk society, and proactive learning is one of the features of this form of society. Indeed, it could be argued that if the learning society emphasizes response to externally imposed change, it is an adaptive society, with people merely learning nonreflectively to discover the harmony of nonlearning, ritualistic activity. However, if the learning society is reflective and oriented toward change, then the society is—almost by definition—a risk society.

Conclusion

Learning both produces change and occurs as a result of it; learning can be for the purpose of conformity or for change, it can be nonreflective or reflective. People in contemporary society live in patterned and organized relationships, and any change in one person will mean that the relationships are affected in some way or other. Consequently, some relationships do not survive the effects of learning, and yet it is in those very relationships that the highest values of humanity are manifest. Time does not stand still, and learning occurs throughout the human life span. Wherever action cannot be taken for granted, there is the possibility of new learning and new growth, but if that is always sought individually and in an individuating manner, the richness of human relationship can be lost. This, then, is the paradox of the human condition. In contrast, the survival of organizations, even of the state, may in part depend on nonlearning, or at least on learning that does not produce change.

14

The Political Dimension of Learning

Throughout this book, the concept of power has played a major role. In places, it has been claimed that only in certain egalitarian forms of human relationships can reflective learning be fostered; in others, the problem of people exercising power over people and its negative effects on people and their learning has been cited. Maintaining certain social structures requires a state. Consequently, it is now necessary to examine the relationship between the state and learning.

The adult education literature often treats the state and society as if they are the same thing. Yet the state and society are different, and both should be taken into consideration in analyses of adult education and learning. The sociology of adult education has concentrated on the social element in adult education, as befits sociological analysis of the educational institution, and where appropriate the concept of power has been introduced. But as has been pointed out earlier, power plays an important role in both learning and action. Indeed, the concepts of interest, power, and control have figured quite often in this study. In this chapter, points that were implicit in our earlier discussion are brought out as we consider how learning and education must, by their very nature, have a political dimension.

221

So far, educational theorists have not paid much attention to the concept of the state, even when they have concerned themselves with the politics of adult education (see, for example, Freire, 1985; Evans, 1987; Griffin, 1987; Jarvis, forthcoming). A recent exception is Thomas (1991), although the perspective adopted here differs from the one he utilizes. The first part of this chapter shows why theorists have argued that the state is a necessary phenomenon in modern society. Then it reviews a number of theories of the state and democracy. Finally, the paradox of learning in the political situation is discussed.

The Need for the State

One of the central issues in political theory is the extent to which a need for the state exists. Some, such as anarchists, clearly do not believe it is necessary, while others obviously do. Marxists believe that since the ruling classes use the apparatus of the state for their own ends, the state itself should disappear and egalitarianism emerge. Statists, both liberal and conservative, contend that the state needs to exist for a variety of reasons, such as the total chaos that would emerge if there were no state — Hobbes's ([1651] 1968) celebrated war of all against all. Another reason commonly adduced is that because the division of labor in society has created a situation of total diversity, the state is necessary in order to unite the whole. The paradoxical aspect of this argument is that the actual exercise of power to unite the whole is also the very process that divides it: it creates a situation of rulers and ruled.

This type of discussion is missing from much adult education literature. In recent years, the idea that adult education should create critical thinkers (Meyers, 1986; Brookfield, 1987) and that it should empower groups and individuals has become a dominant theme in American adult education literature. Indeed, the whole theory of autonomous and self-directed learners has assumed that all are free to pursue their own interests in whatever way they wish, although it has been argued here that there are constraining forces on action, even if the will is still free. There has also been a great deal of theorizing about adult learning, much of which is based on an individualistic conception of the person in which little or no consideration has been given to the person in society, let alone the person in a state. Such an approach is a weak form of liberalism; it is apolitical and oversimplistic, because if every adult were a self-directed learner and a critical thinker, the stability of society would be threatened. Indeed, this is one of the paradoxes of learning — that if everyone were to engage in it in a reflective and critical manner all the time, the basis of society would be undermined. Learning can be adaptive and conservative in its outcome, but it can also be subversive in some situations. Hence, it might be better for the survival of society if people were to engage in nonreflective learning. If everybody were reflective, innovative learners, society would need the state, as Hobbes postulated in *Leviathan*, to create stability and unity.

Thus it becomes necessary to explore the concept of the state before this analysis proceeds any further. For some, the state is the social institution that claims the monopolistic legal right to employ force within a specified territory (see Weber, 1964, p. 156). However, this definition is too restrictive, because it limits the state to the exercise of legitimate force, and obviously its functions are broader than this. Yet it points to a significant feature about the nature of the state for Marxists that is implicit in the above discussion — that it is essentially a repressive institution, even in its reformist manifestations. Indeed, it might need to exist to ensure that society does not collapse into the chaos that might result if the individual exercise of freedom was practiced by all its members. Marx and Engels ([1848] 1947, p. 82) focus on this very point of repressiveness when they view the state in class terms: "The bourgeoisie has at last, since the establishment of Modern Industry and of the world market, conquered for itself, in the modern representative State, exclusive political sway. The executive of the modern State is but a committee for managing the common affairs of the whole bourgeoisie."

While Marx and Engels might be correct for the most part, Taylor (1967, p. 29) points out that this is an overstatement, because the state has a life of its own and has its own interests

to sustain. It cannot totally repress one class, or else it will un-
leash forces that will result in instability and ultimately in some
form of revolution. Nevertheless, even by Marx and Engels's
lifetime, the bureaucratic state was beginning to appear, and
as may be seen in the preceding quotation, they actually view
the state as managing the public space of the people.

Political theorists have generally grasped the fact, however, that "no state can sustain itself through brute force alone"
(Hoffman, 1988, p. 73), and so coercion must go hand in hand
with consent. It is this element in the nature of the state that
is crucial for educational theorists. Indeed, Marxists have highlighted the fact that the state tries to gain consent by repres-
sion, through mechanisms other than blatant force. Althusser
(1972, pp. 251–255) points to the fact that the state controls the
ideological apparatus as well as the repressive apparatus of force.
He proposes that there are at least eight state ideological apparatuses: religion, education, the family, law, politics, trades
unionism, the media, and culture. Through each of these people can be socialized, albeit sometimes unknowingly, into con-
senting to the views of the state's ruling elite. While Althusser
perhaps overstates his case, since it is possible for each of these
to operate in such a way as to produce consent, they may also
each create innovative situations where critical reflective learning is conducive to change. Therefore, the ideological apparatus is very significant for the survival of the state. It is here that
Gramsci's (Joll, 1977) important concept of hegemony enters
the debate. Indeed, it could be argued that those who control
the state are in a strong position only when the ideological apparatus functions effectively and produces consent, but the elite
are weak when they have to show that they control the legitimate use of force, which is their last defense. Hence consent
must be produced and it might have to be produced coercively,
or even in a Machiavellian manner, in order not to utilize the
forces of coercion openly. For a government to survive, therefore, the state must not appear coercive but rather passive and
even permissive.

The significance of this conclusion is that if the state functions in a Machiavellian manner, people might have a false per-

spective on it, and ultimately they develop a false or distorted consciousness about their own interests. This false consciousness is something that Marx called attention to in his discussion of false class consciousness, for he maintained that the bourgeoisie controls the state in its own selfish interests. This has also been a concern of critical theorists in more recent years, since they claim that the people might not always be aware of their own interests. However, it was suggested earlier that false consciousness might more readily occur in less pluralistic societies, so that while the Marxist analysis is still relevant to many totalitarian societies, the so-called false consciousness might actually be a form of ignorance in pluralistic societies. The fact that pluralism does allow for different interpretations of reality might also mean that the state is even more necessary to hold the diversity together in some form and even to control people's learning to some extent.

The state, then, appears to be a necessary evil. Without it there might be chaos, but with it there is social division and the possibility, even the probability, of some form of deception of the people. It is a controllable social institution. Those who exercise power in it must gain, but not necessarily appear to seek, the consent of the people in society if they are to survive in their elite capacity. At the same time, they claim the right to exercise force to ensure the survival and smooth functioning of society if they fail to gain that consent—which is a very strange paradox. In short, the very existence of the state is an implicit denial of the possibility of total democracy.

Theories of the State and Democracy

From the above discussion, it is clear that there is no one theory of the state, not even an agreed-on definition. However, Dunleavy and O'Leary (1987, pp. 1–6) distinguish between organizational definitions and functional ones. We will take the former approach, since functionalist definitions generally fail to provide a theoretical base on which other analyses might be constructed. Dunleavy and O'Leary's (1987, p. 1) organizational definition holds that "the state is a set of governmental institutions." While the idea that the state is about institutions is accepted, this definition is slightly tautological, since it relates the state to institutions of government. It is suggested here that the state is a set of public institutions through which the government exercises power. Government, then, is "the process of making rules, controlling, guiding, or regulating" (Dunleavy and O'Leary, 1987, p. 1), but ultimately this definition of the state indicates that ultimately all power comes from the people, since the institutions are public.

Nonstatists contend that there are still some societies that have no state, since all the people meet to discuss and make decisions that affect them. In this instance, then, the power resides with the assembly of citizens who make the decisions. However, such a democratic form of decision making is perhaps impractical in modern society. Therefore, other theories about the way that social institutions can be controlled have emerged.

Anarchism holds that at some stage, humankind will be mature enough to live in harmony without rulers. This is an idealistic position, one to which humankind might aspire but has probably not attained. This form of society is implicit in some of Buber's ideals.

Other positions have adopted a minimal state approach — that is, that people should be left as free as possible, with the state intervening only occasionally. Classical liberalism is the epitome of this approach; it regards society as a collection of individuals having their own human rights. Within it the state only functions to protect life, limb, and property, while in all other matters the individuals are free to act legally as they wish (Mann, 1983; Grey, 1986). However, society has changed since this position was formulated. Individuals now seem less significant than do parties and organizations (Weber, 1971). In the 1960s, classical pluralism — in which the state was regarded as neutral, although it had to arbitrate between the political and economic power bases within society — emerged. The state only intervened in response to the pressures of the plurality of social institutions and also in response to pressure exerted by interest groups formed for that specific purpose, and it was the prerogative of any individual to form such a group to agitate in society.

Having such rights ensured that democracy apparently existed and that the people were free to act within it.

Classical pluralism faced a number of problems during the early 1970s because of the slowing down of economic growth and the increase in social unrest. This led to a general feeling that some forms of unorganized social protest was not in the best interest of the people and that it was necessary for the state to have a professionalized decision-making process that provided "a substitute for external political controls in many areas of state activity where the conventional pluralist emphasis on party politics and interest groups would [have been] inappropriate" (Dunleavy, 1981, p. 205). Because society is so complex, this neo-pluralist argument was plausible, but the state could be seen to be active in the affairs of people, providing the expert and the professional to act in the nation's best interest. A certain credibility was attached to this position, since the government of the day had a reformist stance, which enabled such claims to appear plausible. (This was certainly true in the United Kingdom, and for a short time there was government with a reformist position in the United States.) Additionally, the state was seen to be active in debates with the elites of each segment of society. The state became a pluralism of elites, but it was one in which for the most part consensus was achieved, and the state was seen to be open and reasonably democratic (Mills, 1959).

However, this approach to the state was not to last long. In the late 1970s, liberal antipluralism — a natural successor in the process of social change from the 1960s — came to the fore. In this theory of the state, there is a rhetoric of a return to classical liberalism in curtailing the activities of the state, from its interventionist approach of the earlier period, even if only intervention by elites. The major change, however, was in the methodological rationale employed to justify its apparently restricted activities: the incorporation of the theories of classical non-Marxist economics and the workings of the market now provided the rationale for not intervening. The market forces were left to provide the apparent workings of democracy, since the market seems to function on an exchange of equivalents, and so the "relations of production can do without a traditional authority legitimated from above" (Habermas, 1976, p. 22). This is consistent with the liberal view of the state, but the view of the market is rather idealistic, since it is an exchange in which the powerful nearly always win but in which the weak can have a try, so that society appears to have a semblance of democracy. Now it is the elite of one segment of society, the economic sector, that prevails in society, and the government does not need pressure groups because it claims to represent the will and interests of the people as a result of elections, and so it claims that it must be left to govern in those areas where the market does not rule. However, one of the problems with this approach is that the market is so obviously biased in favor of the interests of the powerful that the consensus achieved through the ideological apparatus appears much more fragile, and people are apparently more aware of the biases within the operations of the state.

In contrast to this emphasis on market forces, another approach to governing is that of central planning. The outcome of this has been interventionism of a reformist nature, but its extreme form is the totalitarian state, such as those of Eastern Europe that have recently collapsed. In the totalitarian state, the elite rule totally. This is depicted by Bentham's *Panopticon* (see Bauman, 1988) or Huxley's critique *Brave New World* (1955), which was first published in 1932. Bentham's vision is of an institution in which the supervisors could see the inmates without ever being seen and know them without ever being known. Likewise, the supervisors are viewed by the headkeeper who they can never see. The outcome, for Bentham, is total conformity and peace and calm but no individual freedom. But as Huxley shows, this state of affairs is unreal, since however sophisticated the social or genetic engineering, individualism will always somehow emerge, and then the totalitarian social system will itself be under attack. Rulers have, at different times in history, tried to create such societies with little success.

All the theories fall somewhere between the two extremes of anarchism and totalitarianism. Marxism has traditionally maintained that it does not really matter which form of government a state has; its workings are always the same. The elite use the apparatus of state for their own ends, so that the state is an evil that has to be overthrown. As humankind matures, it will then learn to live in a classless — that is, stateless — society. Until that time of maturity, however, the culture of the proletariat must prevail; after the revolution, the dictatorship of the proletariat will ensure the transition to a classless (and stateless) society. But the concept of the dictatorship of the proletariat is itself an indication that society needs a state. Marx was an idealist, however, and his view of the classless society demands as much maturity from human beings as does the pure anarchist state.

These, then, are some of the major theories of the way that the state functions. It is clear that the major issue is the extent to which the power of the state is controlled by the people. The idea that most of these forms of state are democratic is frequently asserted, and before the argument of this chapter can proceed any further, it is necessary to clarify this point.

The concept of democracy is rather a loose one, but in its broadest sense, it refers to the fact that in some manner the people have power or authority in society. But certain questions need to be asked: Who are the people? Do they actually exercise power? How do they exercise power? In response to these questions, it can be shown that throughout history, the criteria for a "person" have changed — from male citizen to landowner to educated person to all adults over twenty-one years of age to all adults over eighteen years of age. It is not beyond the realm of imagination to see it change yet again. The extent to which people have ever exercised power is itself debatable, but certainly they have sometimes participated in the selection process for the ruling elite and occasionally have exercised more power in revolutionary-type situations.

This discussion illustrates the point that the concept of democracy is problematic, as Arblaster (1987, p. 6) notes: "To suppose that this century can fix the definition of democracy or, even more arrogantly, that it is in this century that democracy has been finally and definitely realised, is to be blind not only to the probabilities of the future but also to the certainties of the past. Hence, any study of what democracy is, any attempt to discover its essence or meaning, must necessarily be an historical study at least in part."

However, it has to be recognized that throughout history many enlightened and educated persons have suggested that democracy is not even a good form of government. Aristotle certainly had his doubts, as did John Stuart Mill ([1859] 1944), who claimed that those governments throughout history that have exhibited sustained mental abilities have been aristocratic and elsewhere that "no government by a democracy or numerous aristocracy, either in its political acts or in its opinions, qualities, and tone of mind which it fosters, ever did or could rise above mediocrity" (p. 124). Recently, one of the thinkers of the new right has made similar claims: "No conservative . . . is likely to think that democracy is an essential axiom of his politics" (Scruton, 1980, p. 56). However, throughout his writing, Mill claimed that education is one of the ways to enlightenment. Thus he advocated that while everybody should have the right to vote for their leaders, the educated should have more than one vote in order to ensure good government, although he certainly did not see this as democratic.

It is ironic that one of the most influential defenders of education in nineteenth-century England did not regard democracy as necessarily a good form of government and called for more education in order to produce a more enlightened voter, whereas educational theorists tend to see democracy as a good form of government that should be supported. Implicit here are a number of assumptions about the relationship between education, learning, and wise decision making — relationships that educators need to explore in greater depth.

It can be seen that the varying theories of the state differ in relation to how much power is given to the people and therefore in their degree of democracy. If it is an ideal that the people should be able to exercise power, then Mill's argument that the people should be knowledgeable about the things over which they endeavor to govern is convincing. By contrast, it could be argued that contemporary society has become so complex that often the politicians are also fairly ignorant about the areas of society over which they rule. This might call for some reforms in both local and national government. Be that as it may, the significant issue for this discussion is the nature of the state and the way that people's learning relates to it.

The State and Learning

By its very existence, the state must exercise control. It does this through force or through the manipulation of the public institutions, including education — often with the claim that it is in the national interest or for the public good. The extent to which these claims are valid has to do with the nature of the political party that is apparently in control of the state apparatus. Certainly the Marxist theorists have some grave doubts about this. Althusser (1972, p. 258; original italics) comments as follows: "I believe that the ideological apparatus which has been installed in the *dominant* position in mature capitalist social formations as a result of a violent political and ideological class struggle against the old dominant ideological State apparatus is the *educational ideological apparatus.*" Althusser points out that Lenin desperately sought to control the ideological apparatus, especially the educational one, to secure the transition of Russia to socialism. Whatever the complexion of the ruling elite, education may be used to the same effect, and so may the media, and the law, and so on.

To rule a society, the public institutions, or the apparatus of state, have to be controlled by the forces of government. They need to use the institutions to convince people that what they are doing is in the public interest, that "there is no other way," and that they are the legitimate government. In other words, they want people who will believe their claims, who will learn the message that is presented to them unreflectively and uncritically. The paradox is that this is true whatever the form of government, whether it is democratic or totalitarian. For stability, at least of one form of government, it needs a people that will learn and accept unreflectively the message that it presents. If too many people reflect and criticize the position of government, this poses a threat to those who exercise power.

In addition, for new people coming into the country, the state is forced to introduce certain forms of education that will ensure that they learn unreflectively what it means to be an American, a Canadian, and so on — Americanization education (Carlson, 1987), Canadianization education. Carlson subtitles his book *A Quest for Conformity*. The exercise of power has almost always demanded that people learn what they are told and conform in their actions to the stipulated modes of behavior. Throughout history whose who do not conform have suffered for their nonconformity.

But the paradox is, as Mill points out, that if the people are to play their part in civil society, they must be knowledgeable. Perhaps it could be claimed that they must be reflective thinkers; Brookfield (1987) argues that they need to be critical, although reflectivity incorporates the concept of critical thought. Hence, while the government might need unreflective learners among the population so that it might govern without the use of force, the ideal of democracy demands that the people be reflective learners in order to represent their interests in the political process.

The fact that learning is both reflective and nonreflective is a paradox. In its reflective form, it may result in people reaching conclusions other than those to which their governments adhere. There is a real sense in which change — and even progress — can occur only because people have thought new thoughts and have learned new things and have either introduced them into the procedures of society through common agreement or have had to enter a conflict with those who exercise power to create a change situation. Society needs this form of learning if it is to progress and become a more human place for people to live and realize their own humanity. Indeed, if society is to be democratically governed, it needs a people who are thinking and learning reflectively. But it also needs the procedures that allow the state to function smoothly while the people debate diverse outcomes of learning.

But it could be claimed that the modern manifestation of democracy is not that people actually have power but that they have the freedom to debate the complex political issues of their day and to influence the decision-making process through their actions. In this sense, not only do they have the freedom to learn, but they also have the freedom to act on the outcomes of their learning, either through the representation of interest or through the election of those who will exercise power over them. But herein lies the paradox. People who have power exercised over them are no longer completely free and their learning and their action are most likely to be curtailed, even if only in part, by those who control the public institutions. Through that control, the rulers may endeavor to manipulate the knowledge that is transmitted by the institutions to ensure that the people think that they have elected a "good" government. This, then, is the inevitable paradox of the state. For people to be totally free to learn and act in accord with their own authenticity they have to create a stateless society, but humankind is not sufficiently mature for that.

Additionally, as Habermas (1989) has demonstrated, the public sphere has been transformed and the democratic debate finds less place in contemporary society than it used to. Now the media appear to carry the debate while at the same time often influencing people, since they learn uncritically from its presentations. People think that they participate in the public debate because they see it on television and so the media convey a representation of democracy, but whether this is the reality is questionable.

Consequently, it can be seen that reflective learning, the very phenomenon that helps individuals to mature, is necessary but is itself a potentially subversive phenomenon within the state, especially those states that seek to control everything from the center (that is, totalitarian societies). The 1980s saw the emergence of new right governments that have also endeavored to stifle free thought and reflective learning, and so the voluntary organizations that can present alternative interpretations of social phenomena and foster critical thought about them assume a major role in the development of democracy in contemporary society. The interest groups, having their educative functions and often typified as radical adult education (Lovett, 1988), present an important plurality of perspectives that is important if freedom of choice is to exist. They exist as significant alternatives to the public institutions, making it possible for citizens to learn about the affairs of state since the public institutions have been largely controlled by the elite. But the alternatives are often presented by those who exercise power as odd folk riding their hobbyhorses. The importance of reflective learning, then, lies not only in analyzing the content of the message but also in examining the way that it is presented, since the medium has become the message in information society. It is significant that in the more totalitarian states, such public representation of interests is not tolerated at all, but in Western society it is regarded as a legitimate political manifestation of interests.

Conclusion

This chapter has illustrated the double paradox of learning within the state—the state apparently needs unreflective learners to achieve stability but reflective learners if it is to survive without some form of revolution. In other words, for a government to achieve stability, it requires a compliant population that will learn unreflectively and conform. Learning, however, is more complex than that—people are free to learn reflectively and arrive at conclusions that are not conformist. This process is potentially subversive to those who exercise the powers of the state. At the same time, for the democratic state to survive, it must always have the potential to be influenced and changed by its citizens. Reflective learning and experimental action are the ways they can engage in these activities. Thus reflective learning is both a democratic undertaking and a potentially subversive activity.

15

Implications
for Teaching
and Education

This book has explored many paradoxes of learning. They have revolved around the problems of becoming being a person and of being an individual in society. They have referred to autonomy and free will, to meaning and truth, to working and aging, and to power and the state. But they all have implications for educators. Until recently (Bateman, 1990; Brookfield, 1990), learning constituted the main focus of research in adult education, although it has never been quite so prominent in initial education studies. However, adult education has treated teaching in such a manner as to suggest that Rogers's (1969, p. 103) dictum that teaching is an overrated function had been accepted. Indeed, the term *teaching* occurs nowhere in the index of Merriam and Cunningham's *Handbook of Adult and Continuing Education* (1989). But while teaching disappeared from the academic limelight of adult education, it was naturally still going on, and it is now rightly beginning to reassert its place in the spectrum of inquiry into the education of adults.

In this final chapter, some of the implications of the preceding discussion will be expanded in relation to teaching and education. A number of significant issues will be discussed. We begin with the ethical problem of teaching itself, move on to

teaching methods and styles within the context of human relationships, and conclude with a discussion of the paradoxes of
learning.

Teaching: An Ethical Problem

One of the results of the Rogerian approach to teaching has been
the emphasis placed on self-directed learning and the assumptions of human freedom and individuality — features that reflect
American cultural values. Individuals should, according to this
viewpoint, be free to do their own thing for their human essence to evolve freely from the human existent. Since the driving force of this process is human learning, any interference in
it raises profound problems of an ethical nature. But this is just
what education is involved in and what teachers do, sometimes
without considering these ethical questions. Education seeks to
control learning in some way, to direct it and to ensure that
it is harnessed in the interests of the state or the organization;
it reflects the institutionalization of learning. Mill ([1859] 1962,
p. 239) makes this point in respect to the state: "The objections
which are urged with reason against State education do not apply to the enforcement of education by the State, but to the State's
taking upon itself to direct that education; which is a totally
different thing. That the whole or any part of the education of
people should be in State hands, I go as far as anyone in depre-
cating." For Mill, then, the control of the educational process
is problematic, and the last thing he wanted was for people to
be molded into a mass. People have to be free to learn — perhaps
without any interference — although Mill would have claimed
that this should occur without any state interference. The difficulty with this is that although learning is a natural phenomenon, what is learned may not always be useful or relevant within
contemporary society, so that learning should perhaps be guided
and help should be given, especially to those who are disadvan-
taged and least able to learn the most appropriate things. However, this claim does raise the problems of people not knowing
what is in their own best interest and the extent to which they
should be assisted in discovering it. It also contrasts education

as a state-initiated institution with learning, which is a natural human phenomenon. Teaching, then, always treads this delicate line between the best interests of the learners and the needs of society, and the extent to which teachers should assist those least able to learn the most appropriate things for themselves. Hence, for instance, considerable financial support has been given to basic education by governments, but even this support is no doubt given out of a mixture of motives — bureaucratic governments need a literate population, but they also give money to help the illiterate learn to read and write and to improve their position in society.

Learning is about becoming a person in society, about transforming the experiences of living into knowledge, skills, and attitudes so that human individuality might develop, and teaching can assist this endeavor. But paradoxically, learning is also about adapting and becoming a conforming member of society; not surprisingly, teaching can assist in this also. The paradoxes of learning are reflected in the contradictions of teaching. While the direction of that process is partially affected by the biases built into the cultural system, it is also affected by those who are intermediaries between the learners and the system. Parents and significant others are the earliest intermediaries, and it is perhaps no accident that in young children's education, teachers are often regarded as in loco parentis; they are the significant intermediaries between the learners and the external world. Their understanding of that world and the way they mediate between it and the children affect the development of the children as persons quite profoundly. Naturally, this concept of in loco parentis declines in significance as the children grow, but teachers still remain mediators between the world and the learners.

Teachers and human resource developers occupy space between the sociocultural world and the learners; they perform a hermeneutic function of interpreting that milieu for the learners. Moreover, the learners rarely own or control the space in which the teaching and learning occur. Teachers and human potential developers, by virtue of their position in the school or the employing organization, control that space even though they seldom own it, and by their control they affect the process of learning and therefore the direction of the learners' development. However, the question of how they manage the space and in whose interests they see themselves acting are fundamental questions that concern the way education functions.

Whatever the age or the stage of development of the learners, the role of teacher is therefore one of considerable moral responsibility. Sometimes this moral responsibility is abrogated, or not even recognized, as the teaching role serves the ends of contemporary society. Teachers become significant in assisting students acquire certain certificates, human resource developers in ensuring that the learners acquire the requisite skills, and so on. Once teaching is located in the having mode rather than the being one, many of its moral elements can be negated. However, learning occurs in the process of becoming, it is a being phenomenon; thus it is necessary to recognize its significance and its ethical implications.

Few studies have been conducted on the ethics of teaching; those that have been are mostly about teaching schoolchildren (see Strike and Soltis, 1985; Goodlad, Soder, and Sirotnik, 1990). At the same time, the ethical issues are apparent in studies on critical pedagogy (Giroux, 1981; Carr and Kemmis, 1986; Livingstone and contributors, 1987; Young, 1990). Only Caffarella (1988) addresses the problem for teachers of adults, but unfortunately even she does not see teaching in itself as an ethical problem. In her comparison of two different approaches to teaching, she hints at the fundamental problem, but she never actually discusses it.

Teachers exercise control over the space that their learners occupy, whether they like it or not. Thus they influence the learning process to a considerable degree. A number of questions need to be posed at this point. First, to what extent does anyone have that right to influence the process of development so directly? Second, if people do have that right, are they suitable persons to hold that responsibility? Third, are they fully aware of the significance of the teaching and learning process so that they can exercise the role in the most responsible manner? And fourth, do they relate their teaching to the process of human becoming or only to that of acquiring knowledge and skills?

This is not the place to explore these questions in great detail, although they cannot be neglected here entirely. In contemporary society, teaching has assumed a role performed by the priests and elders in bygone generations and in nonindustrialized societies, when they sought to pass on to the next generation the cultural knowledge that the people regarded as sacred or essential. As the body of knowledge necessary to function in this world has grown, it has become impractical for its transmission to be restricted to those who traditionally undertook the task. Teaching has become a full-time occupation with children and is becoming so with adults in a variety of different walks of life, and it has become essential for the smooth functioning of society. Some of the ethics associated with smooth functioning are questionable, however, because if the social system is in any way short of perfection, if it contains immoral biases, should teachers try to mediate it effectively? Even if society were perfect, should teachers then seek to mediate it? If that mediating process involves learners acquiring knowledge and skills and learning them in a nonreflective manner, then it becomes questionable whether teachers should ever be effective mediators, because they might hinder the growth and development of the learners. Indeed, education is in danger of becoming a process of indoctrination (Snook, 1972), unless the teaching style is nonauthoritarian. Here then is a fundamental paradox — the more effective the process of mediating, the greater the chance that the learners will learn unreflectively and perhaps not grow and develop as they might. Should teachers, therefore, be prepared to change their approach and help the learners grow and develop? Should they even be ready to ask whether their primary task is to provide experiences where the learners have the opportunity to learn for themselves under guidance and stimulation, rather than engage in the transmission of knowledge and skills? Is teaching essentially a process of creating reflective, or even critical, thinkers? (Brookfield, 1987). This is not the role that people in general associate with teachers, and this is perhaps because learning is socially defined in its unreflective mode. Additionally, teaching is usually defined by this didactic function. But the process of providing learners with the freedom to learn is not a position that would be particularly tenable politically, since it is important that learning is managed if society, and the organizations within which people function, is to remain stable (Thomas, 1991).

Teaching, then, is confronted with a moral paradox. Given that teaching is regarded as essential and that it is also actually performing this mediating role, it becomes necessary to inquire whether those who are doing it are aware of the complexities of the process in which they are involved and whether they are exercising their responsibility in a way most likely to help the learners become more fully human. Helping learners develop their humanity through the teaching and learning process is a moral one; it involves all aspects of human relationships, including teaching styles and methods as well as the whole of the classroom conduct. Naturally, many who enter teaching do so because they recognize the profound significance of their role, and while the rather crude term *human resource developer* has implications that some occupational trainers recognize (namely, that the human being is a resource that has to be developed to maximize return on capital investment), the question still remains in whose interests the human resources are being developed. Underlying all teaching, therefore, are political questions (Giroux, 1981), and they are intimately related to the paradoxes of learning.

Methods and Styles of Teaching

Teachers are often expected to have "all the answers," and so many learners, both adult and children, participate in education expecting to be told by the teachers what to learn and what to do. Indeed, they frequently put considerable pressure on teachers to provide them with "the answers," so that all that they have to do is memorize them. This is a general expectation in society as well. "Good" teachers are expected to know all the answers and merely provide them for the learners to learn. This is another sign of the having society—teachers have a commodity that they can share with their learners. Teachers are expected to have authority and to provide answers in a didactic manner, and as a result of memorizing and practicing, the learners can acquire that knowledge, pass an examination, and gain some form of certification.

But, it might be asked, is this the nature of teaching? Is the teacher there to provide information for learners to learn in a nonreflective manner? Is there always just one truth, or one meaning, or one piece of information to be transmitted? One of the symbols of modern society is that there are alternative values and ways of behaving. For the teacher to provide one interpretation only is to deny the learners the freedom to make their own choices and to discover for themselves. Consequently, it may be seen that certain methods and styles of teaching lend themselves more to learners experiencing freedom than do others. Since teaching styles are about human relationships in the teaching and learning transaction, they represent the focus of this section.

Perhaps the most significant piece of research that has affected understanding about teaching styles was developed by Lippett and White (1958), in a project directed by Kurt Lewin in the 1930s. They examined leadership styles of youth leaders in ten youth clubs in the United States. Basically they discovered three styles: authoritarian, democratic, and laissez-faire. They also discovered that group behavior tended to be consistent with the leadership styles. Authoritarian leaders created group dependence on the leader, with the group disintegrating when the leader was not present; democratic styles created harmonious working relationships whether the leader was present or not; laissez-faire styles resulted in little being achieved whether the leader was present or not. If the learners are dependent on the teacher/leader, then they are looking for a fount of wisdom rather than a situation in which they can reflect and accept or reject. If the learners are in an environment in which they do not feel free to question the knowledge, skills, or attitudes that they are presented, they will most likely adopt a type of learning that can be classified as nonreflective learning. Another response to such a situation, especially if the students do not accept the information that is being presented to them, is simply to reject it; then nonlearning occurs, as can happen in some laissez-faire situations.

Other research in leadership styles suggests similar learning outcomes (see Jarvis, 1983, pp. 114–120). Styles other than the three suggested here — such as paternalistic and even maternalistic ones — could be examined. In any case, the style of teaching is a very important element in any teaching and learning transaction. It may actually determine the type of learning that takes place, since the style establishes the atmosphere within which potential learning situations are experienced. This is especially true for the deferential learner, who is always seeking an authority on whom to rely.

Stock (1974) has summarized some other research on teaching styles in adult education. In his overview of the research, he notes some of the other variables in the process of creating an atmosphere that is conducive to learning, such as the role perception and the personality type of the instructor.

It is maintained here that style is perhaps as important as teaching method because the style helps to create the atmosphere within which the learning occurs. The teaching method might also do this, but most methods can be used with different teaching styles anyway. For example, it is possible to employ the much, and sometimes wrongly, maligned lecture method in either a democratic or an authoritarian style, and it may be utilized by a warm and enthusiastic teacher or a cold and unemotional one (Stock, 1974). If the lecturer presents material that the learners are expected to learn and does so in a way that shows that this is the expectation, then the most likely outcome is that, overtly at least, nonreflective learning will occur. By contrast, if the lecture is employed as a means of conveying ideas that might be considered and if the content is open to discussion by the group — and this aim is also conveyed to the group by means of style — then reflective learning is more likely to occur. Similarly, in a group situation, if the teacher/leader presents the task in an authoritarian and task-oriented manner, the group members might accept what is presented and not reflect upon it, so that nonreflective learning takes place. But if the group leader is an affective leader, working so that the group functions smoothly but not seeking to impose learning outcomes or solutions on the group's problem/learning task, reflective learning might be the result. It would be possible to illustrate this with a variety of methods, and perhaps as significantly, in a variety of educational and noneducational, work and nonoccupational situations. Thus the teaching style is very significant to the learning process, so that it is necessary to concentrate as much on style as on method in the preparation of teachers of adults.

But it might be argued that there are many situations in which the aim of teaching is to have the learners acquire the knowledge, skills, or attitudes presented by the teacher. This could occur if the knowledge that is being presented has been empirically demonstrated to be true, or because the procedure being demonstrated is the one that an organization expects to be put into practice, or because it is important to the learner to learn it for the learner's own good. Each of these three situations raises an important point about the relationship between curriculum content and teaching style and method. First, if the knowledge that is being presented has been proven to be true, then the teacher should have no fear of being found to be incorrect if the students are encouraged to consider the material critically. After all, it has been noted throughout this study that one of the outcomes of reflective learning is conformity. Reflective learning does not mean that everything must change every time learning occurs. Indeed, if the information being presented is correct, its correctness will again be established through the learning, but if it were not, then the learning process will have demonstrated the information to have been false. Since truth must be one of the aims of education, education will itself have benefited from the process. The second point concerns organizational procedure. If the procedure is efficient, then the organization has nothing to fear from reflective learning for the same reasons, but its procedures may be improved if reflective learners devise more appropriate solutions. The same type of argument also applies to the third point. However, the problem might be that it is not the knowledge or the organizational procedure that is being questioned in this discussion, but the self-image of the teacher or of somebody else who holds a position of authority, so that what is presented by the teacher has to be learned by the learners.

It is suggested here that reflective learning is something that adult educators should encourage and that this is often done as effectively through teaching style as through teaching method. It might finally be asked what authority the educator of adults has. It would certainly be wrong to claim that the educator has no authority: there is authority attached to the role of teacher itself within the framework of the formal educational institution, and as an expert, the teacher has the authority of the expert in being able to assist the students in their reflection. The students will vest authority in the teacher, an authority that the authoritarian teacher may never discover or receive. If the teacher is not an expert, the only authority the teacher can expect is that of the teacher's office.

One other factor to consider in this discussion about teaching style pertains to the relationship between teacher and learners and between learners and learners. Good relationships are crucial in the process of teaching and learning, since all learning stems from experience. Most experiential learning paradigms, however, are in the primary mode of experience, but all relationships have a primary mode — people interacting with people. But in teaching, communicative interaction also occurs, which is secondary experience. Much of the information in the teaching and learning transaction is transmitted linguistically, so that learners have experiences in both modes simultaneously. Thus they will learn from both types of experiences at the same time. Educators must ensure that the primary experience enables the learning outcomes to be favorable to learning, in the same way that the secondary experience is designed by the teachers to produce such an outcome. In other words, the humanistic concerns of the teacher and the skills in providing the experience in which communicative interaction occurs are as significant as is the subject knowledge. This means that teachers have to be concerned about creating relationships within which reflective learning can occur through the recognition of the humanity of the learners. Freire (1972b, p. 53), for example, suggests that "through dialogue, the teacher-of-the-students and the students-of-the-teacher cease to exist and a new term emerges: teacher-student with students-teachers. The teacher is no longer merely the one-who-teaches, but one who is himself taught in dialogue with the students, who in their turn while being taught also teach. They become jointly for the process in which all grow."

Teaching and reflective learning and human growth and development are all facilitated in the process of genuine human interaction. Teaching is a humanistic enterprise, and only in human relationships is it possible to establish the best conditions for human growth. Distance learning, however, does not usually include planned primary experiences of human interaction, and part of the skill of the writer of such material is to create an experience through the written word that approximates it. Once again, this is as much about style as it is about content knowledge. However, ultimately teaching must relate to the paradoxes of learning itself.

The Paradoxes of Human Learning

Throughout this study these paradoxes have been clear: learning may be nonreflective or reflective; it may be innovative and creative or it may be conformist and reproductive; it may occur through two totally different modes of experience; and it may relate to the cognitive, the affective, or the psychomotor. One word — *learning* — is used to cover all the possible implications, and that word is socially defined in such a way as to refer to only the lower orders of learning rather than the higher ones; and teaching is thus understood to produce the lower order learning outcomes. Even more problematic, it is these lower orders that constitute the basis of a great deal of examination of student learning, and the reason for this is that such learning is more easily assessable. It is easier to examine what students know in factual terms and also what skills they have acquired than it is to test their understanding and their growth and development. It is easier to appraise a teacher who gives a lecture than one who creates an invigorating but sometimes chaotic atmosphere, and yet it may be in the latter situation that growth and development occur just because the constraints have been minimized and students feel free to question and examine ideas for themselves.

However, providing such an environment in the teaching and learning transaction may produce little change, since the learners may return to a structured environment in which inertia reigns supreme, either because those in power do not wish things to change or because others within the situation prefer the status quo. In these situations, the learners are unable to act in other than repetitive ways, although they would like to be experimental and creative. Such a situation may breed dissatisfaction with the organization. Because learning is so paradoxical, the outcomes of teaching must also be problematic.

Conclusion

This book opened with the story of the Garden of Eden, a profound philosophical myth that encapsulates the paradoxes of human learning. When the inhabitants of the Garden lived in harmony with nature, there were no questions and they could learn nothing, neither good nor evil. Similarly, while people can act with presumption in harmony with their sociocultural milieu, they feel that they have no need to learn, and they do not question its morality. The possibility of learning more is always there, but they do not take advantage of it. Indeed, in the story power is exercised to try to keep the inhabitants of the Garden from learning. It might be argued that ignorance is bliss and that keeping people in ignorance may sometimes be morally acceptable, so that in the story the very first learning act was one of disobedience. Thus learning is always problematic. The story of the garden portrays the moral paradox of learning — it cannot be value free, for the outcomes of learning may be good, but they can also be evil. Through learning, people grow and develop and sometimes this has good consequences, but in other cases they are not necessarily good. For humankind must grow and take moral responsibility for its own learning. Being poses questions that demand answers, but gradually humankind learns that no answers give absolute authority and certainty. But being finds living in uncertainty problematic, as humankind discovers that beyond answers to the questions lie more questions and answers, and yet more questions lie beyond and these also demand answers. Learning, then, typifies the human condition and is part of the human quest — one that is bound to remain unsatisfied within the bounds of time. Beyond time there is a vision of utopia (Levitas, 1990), but unfortunately this is as problematic as the human condition itself. Consequently, learning remains a symbol of the paradox of the human condition.

References

Alanen, A. "Efficient Service as the Professional Ideal of Adult Educators." *Adult Education in Finland,* 1988, *25*(4), 2–13.

Allman, S. "Self-Help Learning and Its Relevance for Learning in Later Life." In E. Midwinter (ed.), *Mutual Aid Universities.* London: Croon Helm, 1984.

Althusser, L. "Ideology and the Ideological State Apparatus." In B. R. Cosin (ed.), *Education, Structure and Society.* Harmondsworth, England: Penguin Books, 1972.

Arblaster, A. *Democracy.* Milton Keynes, England: Open University Press, 1987.

Argyris, C. *Reasoning, Learning, and Action: Individual and Organizational.* San Francisco: Jossey-Bass, 1982.

Argyris, C., and Schön, D. A. *Theory in Practice: Increasing Professional Effectiveness.* San Francisco: Jossey-Bass, 1974.

Argyris, C., and Schön, D. A. *Organizational Learning: A Theory of Action Perspective.* Reading, Mass.: Addison-Wesley, 1978.

Asch, S. E. "Opinions and Social Pressure." *Scientific American, 193,* 1955.

Aslanian, C., and Brickell, H. *Americans in Transition: Life Changes as Reasons for Adult Learning.* New York: College Entrance Examination Board, 1980.

Bateman, W. L. *Open to Question: The Art of Teaching and Learning by Inquiry*. San Francisco: Jossey-Bass, 1990.

Bauman, Z. *Freedom*. Milton Keynes, England: Open University Press, 1988.

Beard, R. *Teaching and Learning in Higher Education*. (3rd ed.) Harmondsworth, England: Penguin Books, 1976.

Berger, P. L. *Invitation to Sociology*. Harmondsworth, England: Penguin Books, 1966.

Berger, P. L. *The Social Reality of Religion*. London: Faber and Faber, 1969.

Berger, P. L., Berger, B., and Kellner, H. *The Homeless Mind*. Harmondsworth, England: Penguin Books, 1974.

Berger, P. L., and Luckmann, T. *The Social Construction of Reality*. New York: Doubleday, 1966.

Bergson, H. *Mind-Energy*. London: Macmillan, 1920.

Bernstein, B. *Class, Codes, and Control*. London: Paladin, 1971.

Beynon, H. *Working for Ford*. Wakefield: E. P. Publishing, 1975.

Bohm, D. *Unfolding Meaning*. London: Routledge and Kegan Paul, 1985.

Bosquet, N. "The Prison Factory." *New Left Review*, 1972, *73* (entire issue).

Boud, D., Keogh, R., and Walker, D. (eds.). *Reflection: Turning Experience into Learning*. London: Kogan Page, 1985.

Bourdieu, P. "Cultural Reproduction and Social Reproduction." In R. Brown (ed.), *Knowledge, Education and Cultural Change*. London: Tavistock, 1973.

Bowles, S., and Gintis, H. *Schooling in Capitalist America*. London: Routledge, 1976.

Bradshaw, J. "The Concept of Social Need." In M. Fitzgerald, P. Halmos, J. Muncie, and D. Zeldin (eds.), *Welfare in Action*. London: Routledge, 1977.

Brinkerhoff, R. O. *Achieving Results from Training: How to Evaluate Human Resource Development to Strengthen Programs and Increase Impact*. San Francisco: Jossey-Bass, 1987.

Brookfield, S. D. *Developing Critical Thinkers: Challenging Adults to Explore Alternative Ways of Thinking and Acting*. San Francisco: Jossey-Bass, 1987.

Brookfield, S. D. "Conceptual, Methodological, and Practical Ambiguities in Self-Directed Learning." In H. B. Long and

Associates, *Self-Directed Learning: Application and Theory*. Athens: Department of Adult Education, University of Georgia, 1988.

Brookfield, S. D. *The Skillful Teacher: On Technique, Trust, and Responsiveness in the Classroom*. San Francisco: Jossey-Bass, 1990.

Brookfield, S. D. (ed.). *Self-Directed Learning: From Theory to Practice*. New Directions for Adult and Continuing Education, no. 25. San Francisco: Jossey-Bass, 1985.

Buber, M. *I and Thou*. (2nd ed.) Edinburgh: Clarke, 1959.

Buber, M. *Between Man and Man*. Glasgow: Fontana Library, 1961.

Caffarella, R. S. "Ethical Dilemmas in Teaching Adults." In R. Brockett (ed.), *Ethical Issues in Adult Education*. New York: Teachers College Press, 1988.

Caffarella, R. S., and O'Donnell, J. M. "Research in Self-Directed Learning: Past, Present, and Future Trends." In H. B. Long and Associates, *Self-Directed Learning: Application and Theory*. Athens: Department of Adult Education, University of Georgia, 1988.

Candy, P. C. "The Transition from Learner Control to Autodidaxy: More Than Meets the Eye." In H. B. Long and Associates, *Advances in Research and Practice in Self-Directed Learning*. Norman: Research Center for Continuing Professional and Higher Education, University of Oklahoma, 1990.

Candy, P. C. *Self-Direction for Lifelong Learning: A Comprehensive Guide to Theory and Practice*. San Francisco: Jossey-Bass, 1991.

Carlson, R. A. *The Americanization Syndrome? A Quest for Conformity*. London: Croon Helm, 1987.

Carnevale, A. P., Gainer, L. J., and Villet, J. *Training in America: The Organization and Strategic Role of Training*. San Francisco: Jossey-Bass, 1990.

Carr, W., and Kemmis, S. *Becoming Critical*. London: Falmer Press, 1986.

Cattell, J. R. "Theory of Fluid and Crystallised Intelligence: A Critical Experiment." *Journal of Educational Psychology*, 1963, *54*(1).

Cervero, R. M. "Changing Relationships Between Theory and Practice." In J. M. Peters, P. Jarvis, and Associates, *Adult Education: Evolution and Achievements in a Developing Field of Study*. San Francisco: Jossey-Bass, 1991.

Chené, A. "The Concept of Autonomy: A Philosophical Discussion." *Adult Education Quarterly,* 1983, *34*(1), 38–47.

Clayton, V. P., and Birren, J. E. "The Development of Wisdom Across the Lifespan." In P. B. Baltes and O. G. Brims, Jr. (eds.), *Lifespan: Development and Behavior in the Context of the Human Lifespan.* New York: Academic Press, 1980.

Cohen, A. P. *The Management of Myths.* Manchester: Manchester University Press, 1975.

Collins Dictionary of the English Language. London: Collins, 1979.

Cooper, D. E. *Authenticity and Learning: Nietzsche's Educational Philosophy.* London: Routledge, 1983.

Cross, K. P. *Adults as Learners: Increasing Participation and Facilitating Learning.* San Francisco: Jossey-Bass, 1981.

Crutchfield, R. S. "Conformity and Character." *American Psychologist,* 1955, *10.*

Dahlgren, L.-O. "Outcomes of Learning." In F. Marton, D. Hounsell, and N. Entwistle (eds.), *The Experience of Learning.* Edinburgh: Scottish Academic Press, 1984.

Daloz, L. A. *Effective Teaching and Mentoring: Realizing the Transformational Power of Adult Learning Experiences.* San Francisco: Jossey-Bass, 1986.

Dearden, R. F. "Autonomy and Education." In R. F. Dearden, P. H. Hirst, and R. S. Peters (eds.), *Education and the Development of Reason.* 3 vols. London: Routledge, 1972.

Dewey, J. *Democracy and Education.* New York: Free Press, 1916.

Dewey, J. *Experience and Education.* New York: Macmillan, 1938.

Dunleavy, P. "Alternative Theories of Liberal Democratic Politics." In D. Potter and Associates (eds.), *Society and the Social Sciences.* Milton Keynes, England: Open University Press, 1981.

Dunleavy, P., and O'Leary, B. *Theories of the State.* London: Macmillan, 1987.

Durkheim, E. *The Division of Labor in Society.* New York: Free Press, 1964.

Entwistle, H. *Antonio Gramsci.* London: Routledge, 1979.

Evans, B. *Radical Adult Education: A Political Critique.* London: Croom Helm, 1987.

Evans-Pritchard, E. E. *Witchcraft, Oracles, and Magic Amongst the Azande.* Oxford, England: Clarendon Press, 1936.

References
253

Faure, E. (Committee chair). *Learning to Be.* Paris: UNESCO, 1972.

Feigenbaum, E. A., and McCorduck, P. *The Fifth Generation.* New York: Signet, 1984.

Freire, P. *Cultural Action for Freedom.* Harmondsworth, England: Penguin Books, 1972a.

Freire, P. *The Pedagogy of the Oppressed.* Harmondsworth, England: Penguin Books, 1972b.

Freire, P. *Education for Critical Consciousness.* London: Sheed and Ward, 1974.

Freire, P. *Pedagogy in Process.* London: Writers and Readers Publishing Cooperative, 1978.

Freire, P. *The Politics of Education.* South Handley, Mass.: Bergin and Garvey, 1985.

Fromm, E. *Man for Himself.* London: Routledge, 1949.

Fromm, E. *Marx's Concept of Man.* New York: Ungar, 1966.

Fromm, E. *To Have or to Be?* New York: HarperCollins, 1976.

Fromm, E. *Fear of Freedom.* London: Routledge, 1946.

Gadamer, H.-G. *Truth and Method.* London: Sheed and Ward, 1975.

Gadamer, H.-G. *Philosophical Hermeneutics.* Berkeley: University of California Press, 1976.

Geuss, R. *The Idea of Critical Theory.* Cambridge, England: Cambridge University Press, 1981.

Gibbs, G. *Teaching Students to Learn.* Milton Keynes, England: Open University Press, 1981.

Giddens, A. *Central Problems in Social Theory: Action, Structure, and Contradiction in Social Analysis.* London: Macmillan, 1979.

Giddens, A. "Reason Without Revolution." In R. J. Bernstein (ed.), *Habermas and Modernity.* Cambridge, England: Polity Press, 1985.

Giroux, H. A. *Ideology, Culture and the Process of Schooling.* London: Falmer, 1981.

Goffman, E. *The Presentation of Self in Everyday Life.* Harmondsworth, England: Penguin Books, 1959.

Goffman, E. *Asylums.* Harmondsworth, England: Penguin Books, 1968a.

Goffman, E. *Stigma.* Harmondsworth, England: Penguin Books, 1968b.

Goffman, E. *Relations in Public*. Harmondsworth, England: Penguin Books, 1971.

Goffman, E. *Interaction Ritual*. Harmondsworth, England: Penguin Books, 1972.

Goodlad, J. I., Soder, R., and Sirotnik, K. A. (eds.). *The Moral Dimensions of Teaching*. San Francisco: Jossey-Bass, 1990.

Grey, J. *Liberalism*. Milton Keynes, England: Open University Press, 1986.

Griffin, C. *Adult Education as Social Policy*. London: Croom Helm, 1987.

Habermas, J. *Knowledge and Human Interests*. London: Heinemann, 1972.

Habermas, J. *Legitimation Crisis*. London: Heinemann, 1976.

Habermas, J. *The Theory of Communicative Action*. Vol. 1. London: Heinemann, 1984.

Habermas, J. *The Theory of Communicative Action*. Vol. 2. Oxford, England: Polity Press, 1987.

Habermas, J. *The Structural Transformation of the Public Sphere*. Cambridge, England: Polity Press, 1989.

Habermas, J. (ed.). *Observations on "The Spiritual Situation of the Age"* (A. Buchwalter, trans.). Cambridge, Mass.: MIT Press, 1987.

Hall, C. S. *A Primer of Freudian Psychology*. London: Allen & Unwin, 1954.

Hanfling, O. *The Quest for Meaning*. Oxford: Blackwell, in association with the Open University, 1987a.

Hanfling, O. (ed.). *Life and Meaning*. Oxford: Blackwell, in association with the Open University, 1987b.

Harré, R. *Social Being*. Oxford, England: Blackwell, 1979.

Hayek, F. A. *The Road to Serfdom*. London: Routledge, 1944.

Heidegger, M. *Being and Time*. London: SCM Press, 1962.

Heidegger, M. *What Is Called Thinking?* New York: HarperCollins, 1968.

Heller, A. *Everyday Life*. London: Routledge, 1984.

Hiemstra, R. "Self-Directed Learning: Individualized Instruction." In H. B. Long and Associates, *Self-Directed Learning: Application and Theory*. Athens: Department of Adult Education, University of Georgia, 1988.

Hobbes, T. *Leviathan*. Harmondsworth, England: Penguin Books, 1968. (Originally published 1651.)

Hoffman, J. *State, Power and Democracy.* Sussex, England: Wheatsheaf, 1988.

Houle, C. O. *The Inquiring Mind.* (2nd ed.) Norman: Research Center for Continuing Professional and Higher Education, University of Oklahoma, 1988.

Huxley, A. *Brave New World.* Harmondsworth, England: Penguin Books, 1955.

Illich, I. *Disabling Professions.* London: Marion Boyars, 1977.

Illich, I., and Verne, E. *Imprisoned in the Global Classroom.* London: Writers and Readers Publishing Cooperative, 1976.

Jarvis, P. "Towards a Sociological Understanding of Superstition." *Social Compass,* 1980, *27,* 285–295.

Jarvis, P. *Adult and Continuing Education: Theory and Practice.* London: Croom Helm, 1983a.

Jarvis, P. "The Lifelong Religious Development of the Individual and the Place of Adult Education." *Lifelong Learning: The Adult Years,* 1983b, *6*(9), 20–23.

Jarvis, P. *Professional Education.* London: Croom Helm, 1983c.

Jarvis, P. *The Sociology of Adult and Continuing Education.* London: Croom Helm, 1985.

Jarvis, P. *Adult Learning in the Social Context.* London: Croom Helm, 1987.

Jarvis, P. "Learning as a Religious Phenomenon." In P. Jarvis (ed.), *New Directions in Adult Religious Education.* Guildford, England: Department of Educational Studies, University of Surrey, 1989.

Jarvis, P. "After the Crisis: The Promise of Adult Education." In F. Pöggeler and Y. Kalmon (eds.), *Adult Education in Crisis Situations.* Jerusalem: Magnes Press, Hebrew University, 1991.

Jarvis, P. *The State and the Education of Adults.* London: Routledge, forthcoming.

Joll, J. *Gramsci.* Glasgow: Fontana, 1977.

Kelly, G. A. *A Theory of Personality: The Psychology of Personal Constructs.* New York: W.W.Norton, 1963.

Kerr, C., Dunlop, J. P., Harbison, F., and Myers, C. A. *Industrialism and Industrial Man.* Harmondsworth, England: Pelican, 1973.

Kidd, J. R. *How Adults Learn.* (Rev. ed.) Chicago: Association Press, 1973.

Knowles, M. S. *Self-Directed Learning*. Chicago: Follett, 1975.

Knowles, M. S. *The Modern Practice of Adult Education*. (2nd ed.) Chicago: Association Press, 1980.

Knowles, M. S. *The Making of an Adult Educator: An Autobiographical Journey*. San Francisco: Jossey-Bass, 1989.

Kohl, H. *36 Children*. Harmondsworth, England: Penguin Books, 1971.

Kolb, D. A. *Experiential Learning*. Englewood Cliffs, N.J.: Prentice-Hall, 1984.

Kontiainen, S. "Individual Models of Adult Learning." *Use of Conceptual Models in Case Studies*. Research bulletin no. 78. Helsinki: University of Helsinki, 1991.

Lacey, A. R. *Bergson*. London: Routledge, 1989.

Lengrand, P. *An Introduction to Lifelong Education*. London: Croom Helm, 1976.

Levitas, R. *The Concept of Utopia*. New York: Allan, 1990.

Lewin, K. "Group Decisions and Social Change." In G. Swanson, T. Newcomb, and E. Hartley, *Readings in Social Psychology*. Troy, Mo.: Holt, Rinehart & Winston, 1952.

Lindley, R. *Autonomy*. London: Macmillan, 1986.

Lippitt, R., and White, R. K. "An Experimental Study of Leadership." In E. Maccoby, *Readings in Social Psychology*. New York: Holt, Rinehart & Winston, 1958.

Livingstone, D. W., and contributors. *Critical Pedagogy and Cultural Power*. London: Macmillan, 1987.

Locke, J. *An Essay Concerning Human Understanding*. London: Dent, 1977. (Originally published 1690.)

London, M. *Change Agents: New Roles and Innovation Strategies for Human Resource Professionals*. San Francisco: Jossey-Bass, 1988.

Long, H. B. "Self-Directed Learning Reconsidered." In H. B. Long and Associates, *Self-Directed Learning: Application and Theory*. Athens: Department of Adult Education, University of Georgia, 1988.

Long, H. B. "Self-Directed Learning: Emerging Theory and Practice." In H. B. Long and Associates, *Self-Directed Learning: Emerging Theory and Practice*. Norman: Research Center for Continuing Professional and Higher Education, University of Oklahoma, 1989.

Long, H. B. "Changing Concepts of Self-Direction in Learning." In H. B. Long and Associates, *Advances in Research and Practice in Self-Directed Learning*. Norman: Research Center for Continuing Professional and Higher Education, University of Oklahoma, 1990.

Lovett, T. (ed.). *Radical Approaches to Adult Education: A Reader*. London: Croom Helm, 1988.

Lovett, T., Clarke, C., and Kilmurray, A. *Adult Education and Community Action*. London: Croom Helm, 1983.

Luckmann, T. *The Invisible Religion*. London: Macmillan, 1967.

McCarthy, T. *The Critical Theory of Jürgen Habermas*. Cambridge, Mass.: MIT Press, 1981.

McGiveny, V. *Access to Education for Non-Participant Adults*. Leicester, England: National Institute of Adult Continuing Education, 1990.

McKenzie, L. *Adult Education and Worldview Construction*. Malabar, Fla.: Krieger, 1991.

McKnight, J. "Professionalized Service and Disabling Help." In I. Illich, *Disabling Professions*. London: Boyars, 1977.

Macquarrie, J. *Existentialism*. Harmondsworth, England: Pelican, 1973.

Mann, M. *Macmillan Student Encyclopedia of Sociology*. London: Macmillan, 1983.

Mannheim, K. *Ideology and Utopia*. London: Routledge, 1936.

Mannings, R. *The Incidental Learning Research Project*. Bristol, England: Folk House, 1986.

Marcel, G. *Being and Having*. Gloucester, Mass.: Peter Smith, 1976.

Marsick, V. J. (ed.). *Learning in the Workplace*. London: Croom Helm, 1987.

Marsick, V. J., and Watkins, K. *Informal and Incidental Learning in the Workplace*. London: Routledge, 1990.

Marx, K., and Engels, F. *The German Ideology*. London: Lawrence and Wishart, 1970. (Originally published 1846.)

Maslow, A. H. *Religious Values and Peak Experiences*. Columbus: Ohio State University Press, 1964.

Maslow, A. H. *Toward a Psychology of Being*. (2nd ed.) New York: Van Nostrand Reinhold, 1968.

Mead, G. H. *Mind, Self, and Society*. Chicago: University of Chicago Press, 1934.

Merriam, S. "Reminiscence and Life-Review: The Potential for

Educational Intervention." In R. Sherron, and B. Lumsden (eds.), *Introduction to Educational Gerontology.* Washington, D.C.: Hemisphere, 1985.

Merriam, S. B., and Caffarella, R. S. *Learning in Adulthood: A Comprehensive Guide.* San Francisco: Jossey-Bass, 1991.

Merriam, S. B., and Cunningham, P. M. (eds.). *Handbook of Adult and Continuing Education.* San Francisco: Jossey-Bass, 1989.

Merton, R. K. *Social Theory and Social Structure.* New York: Free Press, 1968.

Meyers, C. *Teaching Students to Think Critically: A Guide for Faculty in All Disciplines.* San Francisco: Jossey-Bass, 1986.

Mezirow, J. "Perspective Transformation." *Studies in Adult Education,* 1977, *9*(2), 153–164.

Mezirow, J. "A Critical Theory of Adult Learning and Education." *Adult Education,* 1986, *32*(1), 3–24.

Mezirow, J. "Context and Action in Adult Education." *Adult Education Quarterly,* 1985, *35*(3), 142–151.

Mezirow, J. "Transformation Theory." Proceedings of the 29th Annual Adult Education Research Conference. Calgary, Canada: Faculty of Continuing Education, University of Calgary, 1988.

Mezirow, J. *Transformative Dimensions of Adult Learning.* San Francisco: Jossey-Bass, 1991.

Mezirow, J., and Associates. *Fostering Critical Reflection in Adulthood: A Guide to Transformative and Emancipatory Learning.* San Francisco: Jossey-Bass, 1990.

Mill, J. S. *Utilitarianism, Liberty, and Representative Government.* London: Dent, 1944. (Originally published 1859.)

Mill, J. S. *On Liberty.* London: Fontana, 1962. (Originally published 1859.)

Mills, C. W. *The Sociological Imagination.* Harmondsworth, England: Pelican, 1959.

Mocker, D. W. and Spear, G. *Lifelong Learning: Formal, Non-Formal, Informal, and Self-Directed Learning.* Columbus: ERIC Clearinghouse, Ohio State University, 1982.

Moody, H. "Late Life Learning in an Information Society." In D. Peterson, J. Thornton, and J. Birren (eds.), *Education and Aging.* Englewood Cliffs, N.J.: Prentice-Hall, 1986.

Nadler, L., and Wiggs, G. D. *Managing Human Resource Development: A Practical Guide.* San Francisco: Jossey-Bass, 1986.

Nozick, R. *Anarchy, State, and Utopia.* Oxford, England: Blackwell, 1974.

Nyiri, J. C. "Tradition and Practical Knowledge." In J. C. Nyiri and B. Smith (eds.), *Practical Knowledge.* London: Croom Helm, 1988.

O'Dea, T. *The Sociology of Religion.* Englewood Cliffs, N.J.: Prentice-Hall, 1966.

Ottmann, H. "Cognitive Interests and Self-Reflection." In J. B. Thompson and D. Held (eds.), *Habermas: Critical Debates.* London: Macmillan, 1982.

Passmore, J. "On Teaching to Be Critical." In R. S. Peters (ed.), *The Concept of Education.* London: Routledge, 1967.

Paterson, R. K. *Values, Education, and the Adult.* London: Routledge, 1979.

Peters, R. S. "Education as Initiation." In R. D. Archambault (ed.), *Philosophical Analysis and Education.* London: Routledge, 1965.

Peters, R. S. *Ethics and Education.* London: Allen & Unwin, 1966.

Peters, R. S. "Education and the Educated Man." In R. F. Dearden, P. H. Hirst, and R. S. Peters (eds.), *Education and the Development of Reason.* 3 vols. London: Routledge, 1972.

Peters, R. S. *Education and the Education of Teachers.* London: Routledge, 1977.

Peterson, D. A. *Facilitating Education for Older Learners.* San Francisco: Jossey-Bass, 1983.

Piaget, J. *The Child's Conception of the World.* London: Routledge, 1929.

Plato. *Republic.* (F. M. Cornford, trans.). Oxford, England: Clarendon Press, 1949. (Written fourth century B.C.)

Plato. *Protagoras and Meno.* (W.K.C. Guthrie, trans.). Harmondsworth, England: Penguin Books, 1956. (Written fourth century B.C.)

Reber, A. S. *Dictionary of Psychology.* Harmondsworth, England: Penguin Books, 1985.

Reischmann, J. "Learning 'en passant': The Forgotten Dimension." Paper presented at the annual meeting of the American

Association of Adult and Continuing Education, Hollywood, Fla., Oct. 1986.

Riesman, D. *The Lonely Crowd: A Study of the Changing American Character.* New Haven, Conn.: Yale University Press, 1950.

Robinson, D. G., and Robinson, J. C. *Training for Impact: How to Link Training to Business Needs and Measure the Results.* San Francisco: Jossey-Bass, 1989.

Rogers, C. R. *On Becoming a Person.* London: Constable, 1961.

Rogers, C. R. *Freedom to Learn.* Columbus, Ohio: Merrill, 1969.

Rogers, E. H. *Diffusion of Innovations.* New York: Free Press, 1962.

Rorty, R. *Contingency, Irony, and Solidarity.* Cambridge, England: Cambridge University Press, 1989.

Ryan, A. *Property.* Milton Keynes, England: Open University Press, 1987.

Ryle, G. *The Concept of Mind.* Harmondsworth, England: Penguin Books, 1963.

Ryle, G. *On Thinking.* Oxford, England: Blackwell, 1983.

Sartre, J.-P. *Being and Nothingness.* (H. Barnes, trans.). London: Routledge, 1958.

Schön, D. A. *The Reflective Practitioner.* New York: Basic Books, 1983.

Schön, D. A. *Educating the Reflective Practitioner: Toward a New Design for Teaching and Learning in the Profession.* San Francisco: Jossey-Bass, 1987.

Schutz, A. *On Phenomenology and Social Relations.* Chicago: University of Chicago Press, 1970.

Schutz, A. "The Stranger." In B. Cosin, J. R. Dale, G. M. Esland, and D. Swift (eds.), *School and Society.* London: Routledge, 1971.

Schutz, A., and Luckmann, T. *The Structure of the Lifeworld.* London: Heinemann, 1974.

Scruton, R. *The Meaning of Conservatism.* London: Macmillan, 1980.

Seaver, P. S. *Wallington's World.* London: Methuen, 1985.

Seeman, M. "On the Meaning of Alienation." In L. A. Coser and B. Rosenberg (eds.), *Sociological Theory.* New York: Macmillan, 1964.

Simmel, G. "The Metropolis and Mental Life." In K. Thompson

and J. Tunstall (eds.), *Sociological Perspectives.* Harmondsworth, England: Penguin Books, 1971. (Originally published 1908.)

Smith, P., and Jones, O. R. *The Philosophy of Mind.* Cambridge, England: Cambridge University Press, 1986.

Snook, I. A. (ed.). *Concepts of Indoctrination.* London: Routledge, 1972.

Stock, A. "Teaching Styles and Learning." *Studies in Adult Education,* 1974, *6*(2).

Strauss, A. (ed.). *George Herbert Mead on Social Psychology.* Chicago: University of Chicago Press, 1964.

Strike, K. A., and Soltis, J. F. *The Ethics of Teaching.* New York: Teachers College Press, 1985.

Taylor, A.J.P. "Introduction." In (1967 ed. of) K. Marx and F. Engels, *Communist Manifesto.* Harmondsworth, England: Pelican, 1967.

Teilhard de Chardin, P. *The Phenomenon of Man.* London: Fontana, 1965.

Tennant, M. "Lifespan Developmental Psychology and Adult Learning." *International Journal of Lifelong Education,* 1990, *9*(3), 223–236.

Thomas, A. M. *Beyond Education: A New Perspective on Society's Management of Learning.* San Francisco: Jossey-Bass, 1991.

Thompson, J. *Learning Liberation: Women's Responses to Men's Education.* London: Croom Helm, 1983.

Thompson, J. B., and Held, D. (eds.), *Habermas and His Critics.* London: Macmillan, 1982.

Thornton, J. "Lifespan Learning and Education." In D. Peterson, J. Thornton, and J. Birren (eds.), *Education and Aging.* Englewood Clifs, N.J.: Prentice-Hall, 1986.

Tönnies, F. *Community and Society.* New York: HarperCollins, 1963.

Tough, A. *The Adult's Learning Projects.* (2nd ed.) Toronto: Ontario Institute for Studies in Education, 1979.

Tuijnman, A. *Recurrent Education, Earnings, and Well-Being.* Stockholm: Almqvist and Wiksell International, 1989.

Ward, K. *Divine Action.* London: Collins, 1990.

Warnke, G. *Gadamer: Hermeneutics, Tradition, and Reason.* Stanford, Calif.: Stanford University Press, 1987.

Weber, M. *The Theory of Economic and Social Organizations.* New York: Free Press, 1947.

Weber, M. "Class, Status, Party." (Originally published 1922.) In K. Thompson and J. Tunstall (eds.), *Sociological Perspectives*. Harmondsworth, England: Penguin Books in association with the Open University Press, 1971.

Weber, M. *Economy and Society.* 2 vols. Berkeley: University of California Press, 1978. (Originally published 1922.)

Whitworth, J. M. *God's Blueprints*. London: Routledge, 1975.

Wlodkowski, R. J. *Enhancing Adult Motivation to Learn: A Guide to Improving Instruction and Increasing Learner Achievements.* San Francisco: Jossey-Bass, 1985.

Wrong, D. *Skeptical Sociology*. London: Heinemann, 1976.

Young, R. *A Critical Theory of Education.* New York: Teachers College Press, 1990.

Index

A

Action: aspects of conscious, 50–67; and communicative interaction, 65–67; concept of, 51–52; conclusion on, 67; consciousness in, 52–57; forms of, 60–65; freedom of, 126–130; and learning, 78–83; learning and thought related to, 80–82; typology of, 57–65

Adam, 7

Adaptation, and action, 57

Adult education: certification in liberal, 150–151; teaching in, 235–247

Adulthood: maturity gradient in, 164; and personhood, 107–108; and self-direction, 119–120

Africa, language in postcolonial, 39–40

Aging: aspects of wisdom and, 195–208; background on, 195–196; conclusion on, 208; and everyday learning, 196–202; mind and body in, 199; process of, 197; and responses to learning, 205–208; wisdom and practical knowledge in, 202–205

Aims and objectives, in learning sequence, 138–139

Alanen, A., 189

Alienation: and conscious action, 64–65; and learning, 79; in workplace, 183

Allman, S., 107

Althusser, L., 29–30, 224, 231

Anomic nonaction: and consciousness, 58–59; and reflection, 82; and rejection of experience, 73

Arblaster, A., 229

Argyris, C., 53, 60, 61, 62, 63, 76, 184, 216, 219

Aristotle, 230

Arrogance, and meaning, 172

Asch, S. E., 59

Aslanian, C., 129, 175, 212–213

Assessment: of education, 190; in learning sequence, 141

Authenticity: and autonomy, 110; Dadaist, 103–104, 105–106, 115, 212; and dialogue, 166; growth related to, 111–117; and inauthenticity, 115–117; interactive, 104–105, 111, 118; and meaning, 159; models of, 103–105; and nonreflective learning, 115–117;

Polonian, 103–104, 105, 115, 160, 212; and reflective learning, 113–115

Authority: and meaning, 172–173; and teaching styles, 244

Autodidaxy, and free will, 133. *See also* Self-directed learning

Autonomy: authenticity and self-directed learning related to, 110, 119–142; background on, 119–121; conclusion on, 141–142; elements of, 120; and free will, 121–126; and freedom of action, 126–130; paradox of, 141–142; and rationality, 110; and self-directed learning, 130–141

Availability, and authenticity, 104

Awareness. *See* Consciousness

B

Bad faith, and consciousness, 88

Bateman, W. L., 235

Bauman, Z., 228

Beard, R., 75

Behavior patterns, paradox of, 211

Being: and action, 60; and becoming, 101–118; conclusion on, 153–154; consciousness of, 106–107; education as, 149–153; and existence, 34–36; and experience, 147; and having, 143–154; learning as base of, 3, 10, 105–107, 147–149; and needs hierarchy, 143–144, 147; paradox of, 154; physical or personal, 36

Bentham, J., 228

Berger, B., 48, 53, 54, 103, 179, 180

Berger, P. L., 18, 23, 48, 52, 53, 54, 57, 78, 103, 179, 180, 201

Bergson, H., 44, 62, 197–198

Bernstein, B., 39, 163

Beynon, H., 182–183

Body: and aging, 199; and birth of self, 35–36, 38

Bohm, D., 35, 157, 176

Bosquet, N., 182

Boud, D., 56, 76

Bourdieu, P., 21, 38

Bowles, S., 139

Bradshaw, J., 92

Brazil, conscientization in, 94–95

Brickell, H., 129, 175, 212–213

Brinkerhoff, R. O., 111

Brookfield, S. D., 30, 113–114, 119, 137, 141, 222, 232, 235, 239

Buber, M., 104, 105, 106, 111, 118, 119, 125, 212, 215, 226

Bureaucracy: change agents in, 218–219; work distinct from, 180; in workplace, 178–180

C

Caffarella, R. S., 70, 119, 238

Candy, P. C., 132–133

Capitalism, and having, 145

Carlson, R. A., 231

Carnevale, A. P., 182, 184

Carr, W., 238

Cattell, J. R., 42

Certification, in education, 150–151

Cervero, R. M., 53

Change: agents of, and structure, 215–219; aspects of learning and, 209–220; background on, 209–210; conclusion on, 220; and conformity, paradox of, 24–25, 31, 78; and effects of learning, 213–215; paradox of, 210, 219; and risk, 219–220; and societal inhibitions, 210–213

Chené, A., 120, 138

Civic rituals, and legitimation, 29

Clarke, C., 217

Cohen, A. P., 30

Communication, prerequisites for, 82

Communicative interaction: in adult education, 152; and authenticity, 111–112; and conscious action, 65–67; and disjuncture, 84; and having, 144–145; and learning, 82–83; and meaning, 158, 166–167, 174; and teaching styles, 244–245

Communism, and having, 145–146

Community educator, as change agent, 216–217

Computer analogy, and free will, 122–124, 125

Conformity, and change, paradox of, 24–25, 31, 78

Conscientization, and interest, 94–97

Consciousness: in action, 52–57; of being, 106–107; and birth of self, 37, 43–44; concept of, 53; and false consciousness, 31, 86–89, 225; levels of, 58; and monitoring, 55–56; and personhood, 108; and planning, 54–55; and reflection, 56–57; and retrospection, 56; and self-directed learning, 141

Contemplation: and aging, 203–204; and experience, 77, 80

Control: absolute and delegated types of, 133; paradox of, 133

Cooley, W., 48

Cooper, D. E., 103–104

Creative thinking, and workplace learning, 183. *See also* Experimental/creative action

Critical thinking, and authenticity, 113–114

Cross, K. P., 42

Crusoe, R., 13

Crutchfield, R. S., 60

Culture: aspects of, 17–32; background on, 17–18; concept of, 19; conclusion on, 32; extension of, 30–31; and externalization, 22–27; inequality in, 21–22, 26–27; internalization of, 18–22; and legitimation, 27–32; and mind, 38, 41; pluralistic, 21, 27, 48, 88–89, 97, 168–169, 225; substitution of, 31; and teaching, 239. *See also* Society

Cunningham, P. M., 235

Curriculum: in learning sequence, 139; and teaching styles, 243–244

D

Dahlgren, L. O., 155

Daloz, L. A., 204

Dearden, R. F., 110

Decision making: and free will, 125–126; in learning sequence, 136–137

Descartes, R., 35, 156

Development: paradox of, 22; and personhood, 107–111; in workplace, 110–111

Dewey, J., 9, 53, 108, 109, 167, 205

Dialogue: and authenticity, 166; in education, 151–152; learning through, 114; in teaching, 244–245

Disjuncture: and change, 211–213; and conscious action, 59, 61; and interest and need, 93–94; and learning, 82, 83–84, 196, 200, 206, 207; and learning sequence, 134, 136; and meaning, 157, 165; and nature of learning, 4, 15–16; paradox of, 83–84. *See also* Harmony

Doers, older learners as, 207–208

Dreams, and false consciousness, 91

Dualism: and birth of self, 35, 47; concept of, 6

Dunleavy, P., 225–226, 227

Dunlop, J. P., 189

Durkheim, E., 20, 58, 59, 213

Dyadic relationships, effects of learning on, 214–215

E

Education: aims of, 109–110, 112, 138–139, 152, 189–190; as being and having, 149–153; and developing a person, 107–111; dialogue in, 151–152; learning related to, 10; and legitimation, 30; teaching and, 235–247

Einstein, A., 176

Engels, F., 26, 40, 223, 224

Entwistle, H., 63, 87

Essence: and birth of self, 34–35, 43; and interest and need, 93; manifestation of, 105

Ethical issues, of teaching, 236–240

Europe: learning research in, 70; totalitarianism in Eastern, 228

Evans, B., 222

Evans-Pritchard, E. E., 123
Eve, 7
Existence: and being, 34–36; and
    knowledge related to meaning,
    156–158
Experience: aging and wisdom
    related to, 195–208; and being,
    147; conscious, and learning, 11;
    and free will, 124–125; and intel-
    ligence, 42–43; and meaning,
    155–158; response to, 72–78,
    205–208
Experiences, primary and secondary:
    and action, 82–83, 84; and being
    and having, 148; and birth of
    self, 39; and conscious action, 50,
    65–66; and meaning, 155–156,
    157–158; and nature of learning,
    14, 16; and personhood, 105;
    and teaching, 244; and work-
    place, 180–181
Experimental/creative action: and
    authenticity, 113–115; and con-
    sciousness, 60–61; and learning,
    79
Experimental learning, and experi-
    ence, 77–78, 80
Externalization: dimensions of, 23;
    process of, 22–27

F

Faure, E., 10, 36
Ford Motor Company, repetitive
    work at, 182–183
France: public space in, 127; revolu-
    tion in, 15
Free will: and autonomy, 121–126;
    paradox of, 123
Freedom: and action, 51–52; and
    autonomy, 126–130; and non-
    learning, 74; of professionals,
    187; and self-directed learning,
    131–133
Freire, P., 31, 39–40, 52, 76, 86,
    89, 94–96, 114, 139, 149–150,
    151, 160, 184, 215–216, 222,
    244–245
Freud, S., 15, 20, 46, 62, 91, 130
Fromm, E., 64, 120, 129, 144,
    159–160, 165, 176, 183, 212

Functionalism, and socialization,
    20–21

G

Gadamer, H. G., 76, 84, 111,
    147–148, 166–167, 173
Gainer, L. J., 182, 184
Garden of Eden, 5, 7, 9, 15, 83,
    168, 211, 246
Genetics: and culture, 19, 20–21;
    and nature of learning, 9, 13
Gesture, and birth of self, 37,
    41–42, 46
Geuss, R., 89, 92
Gibbs, G., 140
Giddens, A., 37, 52, 55, 59, 62, 66
Gintis, H., 139
Giroux, H. A., 238, 240
Goffman, E., 210–211
Goodlad, J. I., 238
Gramsci, A., 63, 87, 224
Grey, J., 226
Griffin, C., 222
Growth: aging and wisdom related
    to, 195–208; aspects of personal,
    99–247; authenticity related to,
    111–117; and autonomy,
    119–142; and being a person,
    101–118; being and having
    related to, 143–154; and change,
    209–220; meaning and truth
    related to, 155–176; political
    dimension of, 221–234; teaching
    and, 235–247; and workplace
    learning, 177–194

H

Habermas, J., 3, 21, 22, 31, 53, 55,
    56, 66–67, 81, 83, 87, 90–92, 97,
    105, 111–112, 126, 174, 192,
    227–228, 233
Habitualization: and action, 57–58;
    and aging, 201–202, 204; and
    learning, 78–79; process of, 23,
    25, 28, 31
Hall, C. S., 46
Handouts, rationale for, 149
Hanfling, O., 160
Harbison, F., 189

Harmony: paradox of, 84; sought by older learners, 206–207. *See also* Disjuncture

Harré, R., 20–21, 28, 51

Havighurst, R., 203–204

Having: and being, 143–154; characteristics of, 144–146; conclusion on, 153–154; education as, 149–153; and learning, 147–149; and needs hierarchy, 143–144, 147; paradox of, 154; and teaching, 240–241

Hayek, F. A., 118

Hegel, G.W.F., 183

Heidegger, M., 34–35, 36, 52

Held, D., 92

Heller, A., 12, 23, 24, 116–117, 199–201, 202, 203, 213

Heimstra, R., 138

Hobbes, T., 222, 223

Hoffman, J., 224

Houle, C. O., 122, 137, 139

Human condition, paradoxes of, 104–105, 128, 220, 247

Human resource development: ethical implications of, 237–238, 240; paradox of, 115; and personhood, 110–111, 112, 115; and space for action, 128. *See also* Workplace

Hume, D., 125

Huxley, A., 228

I

Identity, and birth of self, 48

Ignorance, paradox of, 165

Illich, I., 93, 150

Individuality: and birth of self, 41, 43; and free will, 122; and internalization, 22; and meaning, 163, 170; and social context for learning, 13–14

Industrial Revolution, 14, 15, 22

Instinct, concept of, 7–8

Institutionalization, process of, 23–24, 25

Institutions, and legitimation, 29–30

Intelligence, and experience, 42–43

Interaction, and social values, 104–105. *See also* Communicative interaction

Interests: aspects of learning and, 86–97; concept of, 89–92; conclusion on, 97; and conscientization, 94–97; and consciousness, 86–89; forms of, 91; and need, 89–94

Internalization: of identity, 48; process of, 18–22, 24–25

J

Jarvis, P., 4, 9, 11, 13, 14, 19, 33, 68, 77, 92, 140, 149, 153, 165, 184, 201, 222, 242

Jaspers, K. T., 34

Joll, J., 224

K

Kant, I., 125, 193

Keller, H., 46

Kellner, H., 48, 53, 54, 103, 179, 180

Kelly, G. A., 54, 60, 78, 113, 125

Kemmis, S., 238

Keogh, R., 56, 76

Kerr, C., 189

Kidd, J. R., 105, 106

Kilmurray, A., 217

Knowledge: categories of, 90–91; creating or having, 148–149; and existence related to meaning, 156–158; meaning and truth related to, 168–170; practical, 187–188, 202–205

Knowles, M. S., 52, 119–120, 130–131, 136, 153, 201, 202

Kohl, H., 152

Kohlberg, L., 108

Kolb, D. A., 3, 9, 69–70, 76

Kontiainen, S., 70

L

Lacey, A. R., 198

Language: and birth of self, 37, 38–40, 43, 46; in learning sequence, 140–141; and legitimation, 28; and meaning, 162–163; and nonreflective learning, 116

Learning: and action, 68–85; and action/nonaction types, 79;

aspects of nature of, 3–16; background on, 3–5; and being, 3, 10, 105–107, 147–149; categories of, 70–78; and change, 209–220; and communicative interaction, 82–83; conclusions on, 16, 84–85; and conscious experience, 11; cycle of, 69–70; and disjuncture, 82, 83–84, 134, 136, 196, 200, 206, 207; education related to, 10; effects of, 213–215; everyday, and aging, 196–202; and experiences, 14–15, 72–78, 205–208; and free will, 126; and having, 147–149; historical views of, 5–9; incidental, 132, 181; independent, 137; informal, 181; and instinct, 7–9; and interests, 86–97; lifelong, 9–12, 53, 99–247; and meaning, 164–165; model of processes in, 71; moral connotations of, 7; paradoxes of, 4–5, 7, 8, 14, 26, 174, 195–196, 210, 215, 237, 245–246, 247; political dimension of, 221–234; preconscious, 74–75, 80; process of, 167; as recollection, 6, 12, 15; research project on, 68–70; and response to experience, 72–78, 205–208; and risk, 219–220; and social context, 12–16; teaching and, 235–247; transformative, 97, 158, 161–162; in workplace, 180–188. *See also* Nonreflective learning; Reflective learning; Self-directed learning

Legitimation: and meaning, 174–175; process of, 27–32

Lengrand, P., 10

Lenin, V. I., 231

Levitas, R., 117, 247

Lewin, K., 139, 241

Life, concept of, 11–12

Lindley, R., 125

Lippitt, R., 138, 139, 241

Livingstone, D. W., 238

Locke, J., 5, 9

London, M., 117, 218

Long, H. B., 119, 120, 131

Lovett, T., 217, 233

Luckmann, T., 23, 47, 57, 62–63, 72, 78, 81, 157, 158, 160, 164, 169, 201

M

McCarthy, T., 92

McGiveny, V., 5

Machiavelli, N., 224

McKnight, J., 93

Macquarrie, J., 34–35, 51, 104, 119, 120, 146, 156

Managers, workplace learning by, 184–185

Mann, M., 226

Mannheim, K., 13, 40, 140

Mannings, R., 75

Manual workers, workplace learning by, 182–184

Marcel, G., 104, 105, 106, 111, 119, 125, 145, 146, 148–149

Marsick, V. J., 5, 70, 75, 132, 181

Marx, K., 26–27, 31, 32, 40, 64, 87, 91, 94, 102, 183, 222, 223, 224, 225, 228–229, 231

Maslow, A. H., 9, 92, 105, 143, 147, 190

Mead, G. H., 33, 36–38, 41–47, 65

Meaning: aspects of truth and 155–176; background on, 155–156; concepts of, 158–164; conclusion on, 176; existence and knowledge related to, 156–158; and learning, 164–165; and legitimation, 174–175; metaphysical, 159–160; as noun, 162–163; paradox of seeking, 165, 168, 171, 175; perspective, 160–162; schemes, 161–162; sociocultural, 160–162; truth and knowledge related to, 168–170; truth and nonlearning related to, 171–174; and understanding, 165–167; as verb, 163–164

Memorization, and experience, 75–76, 80, 83

Meno, 6, 165

Merriam, S. B., 70, 207, 235

Merton, R. K., 57, 59, 61, 63–64

Method: in learning sequence, 140; of teaching, 240–245

Meyers, C., 113, 222

Mezirow, J., 66, 76, 92, 96–97, 155, 160–162, 164

Mill, J. S., 125, 230, 232, 236

Mills, C. W., 227

Mind: and aging, 199; and birth of self, 36–43; culture and, 38, 41

Mocker, C. W., 138, 140

Monitoring: and consciousness, 55–56; and learning, thought, and action, 80–81

Moody, H., 204, 205, 207

Myers, C. A., 189

Myths, management of, 30–31

N

Nadler, L., 110

Need: concept of, 92–94; hierarchy of, 9, 143–144, 147, 190

Negotiation, in learning sequence, 138, 139

Nietzsche, F., 103

Nonaction: anomic, 58–59, 73, 82; concept of, 52; forms of, 58–60; preventive, 59–60, 82; and reflection, 82

Nonconsideration, and experience, 73

Nonlearning: and authenticity, 115; and communicative interaction, 83; meaning and truth related to, 171–174; paradox of, 81; types of, 72–74

Nonreflective learning: and authenticity, 115–117; and birth of self, 37–38, 47; and communicative interaction, 83; and personhood, 103–107; and retrospection, 82; types of, 74–76; in workplace, 180

Nonresponse, and consciousness, 60

Nonverbal communication, and interaction, 65

Norms: institutionalized, 23–24, 26; and need, 92–93; as rituals, 211

Nozick, R., 118

Nyiri, J. C., 187, 204

O

O'Dea, T., 29

O'Donnell, J. M., 119

O'Leary, B., 225–226

Others: generalized, 45–46; significant, 44–45

Ottmann, H., 90

Outcome, in learning sequence, 141

P

Paradox: of autonomy, 141–142; of behavior patterns, 211; of being and having, 154; of change and conformity, 24–25, 31, 78, 210, 219; of control, 133; of development, 22; of disjuncture, 83–84; of free will, 123; of harmony, 84; of human condition, 104–105, 128, 220, 247; of human resource development, 115; of ignorance, 165; of learning, 4–5, 7, 8, 14, 26, 174, 195–196, 210, 215, 237, 245–246, 247; of meaning, 165, 168, 171, 175; of nonlearning, 81; of power, 232–233; of questioning, 4; of reflection, 56; of reflective learning, 117–118, 147, 219, 223, 232, 234; of relationships, 215; of religion, 29; of self, 49; of society, 12, 17–32, 214; of state, 234; of teaching, 174, 239–240; of transformation, 96

Parsons, T., 20, 21

Participation: for being and having, 153; in learning sequence, 137

Passmore, J., 172

Paterson, R. K., 107–108, 191

Performance, concept of, 51

Person: aspects of being a, 101–118; authenticity and growth of, 111–117; conclusion on, 117–118; developing the, 107–111; in social world, 102–107

Peters, R. S., 36–37, 61, 105, 106–107, 108–110, 113, 152

Peterson, D. A., 9–10

Piaget, J., 22, 28, 108, 164, 168

Planning: and aging, 200; and con-

sciousness, 54–55; and free will,
121–126; and freedom to act,
126–130; and learning, thought,
and action, 80
Plato, 3, 5, 6, 9, 165
Play, and birth of self, 44–45
Power: and action, 52, 59, 62; and
consciousness, 87; and freedom
to act, 128; and inauthenticity,
212; paradox of, 232–233. *See also*
State
Preconscious learning, and experience, 74–75, 80
Presumption, and experience,
72–73, 79, 81
Presumptive action, and consciousness, 62–63
Preventive nonaction: and consciousness, 59–60; and reflection, 82
Professionals, workplace learning by,
178, 185–188

Q

Questioning, paradox of, 4

R

Rationality: and autonomy, 110;
and bureaucracy, 178, 179; and
free will, 122–123, 125; and planning, 54; purposive, 112,
189–193; value type of, 112; and
workplace, 188–193
Reber, A. S., 7
Reflection: and consciousness,
56–57; and learning, thought,
and action, 82; paradox of, 56
Reflective learning: and authenticity,
113–115; and communicative interaction, 83; and conscientization, 96; paradoxes of, 117–118,
147, 219, 223, 232, 234; and
teaching styles, 242–244; types
of, 76–78
Reflective skills learning, and experience, 77, 80
Reflexive action, and consciousness,
62
Reformation, 14

Reification, and language, 28
Reischmann, J., 75
Rejection, and experience, 73
Relationships: and effects of learning, 214–215; paradox of, 215
Relativity, and meaning, 173–174
Religion: and being a person, 102,
103; and birth of self, 47; and
legitimation, 29, 30; and meaning, 161, 165, 166, 171, 175;
myth in, 5, 7, 9, 15, 83, 168,
211, 246; paradox of, 29; and
wisdom, 204
Repetition: and conscious action,
61–62; and learning, 79; in work-
place, 182–183
Retrospection: and aging, 198–199,
200–201; and consciousness, 56;
and learning, thought, and action, 82
Riesman, D., 120, 136, 212
Risk, change and learning related
to, 219–220
Ritual: civic, 29; and conscious action, 63–64; and learning, 79;
norms as, 211
Robinson, D. G., 183
Robinson, J. C., 183
Rogers, C. R., 52, 105–106, 235,
236
Rogers, E. H., 185
Rorty, R., 22
Russia, control in, 231
Ryan, A., 145
Ryle, G., 6, 35, 47, 158, 187, 199

S

Sages, older learners as, 207
Sartre, J. P., 35, 88
Schluchter, W., 192
Schön, D. A., 3, 51, 53, 60, 63, 76,
77, 185–186, 216, 219
Schutz, A., 53, 54, 56, 62–63, 72,
81
Scruton, R., 230
Seaver, P. S., 13
Seeman, M., 64
Self: aspects of birth of, 33–49; and
being, 34–36; birth of, 43–47;

and communicative interaction, 65; concern with, and authenticity, 104; conclusion on, 48-49; elements of, 46; growth of, 99-247; and identity, 48; and meaning, 157, 160, 164; and mind, 36-43; paradox of, 49; and transformative learning, 97; and workplace differentiation, 179-180, 184, 191-192

Self-actualization, and workplace learning, 190-193

Self-directed learning: and autonomy, 130-141; concept of, 130-131; and freedom, 131-133; model of, 135; sequence of, 133-141

Self-reflection: and interest, 91-92; and transformative learning, 97

Simmel, G., 102, 177-178

Sirotnik, K. A., 238

Skills learning, and experience, 75

Skinner, B. F., 7

Snook, I. A., 239

Socialization: and communicative interaction, 65-67; process of, 19-21

Society: aspects of development of self in, 1-97; and authenticity, 117; being and self in, 33-49; change inhibited in, 210-213; concept of, 18; and conscious action, 50-67; interests and learning in, 86-97; learning and action in, 12-16, 68-85; and legitimation, 174-175; and nature of learning, 3-16; paradoxes of, 12, 17-32, 214; persons in, 102-107; pluralistic, 21, 27, 48, 88-89, 97, 168-169, 225; and teaching, 236-237. *See also* Culture

Socrates, 6, 165

Soder, R., 238

Soltis, J. F., 238

Soul, and self, 35, 47

Space: actions in, 51-52, 62; educational, 128, 131; freedom of action in, 126-129; private, 127-129; public, 127; self-

directed learning in, 131-133; and teaching, 237-238; in workplace, 178-180, 186

Spear, G., 138, 140

State: aspects of, 221-234; background on, 221-222; conclusion on, 234; and control, 224-225, 231; democracy and, 229-230, 232-233; and learning, 231-234; liberalism and, 226, 227; market forces and, 227-228; need for, 222-225; paradox of, 234; pluralism and, 226-227; theories of, 225-230; totalitarianism and, 228, 233-234

Stock, A., 242

Strauss, A., 36-38, 41-47

Strike, K. A., 238

Structure, and change agents, 215-219

Sweden, adult education assessed in, 190

T

Taylor, A.J.P., 223

Teaching: aspects of, 235-247; background on, 235-236; being and having in, 152-153; conclusion on, 246-247; ethical issues of, 236-240; function of, 237-239; methods of, 140, 240-245; paradoxes of, 174, 239-240; and paradoxes of learning, 245-246; styles of, 138-139, 240-245

Technology, in workplace, 179-180, 188

Teilhard de Chardin, P., 47

Temple, W., 7

Tennant, M., 110

Thomas, A. M., 222, 240

Thompson, J. B., 92, 96, 215

Thornton, J., 203-204, 205

Thought: action and learning related to, 80-82; creative, 183; critical, 113-114; in learning sequence, 140-141; social nature of, 40-41

Time: and aging, 197-198; freedom to act in, 129-130; and learning, 11-12, 15

Tönnies, F., 214
Tough, A., 120, 185
Transformation: and learning, 158, 161–162; paradox of, 96; and self-reflection, 97
Truth: aspects of meaning and, 155–176; knowledge and, 168–170; nonlearning and, 171–174
Tuijnman, A., 190

U

Understanding, and meaning, 165–167
UNESCO report, 36
United Kingdom: adult learning in, 4–5, 70; political theory in, 227, 230; public space in, 127

V

Verne, E., 150
Villet, J., 182, 184

W

Walker, D., 56, 76
Ward, K., 168

Warnke, G., 166
Watkins, K., 5, 70, 75, 132, 181
Weber, M., 54, 55, 112, 179, 188–189, 192, 223, 226
White, R. K., 138, 139, 241
Whitworth, J. M., 102
Wiggs, G. D., 110
Wisdom: aging and, 195–208; and practical knowledge, 202–205
Wlodkowski, R. J., 136
Women: and conscientization, 96; effects of learning on, 215
Work, bureaucracy distinct from, 180
Workplace: aspects of personhood in, 177–194; background on, 177–178; conclusion on, 193–194; facets of, 178–180; learning in, 180–188; and rationality, 188–193; wisdom in, 205. *See also* Human resource development
Wrong, D., 20, 123

Y

Young, R., 238